*All about
the Second Coming*

All about
the Second Coming

■   ■   ■

Herbert Lockyer

edited by Herbert Lockyer, Jr.

HENDRICKSON
PUBLISHERS

ALL ABOUT THE SECOND COMING
Herbert Lockyer, Sr.
edited by Herbert Lockyer, Jr.

Hendrickson Publishers, Inc.
P. O. Box 3473
Peabody, Massachusetts 01961–3473

ISBN: 1-56563-335-0 cloth
ISBN: 1-56563-334-2 paper

Second Printing — November 2000

*Dedicated to the memory of
my earthly and spiritual father,
Herbert Lockyer, Sr.*

Contents

Introduction

The Second Coming: Our Blessed Hope

The doctrine of the Second Coming—the message Jesus declared regarding His glorious appearance as the blessed and only Potentate—is one of the most abused and distorted of the Bible. Among its friends, it has been held out of proportion to other truths and has suffered many wounds. Within the organized church, some reject it altogether, while others are ignorant of it or indifferent to it, claiming, "I know nothing about it. Neither does anyone else!"

Fortunately, the number of those who are striving to understand the great and glorious truth of the Redeemer's return is growing. While they cannot grasp all that is involved in unfulfilled prophecies, they feel that the human race is moving toward the most stupendous events in the world's history and that international and national events and crises are heavy with prophetic significance.

To handle the Word of truth aright, we must preserve the distinction between Christ's return for His church and His descent to earth to reign. While there is only one *advent,* there are two *events* forming it, namely His coming *for* His saints and then His coming *with* His saints. The two focal points are *rapture* and *reign.*

When our Lord comes down from heaven, He is to tarry in midair, as 1 Thessalonians 4:17 teaches. This will constitute the manifestation of Himself to His church. Then He will descend to the earth as the Prince of the kings of the earth. This aspect corresponds to Zechariah's prophecy about His feet standing on the Mount of Olives (Zechariah 14:4). Thus He comes *for* His saints and then *with* His saints, since His church is to assist Him in His governmental control of the earth.

What does the Bible teach about the coming of Christ for His church—this powerful, practical, purifying doctrine that God's people are studying as never before?

The Fact of His Coming

Jude exhorts us earnestly to contend for the faith that was once delivered to the saints. The question is: Can the rapture and the Second Coming be called a part of this faith? Jude evidently thought it could and therefore emphasizes various aspects of such a truth. Yet we are sometimes labeled "faddists" if we reiterate what the New Testament so clearly teaches. Let us, then, read what the Bible has to say about Christ's coming, taking every reference at its face value. If such a doctrine is not a vital part of the Bible, we have no right to spend any time over it. But if it is the pivotal truth of the future, then are we not guilty of a sinful silence by withholding our vocal testimony?

In seeking to outline the fact of Christ's return, we will confine ourselves to the teaching of the New Testament. To be sure, the Old Testament is as divinely inspired as the New Testament and has as much proof for the second advent of our Lord as for His first advent. But the New Testament gives us the full revelation of this theme. The church is not the subject of a divine revelation in the Old Testament. Christ's mystical body is the mystery hid from the ages and unfolded for us in Paul's writings. It is logical to conclude therefore that those New Testament writers who disclose the truth of the church should likewise dwell upon her rapture.

The New Testament contains over three hundred direct references to our Lord's return—more space than is devoted to any other theme. Let us, then, go through the New Testament books and gather out the various announcements and aspects of this theme, discovering each writer's particular viewpoint.

Solomon once declared that a threefold cord is not quickly broken (Ecclesiastes 4:12). We have such a threefold cord of evidence in the testimony of Christ, the testimony of heaven, and the testimony of the Holy Spirit through the church. Here is the trinity in unity.

The testimony of Christ—declaration: In his memorable message on "the Father's house," Jesus declares that He will return for His own: "I will come back and take you to be with me" (John 14:3). Having given such a promise, He will realize it to the full, for Christ said what He meant and meant what He said. Yet, some affirm that when Christ said "I," He was referring to the Holy Spirit. But if Christ had had the Spirit in mind, He would have said so. Further, such language has no significance if our blessed Lord is not coming to take us home to be with Himself forever.

The testimony of heaven—confirmation: In Acts 1:10–11, two men come from heaven to tell earth what heaven believes about the return of Christ. There is no mistaking their message; it is heaven brought and heaven inspired. "This same Jesus . . . will come back in the same way you have seen him go into heaven."

Here on earth we have varied interpretations of truth. In heaven, however, all truths are viewed from the divine standpoint. These two men, then, coming directly from heaven, bring a message of consolation to the men of Galilee who are so perplexed over the sudden disappearance of Christ. The One who has left them is to return as suddenly as He went away.

The testimony of the Holy Spirit through the church—revelation: The bulk of the revelation about the advent truth is in the twenty-three books from Acts to Revelation. The classic passage is 1 Thessalonians 4:13–18 where, under divine inspiration, Paul gives us details to be found nowhere else in the New Testament. With the establishment and extension of the church, strong emphasis was given to Christ's coming. John's "Apocalypse" has the Holy Spirit and the church uniting in a plea for Christ to return. "The Spirit and the bride say, 'Come'" (22:17). It is common to use this part of the verse as the basis of a gospel invitation, but direct interpretation of the phrase is related to a joint appeal for Christ to come. The Spirit through the church, and the church through the Spirit, are calling to Jesus, "Come!" Three times over in the chapter Christ is found saying, "I am coming soon." And back goes the cry of the Spirit and the church, "Come, come Lord Jesus!"

The last word Jesus utters from the glory concerns His coming. Before the heavens close and divine revelation is completed, Christ reaffirms the message of His appearing. "Yes, I am coming soon" (22:20). Then we have the prayer of John, re-echoed by the church down the ages, "Amen. Come, Lord Jesus!" And the sacred volume closes with a benediction.

The Time of His Coming

To predict dates is to contradict the Word of God and falsify our position. Christ declares, "You do not know when that time will come" (Mark 13:33). How dare anyone journey beyond the limits of this explicit declaration? There is enough of certainty to feed the lamp of our faith and enough of uncertainty to make us careful lest when the Bridegroom comes, our lamps are out.

The day of Christ's coming is unknown. It has been marked off on God's calendar, and there we rest. He tells me that He's coming, and that's quite enough.

In studying the time element, we have three distinct groups of passages. The first group suggests uncertainty (Matthew 24:36–44; Acts 1:7; 1 Thessalonians 5:1–2); the second group indicates speed or imminence (Revelation 3:11); the third implies delay (Matthew 24:48; 25:19; Luke 19:11).

The *fact is* certain, and such is sufficient for our comfort and inspiration. The *time* is uncertain, and such is sufficient for our separation and dedication. Of this we are confident, that Christ is soon to leave the secret place of His glory and return to earth. And ours will be the delight of the old Scottish peasant who said, "I dinna ken when He is coming, but I'll be gey glad to see Him when He comes."

Christ is coming! The Scriptures declare it. Saints believe it. Redeemed souls in glory are awaiting it. Satan accepts it. Sadly, multitudes in the church are ignorant of it! May we be found among the number who, with garments washed and white, are ready to hail Christ's arrival!

The Manner of His Coming

Prophecy is often brought into disrepute through the unwise and unwarranted pronouncements of those who are called not as prophets but as interpreters of God's program for the ages. If prophecy is to win more lives, we must have saner interpreters of the prophetic Word. Surely no other realm of the Bible demands more attention to the Pauline injunction about rightly dividing the Word of Truth than that of prophecy. To strain certain parts of the Holy Writ and find in it prophecies of automobiles, airplanes, clothes rationing, modern engines of warfare, and present-day personages is evidently one way to wrongly divide the Word of Truth.

In the description Paul gives of the return of the Lord in the air, we have a triad of accompaniments: the loud command of the Lord, the voice of the archangel, the trumpet call of God (1 Thessalonians 4:16). Perhaps these three blasts are related to those participating in the rapture. The "loud command" may call the dead in Christ. Just as Lazarus came forth from his grave, so the saved dead will respond en masse to Christ's authoritative voice as the resurrection and the life. The "voice of the archangel" may be connected with those who are alive and remain; the "trumpet call of God" may summon the dead who are raised and the living who are changed to meet the Savior. This recalls the blowing of silver trumpets in Numbers 10. Three blasts guided the journeyings of the Israelites: the first and second gathered the tribes; the third commanded them to march forward.

The Resurrection of the Dead

Only some of the dead will rise: "the dead in Christ will rise first" (1 Thessalonians 4:16). The rest of the dead, the wicked dead, will remain in their graves until the time of the great white throne, when all must be raised for the ratification of the condemnation (Revelation 20:12). Here, then, is a comforting hope: our holy, happy dead are to rise again. Death will not keep its prey. According to the late Dr. A. T. Robertson, the word for "loud command," or "shout," is "an old word meaning to order, command (military command). Christ will come as a conqueror." And, as the Victor over the grave, Christ will command the graves to yield the dust of those who belonged to Him while on earth.

We believe in the resurrection of the body. He who brought the body to dust because of sin will raise the dust in the resurrection of glory. Jesus declares that God is able to raise up children out of stones, and what are stones but solidified dust? If God was able to create the body of Adam out of the dust of the earth, surely He is able to fashion the glorified body of believers out of their buried dust or ashes.

The Transformation of the Living

Next in order comes the transformation of all the living saints. "We who are still alive and are left will be caught up together with them in the clouds" (1 Thessalonians 4:17). "We will not all sleep, but we will all be changed" (1 Corinthians 15:51). So there are millions who may never die. What a wonderful experience it would be to lay aside the mortal for immortality! As a Christian, I do not shrink from death. If I have to go home by the way of a grave, God will grant me dying grace. But what a thrill it would be to be found preaching the gospel, urging sinners to repent, when Christ appears! And because we may go without dying, it is imperative so to live that if our transformation should come the very next moment, all will be well between our hearts and the Savior.

Seeing Him, we are to be changed into His likeness. "When he appears we shall be like him, for we shall see him as he is" (1 John 3:2 RSV). Like Him! What is He like? Well, what was He like when He ascended on high? How old was He? Only thirty-three years of age. He did not come to the end of His earthly sojourn an old decrepit man.

> "Not one gold hair was gray
> Upon His crucifixion day."

In His resurrected form, Jesus retains His youthfulness. "We shall be like him" means we will possess His perennial youthfulness. Ours is to be a body knowing no decay because of age. Now, the bodily infirmities of advancing years often hamper our Christian activities. But with a glorified body like Christ's, we will be able to serve Him unceasingly, day and night, forever.

Continuing his dramatic unfolding of Christ's return, Paul declares that we are to be caught up together to meet the Lord in the air. The phrase "caught up" has the thought of being snatched away out of danger—before tribulation overtakes a guilty world, the Lord removes His own. He removes His church from the hour of temptation that comes upon all the world to try those who dwell upon the earth.

The word "together" is worthy of note. First, it suggests the blissful reunion that our lonely hearts anticipate. Now we are not together. Loved ones have been called home; half of our heart is in heaven. But Christ is coming, and when He appears we will be reunited immediately to those whom we have loved and lost. Caught up together! On the way up to meet Jesus we are to have the joy of meeting our dear ones and then, arm in arm, rise to hail the blessed Lord unitedly.

The word "together" also helps slay the "partial rapture" theory, which implies that not all the saved are to be taken and that those who are not sufficiently holy must be left behind when Christ comes. Such an interpretation is entirely foreign to the concept of the church as a body. Further, our translation does not depend upon our sanctification; it is a vital part of our salvation. If we are not sufficiently holy when Christ comes, we shall suffer in respect to reward, but this is a different matter altogether. All who are Christ's at His coming are to share in the rapture. He will leave no one behind in the Egypt of this world.

Again, if our translation depends upon human merit, how are we to know when we have attained the degree of holiness that guarantees our being taken? Or who is to tell us when we have reached the necessary standard for joyful participation in the coming of Christ? Finally, when is Christ to come for the unholy saved ones left behind? Are there to be several raptures? If so, His descents will have to be numerous, which is, of course, unthinkable. We affirm that every born-again person will rise to meet Christ in the air and that the question of fitness will be dealt with at the "bema" or "judgment seat" (Romans 14:10; 2 Corinthians 5:10).

The word "together" also refers to the perfect unity of the people of God. Now they are not together; theological and denominational barriers keep them apart. Unhappy divisions, bitter estrangements prevent that unity promised to the world by the gospel. In their separate churches it is still the custom to sing, "We are not divided, all one body we," but this is only one more lie many religious people are guilty of singing. When Christ arrives in the air, all saints, irrespective of denominational label, will be caught up simply as sinners saved by grace. Our little systems and sects will end; as one complete body the church will gather around her adorable Lord.

The Meeting in the Air

These days, attention is focused on the air. And with all this air activity, we cannot get away from the fact that the devil is the prince of the power of the air. But his present abode is to become Christ's reception court, since He is to receive us unto Himself.

Those who reject the premillennial interpretation of the rapture affirm that this is the only place where the Bible connects the "air" with the coming and reject building a theory on only one reference. But since every part of the Bible is divinely inspired, one verse is sufficient to confirm our belief that Christ is to tarry in midair and that the saints will rise to meet Him just as the filings leap to the magnet.

The Judgment Seat of Christ

After meeting the Lord in the air, the saints have to meet Him in judgment before they are qualified to serve Him in any judicial or administrative capacity. Because no truth can revolutionize the life and labor of a believer like the judgment seat of Christ, let us attend to the judgment so forcibly emphasized by Paul: "If what he has built survives, he will receive his reward" (1 Corinthians 3:14); "For we must all appear before the judgment seat of Christ, that each one may receive what is due him for the things done while in the body, whether good or bad" (2 Corinthians 5:10); "You, then, why do you judge your brother? Or why do you look down on your brother? For we will all stand before God's judgment seat" (Romans 14:10).

Keep in mind that this judgment is for believers only; the judgment for unbelievers is the great white throne of Revelation 20. Thus, if we are at the first judgment, we shall not be at the second. If we are missing at the first, we must be at the second. And it is our relationship to Christ here on earth that determines the judgment we are to face.

The function of the bema, the judgment seat (2 Corinthians 5:10), varies according to differences among believers. First, it will bring about that rectification so imperative for united, eternal service. Think of it in this light: here are two believers who are not on speaking terms; once bosom friends, they had a falling out and have been estranged for years. Belonging to the same church, they often pass each other but with never a nod of recognition. Because each is truly saved, both will be caught up to meet the Lord. But they cannot be divided forever. There must be a place where all differences are ironed out and we are made to see eye to eye. Since the judgment seat of Christ is not a criminal court but a court of inquiry, we may assume that the Lord and His own are to be alone as disputes are settled and relationships harmonized.

Still, if we are at odds with a brother or a sister in the Lord, it is better to patch things up now than to have the shame of adjusting them in the light of His presence. We may sing about knowing each other better when the "mists have rolled away," but we should strive to become better acquainted with each other as we tarry amid the mists. This is not a time for strained relationships. If we have apologies to seek or give, let us act as Christians inspired by God's forgiving grace.

Further, the judgment seat will determine our place and position in coming glory. "Fire will test the quality of each man's work" (1 Corinthians 3:13), and this test reveals our fitness for cooperation with Christ in His governmental control of earth. While we cannot work for heaven, we can certainly work like slaves for our responsibilities to heaven. Faithfulness to the Lord and His Word is the basis of reward, as the parable of the talents makes clear. We will not all be on the same level in glory. Many will stand before the Judge with a saved soul but a lost life. There will be no souls to their credit, no stars in their crown.

The great majority of Christians lose sight of the fact that they are presently developing themselves for future positions in Christ's kingdom. To reign with Him depends upon the loyalty and faithfulness of life and service here. If we are to have an abundant entrance into His presence, we must experience the more abundant life as we continue serving Him on earth. May God grant to each of us grace to reach for the best! If we want the Master's benediction and promotion to higher service, we must determine to be "good and faithful" until the glorious day breaks.

The Marriage Supper

The marriage supper of the Lamb, as mentioned by John in Revelation 19:7–9, describes the culmination of the fellowship between Christ as the Bridegroom and the church as the bride. With C. I. Scofield, we believe that "the bride, the wife of Lamb" (21:9) is the church identified with the "heavenly Jerusalem" (Hebrews 12:22) and to be distinguished from the adulterous and repudiated "wife" of Jehovah yet to be restored (Isaiah 54:1–10; Hosea 2:1–17), who is identified with the earth (Hosea 2:23). A forgiven and restored *wife* could not be called either a "virgin" (2 Corinthians 11:2–3) or a "bride."

The emphasis here is in the phrase "his bride has made herself *ready*" (19:7). What readiness is this? Not the readiness of salvation, which was made possible on earth, but the readiness of participation. Now there is harmony and union so the bride can go forward with the Bridegroom. Everything has been put right among believers, and between believers and their Lord, hence the nuptial ceremony. And what glorious years and experiences we are to have together! Holy intimacy, perfect love, heavenly harmony, and unclouded fellowship are to characterize the Lord and His own forever!

Seven Principles of Prophetic Study

Prophecy is not a subject we can study at will, as a person might pursue a hobby. We are *commanded* to study prophecy as an aspect of divine revelation. "Do your best to present yourself to God as one approved,... who correctly handles the word of truth" (2 Timothy 2:15). Unless we give our ourselves to an understanding of eschatology, we do not correctly handle the Scriptures.

The study of prophecy, it will be found, both gladdens and saddens. As we contemplate the glorious future of both the church and the Jews, we are thrilled. Truly, the best is yet to be! On the other hand, as we meditate upon the certain and terrible judgment awaiting the godless, sorrow fills our heart.

Prophecy, however, demands the recognition of seven principles, and because of quickened interest in the doctrine of last things, we need to consider these principles for our particular study.

First Principle: It is essential to have had an experience of the regenerating work of the Holy Spirit

The natural man, says the Apostle Paul, cannot receive the things of the Spirit of God—and prophecy is among these things. This unrenewed, unsaved man, even although he is cultured and religious, cannot comprehend the deep things of God, since they can be discerned only by the Spirit. We must therefore be born of and indwelt by the Spirit if we would understand the times (1 Corinthians 2:14). "The LORD confides in those who fear him; he makes his covenant known to them" (Psalm 25:14).

The world's history is made up of covenants, but they can be revealed only to those who are spiritually fit. Except a man be born again, he cannot see anything fascinating in prophetic truths; they are foolishness to him. But to one truly born again, how different such things of God are.

Second Principle: One must believe the Bible to be the prophetic Word

Peter says, "We have the word of the prophets made more certain, . . . as to a light shining in a dark place" (2 Peter 1:19). The Scriptures are the only safe prophetic guide. They alone contain God's blueprint of the future. What a difference it would make to those who are planning programs for a weary world if they recognized this truth! Sadly, however, most of our diplomats and rulers are totally ignorant of what God has recorded about the present and future condition of the world.

Accepting as we do the "harmony of the prophetic Word" (to use Dr. A. C. Gaebelein's phrase), we must remember that only about one-fourth of the Bible is taken up with prophecy. We must preserve the same balance in our presentation of God's full-ordered Word. We must not be guilty of overemphasizing any part but must strive for equal emphasis of each part.

Third Principle: There must be complete reliance upon the Holy Spirit, whose prerogative it is to show us things to come (John 16:13)

As the Author of the sacred Scriptures, the Holy Spirit knows the mind of God concerning past, present, or future matters and can draw aside the veil accordingly. Any phase of truth is revelation. Therefore, prayerfully dependent upon the Spirit, we petition Him, "Teach me what I cannot see" (Job 34:32).

Is this not what accounts for the gifts of clear exposition that many who are ordinary folk manifest regarding the inner significance of the divine program of the ages? What is hid from those who, in their own estimation, are wise and prudent is revealed to all who have childlike trust. "When he, the Spirit of truth comes, he will guide you into all truth" (John 16:13).

Fourth Principle: Grasp the broad prophetic outline

We must never be dogmatic in the interpretation of details. In essential things—unity. In doubtful things—liberty. In all things—charity. As to the texture of prophetic tapestry, it will greatly help to remember that as we distinguish the dispensations, the Scriptures harmonize. Briefly stated, future events are grouped around the return of Christ for His church and her judgment at the bema, the marriage supper, and her share in the governmental control of the earth. Upon the earth, following the rapture will come the completing of the prophetic picture: the Great Tribulation period with its emergence of the antichrist and the false prophet, the grouping of world forces, the persecution of the Jews, the descent of Christ, the dealing with godless powers as He ushers in His reign of one thousand years, the little season, the great white throne, and the new heavens and new earth.

Fifth Principle: When studying prophecy, guard against extremes in interpretations and applications

We only drag the truth into disrepute when we treat the Bible as a prophetic curiosity shop. Prophecy does not consist in choosing dates, forecasting future events, and interpreting signs—seeing airplanes in the flying birds of Isaiah 31:5 and world leaders in the latter part of Daniel 11. In all phases of Bible study we must first discover the interpretation of a text and then make our application. It is against all the rules of Bible interpretation to confine ourselves to application or, as is often the case, to allow the imagination full play when it comes to application.

Stressing a prayerful dependence upon the Holy Spirit as we seek enlightenment, we will, at the same time, follow the guidance of sane and spiritual teachers. The diligent and independent study of prophecy need not preclude appropriating the fruit of minds deeply taught in the Word. Truth comes to us through others, so that we in turn may teach still others. "And the things you have heard me say in the presence of many witnesses entrust to reliable men who will also be qualified to teach others" (2 Timothy 2:2).

Sixth Principle: We must keep our eyes on the Lord Jesus around whom all prophecy moves

"For the testimony of Jesus is the spirit of prophecy" (Revelation 19:10). That Christ is the Key of all Scripture is evident from the fact that in any Scripture He opened He expounded the things concerning *Him-*

self. Sadly, we can be taken up with the dispensations and details of prophecy but miss the One who is coming. Surely the study of prophecy misses its objective if it obscures the face of Him to whom all the prophets gave witness. We may disagree on minor matters, but of this we are confident, Jesus *Himself* is coming again. The study before us is far more fascinating and sanctifying when we keep on looking for Christ, who is the central Figure in the prophetic puzzle. We will find that the sacred writers of Scripture never journey far from Him, who is coming to fulfill all predictions of His future glory.

Seventh Principle: We can secure the utmost spiritual good from the study of prophecy only if we associate it with practical aims

There must be the constant application of the truth to the problems of life. The apostles were not visionaries when they wrote of the future. Christ's coming was always related to some aspect of duty. Without love the gift of prophecy is profitless. "If I have the gift of prophecy . . . but have not love, I am nothing" (1 Corinthians 13:2). Accepting the blessed hope as a part of our faith, we must be strangers to all ungodliness. With the hope of the Second Coming burning within our heart, we must be pure. "Dear friends, now we are children of God, and what we will be has not yet been made known. But we know that when he appears, we shall be like him, for we shall see him as he is. Everyone who has this hope in him purifies himself, just as he is pure" (1 John 3:2–3).

With such a blessed hope in view
We would more holy be;
More like our risen, glorious Lord,
Whose face we soon shall see.

The Order of Events

The book of Revelation is a unified whole that provides a prophetic outline of the course of church history from the apostolic period to its translation at Christ's return and of the subsequent judgments to overtake a godless, guilty world. The style of Revelation is apocalyptic; its great drama unfolds on a scale of peerless grandeur as the earth staggers under the shock of battle and the strokes of judgment. Exposed to view are the unending horrors of the Abyss and the eternal joys of heaven.

The order of events is as follows:

1. The present age will culminate in apostasy and a period of unprecedented trial. The "man of sin" will be fully manifested, will assume political supremacy, and will claim religious homage.

2. The true church of Christ will be raptured to heaven, and the man of sin will establish a covenant with the Jews. But he will violate his agreement with the Jews, gather forces against them from other nations, and seek to destroy God's ancient people.

3. Christ will appear in great glory and will destroy the man of sin and the false prophet. He will cast the devil, who inspired them, into the bottomless pit for a thousand years.

4. The millennial period will then be inaugurated. Sin will be suppressed but not exterminated. Christ will rule with a rod of iron, and universal peace and blessing will be enjoyed.

5. The loosing of Satan will result in the deception of the nations who follow him in earth's last revolt. This will be met by disastrous punishment for the rebels and their leader.

6. The last judgment will be set up, and Christ as the supreme Judge will preside at the condemnation of the ungodly.

7. The eternal age, with its permanent destinies, will begin after Jesus delivers up the kingdom to the Father. Then God will be all in all.

The Sign of the Cross

The book of Revelation is marked with the sign of the cross, the conflict that centers on the person of Christ as the Lamb slain from before the foundation of the world. Revelation highlights suffering faith and enduring hope. The grim struggle between light and darkness is depicted in vivid colors. Little mention is made of love, but much of wrath. Whatever changing events mark the progress of the conflict, the ultimate outcome is never in doubt.

The rivalry between the powers of light and darkness is illustrated in a series of contrasts:

- The servants of God are sealed; the antichrist seals his followers.
- The church is seen as a woman clothed with the sun; the antichrist's apostate church is seen as a woman decked with jewels.
- The Lamb, once slain, is alive again; the beast with a deadly head wound lives again.
- Jehovah is worshiped; the antichrist claims worship.
  Christ has His true prophets; the antichrist has his false prophet.

Because the book is a revelation of Christ, we expect it to be full of Him—and it is! Christ's Person and work dominate its pages. G. Campbell Morgan rightly observes that "any study of Revelation which does not concentrate upon Christ, and does not view all else in relation to Him, must bring the reader into an inextricable labyrinth." Consider the following two points.

1. The entire book revolves around Christ as the Lamb:
- chapter 1: the vision of the Lamb
- chapters 2 and 3: the message of the Lamb
- chapters 4 and 5: the adoration of the Lamb
- chapters 6 to 19: the wrath of the Lamb
- chapter 19:7–10: the marriage of the Lamb
  chapter 19:11–22: the reign of the Lamb

2. Christ is the strong golden thread, uniting the epistle through His kingly names, His strong attributes, and the victories of His First Coming and His Second Coming.
- His names include: Jesus Christ (1:1); Jesus (22:26; etc.); Lord Jesus (22:20; etc.); Lord Jesus Christ (22:21; etc.); the Christ (20:4, 6); the Christ of God (11:15; 12:10); the Lamb (over 20 times); the King of Kings (19:16; etc.); Faithful and True (19:11); the Word of God (19:13); the Unknown Name (19:12); the Root and Offspring of David (22:16); the Bright and Morning Star (22:16).

- His attributes include: He is both divine and human, the possessor of two natures (5:15; 22:16); He is the First and the Last, and everything in between (1:17; 2:8); He is the Living Word of God (19:13); He is the Searcher of Hearts (2:23); He is the Ancient of Days (1:14); He is the object of worship and praise (5:8–14; 7:12).
- His victories include: He is faithful in His witness to God and His Word (1:5; 3:14); He is the Conqueror of Satan (3:21; 5:5; 20:10); He is the Crucified One (5:6, 12; 7:14; 13:8); He is the Atoning One (1:5; 7:14; 22:14); He is the Risen One (1:18; 2:8; 3:21; 22:1–2); He is the Exalted King (1:5; 3:7; 17:14); He is the Coming One (1:7; 19:11, 19; 22:20).

SECTION ONE:
THE PRESENT CHURCH AGE

■　　■　　■

Revelation 1–3

From Pentecost
to the Rapture of the Church

1

Introduction to the Book of Revelation

Revelation 1:1–11

On the island of Patmos . . . on the Lord's Day I was in the Spirit, and I heard behind me a loud voice . . . which said, "Write on a scroll what you see and send it to the seven churches." (Revelation 1:9–11)

> To desert island banished
> With God the exile dwells
> And sees the future glory
> His mystic writing tells. (Ancient Latin Hymn)

Prison literature (including Paul's Prison Epistles and John Bunyan's *Pilgrim's Progress*) enriches the life of the church! Banished to the island of Patmos, John in his lonely cell received the most remarkable revelation ever granted. To the west was Rome, the city of seven hills; to the east were Palestine, the Euphrates River, and Babylon. Amid these geographical surroundings—which figure prominently in Revelation—the Apostle John received his vision.

No one was better fitted than John to act as the appointed channel of this sublime revelation. This is evident from what the Gospels record of his intimate fellowship with Christ. John was Christ's close friend, whom He loved very much. He is also pictured as leaning upon the bosom of Jesus. And it was John who wrote the words of Jesus regarding the Spirit's ability to show the servants of Christ "what must soon take place" (Revelation 1:1; 22:6).

The Setting

In authoritative fashion the apostle begins this section with his own name: "John, To the seven churches in the province of Asia" (1:4). Similarly emphatic is the phrase in verse 9: "I, John." The word *apostello* means "to send forth" and describes a messenger commissioned to undertake some important mission. This is how the term is applied to Christ (Hebrews 3:1). As John begins the communication of the revelation sent to him (1:1), he affirms his authority as an apostle, or "sent one." What he is about to announce was not of his own creation. As a God-sent messenger, John is going to describe "everything he saw" (1:2). In the "I, John" of verse 9, the apostle proclaims the opening of the book containing the Second Coming of Christ. In the "I, Jesus" of 22:20, Christ announces His own Second Coming.

John was a saint and knew much about long periods of communion and meditation; it was during one of these seasons of spiritual reflection, on a Lord's Day, that he found himself transported by the Spirit into the heavenly realms. Thus his own meditative nature, and the sweet and precious memories of Christ, prepared him for extraordinary visions. This transference of the inner being to another realm was also experienced by other Bible saints, who likewise received visions and revelations by a supernatural power, apart from their own natural mind. Their natural powers were held in abeyance while dominated or controlled by the Spirit (see 1 Kings 18:12; Isaiah 6; Ezekiel 3:12, 14; 37:1; Acts 8:39; 2 Corinthians 12).

The combination of the two phrases "on the island of Patmos" and "in the Spirit" (1:9–10) prove that geographical limitations are no hindrance to spiritual vision. Patmos was the sphere, but the Spirit was the atmosphere. The extremely dreary and inhospitable island on the Aegean Sea was no barrier to John's reception of the unveiling of Christ.

All that John saw while in his ecstatic condition was divinely authoritative; hence the constant refrain, "These words are trustworthy and true" (19:9; 22:6–10). What John witnessed he had to write down. Guided by the Spirit, he recorded his sublime revelation. Twelve times John was told to *write*. We may not be able to write volumes, but what we do write can *say* volumes if we record what we receive by the Spirit. What Ezekiel saw in vision he had to transcribe and tell (Ezekiel 12:21–25). With Paul's heavenly revelations it was different: when caught up into paradise, he heard unspeakable words, but his lips were sealed as to what he saw and heard (2 Corinthians 12:1–7). The thorn in his flesh prevented him from exalting above measure in the abundance of his revelations. But in John's case, again and again he warns us about keeping those things he received and recorded (Revelation 1:3, etc.).

How impoverished the church would have been if John had failed to record the revelation granted him by the Holy Spirit! But John obeyed the divine voice and gave the churches of his time this precious unfolding, with the exhortation that it must be read and with the promise that a divine blessing would rest upon all who read the record and obeyed its instructions.

The Recipients of the Letter

The original readers of Revelation were the members of the churches in Asia Minor, which was remarkable for the number and wealth of its cities. The seven churches named in Revelation were important centers from which the gospel spread eastward and westward. Revelation is for the church universal and for all the churches of succeeding generations. Here Christ reveals Himself to "all the churches" (2:23; 22:16). What a mighty spiritual renewal would be experienced today if all churches lived in the light of this final book of the Bible!

From Ephesus, John had directed the churches of Asia Minor in spiritual matters. This continued while he was a prisoner of Rome on the island of Patmos near the end of the reign of Emperor Domitian (probably about A.D. 90). However, Tertullian, one of the early church fathers, felt that Revelation was written during Nero's persecution, around A.D. 64. Modern scholars favor this earlier date.

The purpose of Revelation is indicated in its prologue. The book was written to show us the things that "must soon take place." This corresponds with the activities of the Holy Spirit, which include guiding us into all truth and showing us things to come (see John 16:13).

Although some theologians dispute the Johannine authorship of Revelation, their objections do not move us from the position that John, the beloved disciple (who wrote the Gospel of John and the three Epistles of John), was also the writer of Revelation. The testimony of the early church cannot be ignored. Revelation is quoted with the author's name earlier than any other New Testament book except 1 Corinthians. In his Gospel and Epistles John writes in the third person, but in Revelation he names himself four times (1:1, 4, 9; 22:8) and writes in the first person.

In most cases the writers of Holy Scripture did not title their respective books. The title of Revelation is not "the revelation of Saint John the divine," as if to suggest that the apostle possessed some special sanctity. The book contains "the revelation of Jesus Christ . . . to his servant John (1:1). John was the recipient, not the author, of Revelation. Often the book is referred to as "the Revelations," but while it contains various visions that John received while in the Spirit, these were essentially one, being received in one day, namely, "the Lord's Day" (1:10). The unity of the whole book is expressed in the two opening words, "The revelation."

Some people think we should treat Revelation as an enigma—the more we study it the less we understand it. But this book is a *revelation*. It is not a mystery, not a covering up. The name means an unveiling, an uncovering, a drawing aside of a curtain to show something that can no longer be concealed. True, Revelation is highly symbolic, but there is hardly a symbol in the book that is not explained in some other part of Scripture. In fact, Revelation contains some three hundred allusions to other parts of Scripture. Therefore, we must seek to compare Scripture with Scripture.

What was sealed to Daniel would be made clear at the end-time period of the Gentile age: "Those who are wise shall understand" (Daniel 12:9–10). Events mentioned by Daniel are now fully revealed by God to His servants. To the undiscerning mind much of Revelation may appear dark, inexplicable, impossible to comprehend; but to those who wait upon the Spirit, its plan and purpose are clear. Yet in all our efforts to understand Revelation, we must bear in mind the wise comment of Bishop John Newton (1725–1807) that explaining the book of Revelation perfectly is not the work of one person or of one age, and it probably will not be clearly understood until all has been fulfilled.

The book of Revelation has long been a battleground between differing systems of interpretation.

- *Idealists* deny any historical or prophetical meaning of Revelation. Instead, they regard the book as simply providing symbolic presentations, applicable to all times and eras, of the conflict between good and evil and of the ultimate victory of good.

- *Preterists* relegate everything in Revelation to the past, believing that almost all the prophecies of the book have already been fulfilled. (The bulk of those prophecies relate to the destruction of Jerusalem and the fall of Rome during the early centuries of the Christian era.) However, when prophecy becomes history, it ceases to be prophecy. Revelation is distinctly referred to as *prophecy*.
- *Historicists* interpret Revelation as a progressive study of the fortunes of the church from her commencement to her consummation. Those who hold this continuous-historical view assert that the prophecies are partly fulfilled and partly unfulfilled, with some being fulfilled before our very eyes.
- *Futurists* include two major groups: simple and extreme. The *simple futurists* accept the first three chapters of Revelation as fulfilled, and all that follows as referring to the coming appearance of Christ. The *extreme futurists* regard all of Revelation as referring to the Lord's coming, with the first three chapters being a prediction of the Jews after the first resurrection.
- *Tribulationists* have two schools. Some believe the church is not raptured at the end of chapter 3 but remains on the earth through the first three-and-a-half years of the Tribulation and is not caught up until the last trumpet in Revelation 11:15. Advocates of this interpretation say we must follow the church through the seals and the trumpets. The visible church is to go through the whole of the Tribulation, but the *invisible* church is to be raptured just before the last half of this terrible period of judgment breaks upon the guilty earth. Other tribulationists take the church through the entire Tribulation. They believe that Christ will not return for His own until He comes in glory and power.

What are we to make of these different interpretations? The tribulationists fail to realize that the seals, trumpets, and bowls are related to judgment and apply to Jews and Gentiles. The church, then, cannot be on earth after chapter 3 because it is not the subject of judicial judgment. Rather, *the Lord will save His own from the horrors of the Tribulation:* "Since you have kept my command to endure patiently, I will also keep you from the hour of trial that is going to come upon the whole world to test those who live on the earth" (Revelation 3:10; see also 1 Thessalonians

1:10). Because prophecy is frequently progressive or cumulative, the historical and futurist interpretative systems can be combined. Those who lived in John's day and suffered much at the hands of Rome saw some fulfillment in what John wrote. But the persecutions of the first century did not exhaust John's predictions, for these point on to complete fulfillment. In Revelation 1:19, John himself gives us the words of Christ as a guide to interpreting the book:

- "Write, therefore, what you have seen"—the past—referring to the glorious vision that John speaks of in chapter 1.
- "What is now"—the present—church history as outlined in chapters 2 and 3.
  "What will take place later"—the future—all that is to follow the rapture of the church, as shown in chapters 4–22.

The complete fulfillment of this section is therefore future. Then the predictions and promises of the prophets will be realized, and the kingdom of the Messiah will be set up.

J. B. Phillips outlines five important lessons we can learn from the book of Revelation:

1. The absolute sovereignty of God results in His ultimate purpose to destroy all forms of evil.

2. The inevitable judgments of God will come upon evil, especially the worship of false gods, which include riches, power, and success.

3. The necessity for patient endurance is based on the knowledge that God is in control of all history.

4. The existence of reality (represented under such symbols as the New Jerusalem, apart and secure from the battles and tribulations of earthly life) promises complete spiritual security to those who are faithful to God and His Christ.

5. The glimpse of worship and adoration constantly offered to God and the Lamb demonstrates man's ultimate acknowledgment of the character of God when he sees God as He is.

2

Sevenfold Portrait of the Son of Man

Revelation 1

I saw seven golden lampstands, and among the lampstands was someone "like a son of man." (Revelation 1:12)

In this section John provides an awesome description of the One whose voice he heard. Symbols of function and symbols of character are here identified with the Son of Man, who shares full and complete deity. The seven parts of the full-length portrait of Christ are easily discernible, and all the features (as we shall indicate more fully) are scattered among the churches. This portrait also depicts the vast difference between our Lord's past sorrow and His future sovereignty. At last we see the once-scorned Jesus crowned forever as the King of Kings and Lord of Lords!

The book of Revelation is about the person and power of Christ, with manifold symbols of His activities, functions, and character. Here we see Jesus related to time and eternity, and to the Jew, the Gentile, and the church of God. The first chapter shows Christ as the heavenly One with a human appearance. Deity and humanity are combined, and the heavenly and the earthly are marvelously mingled together (1:9–18). What a vast difference there is between our Lord's past sorrow and His future sovereignty! At last we see Jesus (once the object of shame, scorn, and contempt) crowned with honor and glory.

First: His Garments (Revelation 1:13)

Dressed in a robe reaching down to his feet. (Revelation 1:13)

In the midst of the seven candlesticks, there appears someone "like a son of man," clothed with a garment down to the foot and girt about the breasts with a golden girdle. Christ's position—in the midst of the church (symbolized by the seven candlesticks)—declares Him to be the head and central power of the church. Christ's title—the Son of Man—identifies Him with humanity and judgment.

Christ's clothing declares His kingly authority and the majesty of His priesthood. The allusion is to the beautiful garments of the high priest under the Levitical order and indicates the personal qualities and official position of the priest.

Christ's garment was down to the feet, but it did not cover them. Otherwise John would not have seen their nailprints and worshiped his Lord, whose glorified form was properly clothed. At Calvary Jesus lost all His garments to the gamblers, but now He is clothed in His beautiful robe as the Great High Priest. "His clothes became as white as the light" (Matthew 17:2).

Christ also had "a golden sash around his chest." When the sash, or girdle, is around the loins it implies service (as in John 13:4–5), but around the chest it implies dignified priestly judgment. Being of gold, the sash pictures Christ's deity and His righteous kingship. As for the chest, these can imply either calm and repose or else preparation for judgment.

Robed as the King-Priest, Christ was not seen by John as the Priest of the golden altar with the censer and the burning incense, but rather among the candlesticks with the golden snuffers. It is as though He were inquiring for the last time whether the lamps of the sanctuary would burn worthy of the place, or whether He would be compelled to remove them soon. All the figures of speech that follow express judgment—the revelation of a priest, not at the altar with incense even at the lampstand with oil to feed it, but with snuffers to judge and trim the smoky wicks.

This initial vision was not about the pastoral grace of Christ, but His judicial authority. Thus Revelation must be viewed as a book of judgment. Various "judge" words appear thirteen times in the book. The seven churches are depicted as being in the place of this judgment, which must always begin at the house of God (see 1 Peter 4:17).

Second: His Head and Hair (Revelation 1:14)

His head and hair were white like wool, as white as snow. (Revelation 1:14)

Christ's white, uncovered head easily distinguished the glorified Person being revealed. The whiteness of wool and snow, used by Isaiah to describe the cleansing of the heart from the foulness of sin (Isaiah 1:18), here symbolizes the absolute purity and agelessness of the Savior, whose shed blood alone can cleanse from the vileness of sin and enable us to walk with Him in white garments.

The uncovered, majestic head of the Son of Man conveys the idea of mature experience and of perfected wisdom coupled with immaculate holiness. Daniel had a similar vision of the one who as the Ancient of Days had a garment as white as snow and whose hair was white like wool (Daniel 7:9).

Christ's transfiguration was a preview of the Patmos vision. Peter, James, and John were eyewitnesses of Christ's majesty and were overawed as they saw His face shining with brilliant white light (Matthew 17:2). For a moment they saw His glory as the only begotten of the Father.

With us, white hair is a token of old age, decay, and nearness to the grave. But this is not implied here in Revelation, for the white-haired one whom John saw is ageless, deathless, and eternal. From eternity to eternity Jesus is the same, and His years have no end.

Christ always retains the dew of His youth, yet He has always been venerable in the eternal wisdom and glory He had with the Father from before the foundation of the world. John, who once saw the head and hairs of his Lord crowned with thorns, now beholds them crowned with the diadem of heaven's glory.

Third: His Eyes (Revelation 1:14)

His eyes were like blazing fire. (Revelation 1:14)

The Bible has much to say about the eyes of the Lord, which run to and fro throughout the earth (2 Chronicles 16:9) and are in every place (Proverbs 15:3). Eyes as well as tongues have a way of speaking, and the eyes of the Lord beholding the evil and the good indicate divine discernment, deep penetration, and intimate knowledge. As for the "blazing fire," this represents perfect understanding and the ability to search out the very thoughts, intents, and motives of the heart. Everything is exposed by those piercing eyes, and no one can escape their scrutiny.

All who see the Lord when He returns in His glory will see His eyes flashing forth as a flame of fire (Revelation 19:19). Revelation is a book of fire, for the word "fire" occurs nineteen times in it. Those flamelike eyes of Christ—always fixed on the moving scene of human life, and untiring in reading human hearts and the true meaning of all human events and actions—will burn up all that is alien to their holy gaze when their Possessor comes back to earth in His blood-dipped garments. "Nothing in all creation is hidden from God's sight. Everything is uncovered and laid bare before the eyes of him to whom we must give account" (Hebrews 4:13).

When Christ was on earth, His loving eyes were often wet with tears over the sins and sorrow of those around Him. Surely there is no passage in Holy Scripture so moving and revealing as the one describing Christ's grief over the death of one He loved: "Jesus wept" (John 11:35).

But the eyes that John saw here in Revelation were red with judgment, not tears. How grateful we should be that through grace we will not see the scathing look of those eyes as they search out and destroy all that is antagonistic to the divine will!

Fourth: His Feet (Revelation 1:15)

His feet were like bronze glowing in a furnace. (Revelation 1:15)

Although the glorified Son of Man was "dressed in a robe reaching down to his feet" (1:13), the feet were not hidden but visible, shining like polished brass. Those feet were bare, even as the feet of the ministering priests of Israel had been bare. They were like fine, burnished brass. As Phillips translates it, "His feet shone as the finest bronze blown in the furnace." The idea is that brass becomes white only in a furnace of intense heat. Such brass is almost intolerable to human gaze.

Brass symbolizes not only strength and endurance (Psalm 107:16; Zechariah 6:1; Micah 4:13) but also the firmness of divine judgment, as seen at the brazen altar and the brazen serpent (Exodus 27:1–7; Numbers 21:8–9). As a composite metal produced by fire, brass is the symbol of the wrath of a thrice-holy God upon sin and sinners. As for the feet, they suggest an unfettered, holy walk as well as the powerful triumph of judgment. Those blessed feet that once walked the streets of Jerusalem on errands of mercy, that a sinful woman washed with her tears and cruel men tore with nails at Calvary, are now the feet of the Avenger as He comes to tread down His foes (see Ezekiel 22:17–22).

Fifth: His Voice (Revelation 1:15)

His voice was like the sound of rushing waters . . . out of his mouth came a sharp double-edged sword. (Revelation 1:15–16)

We group voice and mouth because they go together, one being necessary to the use of the other. *Voice* and *sound* in 1:15 are both translated from the same Greek word, *phōnē*. The book of Revelation is a book of the *voice*, which John uses fifty-five times. The thunderous voice that John heard corresponds to the voice of "the Ancient of Days," described by Daniel as "the voice of a multitude" (Daniel 10:6). *Waters* are a symbol of raging, turbulent nations (Revelation 16:4–5; 17:15). When Christ appears in judgment, His clear, distinct, authoritative voice will calm the clamor of earth. No one will be able to resist the overwhelming power and tranquillity of His utterance. When He utters His voice, the earth will melt.

Sixth: His Right Hand (Revelation 1:16)

In his right hand he held seven stars . . . He placed his right hand on me . . . The seven stars that you saw in my right hand. (Revelation 1:16–17, 20)

"The right hand" is used often in Scripture and denotes a position of divine or supreme authority, as well as power and protection (Ephesians 1:20; Hebrews 1:3). We often hear a qualified person referred to as "my right-hand man," implying someone who has authority delegated to him and is indispensable. Being at God's right hand, Christ always acts as His Father would. Holding us in His right hand suggests that we are empowered to serve as He would if He were still here on earth.

What assurance John must have had when, overawed by the dazzling vision of his glorified Lord, he felt Christ's right hand upon him and heard His tender voice say, "Do not be afraid" (1:17). This was the same voice he had heard when he and the other disciples were toiling against the contrary waves and Jesus bade them not to be afraid. John knew a great deal about that compelling right hand of the Master. Had he not seen it heal the leper, raise sinking Peter, touch the wounded ear of Malchus, and break the loaves lifted up in benediction? Now the same hand is stretched out to reassure John that the Master he dearly loved was alive forever and had in His right hand the keys of hell and of death.

The Apostle John informs us that the seven stars in Christ's right hand are the angels of the seven churches. What does this mean? Some interpreters have understood the stars to refer to guardian angels, but this view is difficult to reconcile with angelic warning and reproof (2:4–5) and with angelic promise and encouragement (2:10). Others think the stars or angels represent the ideal embodiment of the church, just as the forces of nature are presented as God's messengers.

The most usual and widely adopted interpretation of the stars or angels of the churches is that they represent the chief ministers or presiding elders of a congregation, the equivalent of bishops or elders (the spiritual overseers of the early church). Some scholars suggest that the term is derived from the Jewish synagogue staff, where the messenger's recognized office was known by the title "angel of the synagogue." Lightfoot's comment should be borne in mind: "It is conceivable, indeed, that a bishop or chief pastor should be called an angel, or messenger of God, or of Christ, but he would hardly be styled an angel of the church over which he presides."

It is assuring to know that all who serve the Lord in responsible positions are in His right hand, the place of possession and security (John 10:28–30). Bible expositor Walter Scott has this to say,

> A scripturally constituted ministry where all was in place, and every endowment of the Spirit was exercised under the Lordship of Christ might well be spoken of as "in His right hand."

The stars are declared to be the angels or representatives of the churches. The angel of the church is the symbolical representative of the assembly seen in those responsible in it, which indeed all really are (1:20). The "stars," as a symbol are the expression of—

1. Countless multitudes (Genesis 15:5)

2. Eminent persons in authority, civil and ecclesiastical (Daniel 8:10; Revelation 6:13; 12:4).

3. Lesser or subordinate powers in general (Genesis 37:9; Revelation 12:1).

All church authority, all ministry, and all spiritual rule in every assembly is vested in Christ. His competency to give or withhold, to preserve and sustain every true minister of God is the fundamental idea in the stars being in His right hand. When the eternal security of believers is in question they are said to be in His hand and in the Father's hand, from whence no power can pluck them. But they are not said to be in His "*right* hand" as here.

Spiritual leaders—we do not say official ones, for all such have not been set in the church of God—are held and maintained in the right hand of the Son of Man. *The right hand* betokens supreme authority and honor (Psalm 110:1; Ephesians 1:20). What a responsible, yet withal honorable position every ruler in the church occupies. Daniel 12:3 points to a future class of Jewish ministers or rulers. Jude 13 refers to a class of Christian apostates.

When Jesus was in the world, going about doing good, His hands were always active in relieving people's physical and material needs. But the only reward He received for the benefactions of His holy hands was to have them torn apart by nails. Now, the ones redeemed by His blood are safe in those hands, which are well able to preserve, protect, and provide for all they hold. Are we among the *stars* in His right hand? If so, then we have the responsibility to shine. This is the night of our Lord's absence from the earth, and we as saints collectively and individually are the light of the world. As light bearers amid gathering darkness, we must reflect something of His glory.

Seventh: His Face (Revelation 1:16)

His face was like the sun shining in all its brilliance. (Revelation 1:16)

John was overwhelmed as he beheld "the brightness of His glory" (compare 2 Thessalonians 2:8; Hebrews 1:3). The things of earth must have become strangely dim as the apostle gazed upon the undimmed glory of Jesus Christ, of which His transfiguration had been but a glimpse. ("His face shone like the sun," Matthew 17:2.) While Christ was on earth, His eternal majesty was veiled, but now John witnesses His imperial glory and magnificence. The face is the window of the soul, and now all that Christ is within Himself shines forth in beauteous glory.

There is, of course, a vast difference between the glory of the sun and that of the planets (1 Corinthians 15:41). The sun does not borrow light from any source, but is a self-contained source of light and power. But the planets are mere reflectors of what they receive from the sun. Jesus has a transcendent glory all His own, and it is emphasized in a threefold way: to the world, He is its Light (John 8:12); to Israel, He is the Sun of righteousness (Malachi 4:2); to the church, He is the bright Morning Star (Revelation 22:16).

In Christ's humiliation, His face was marred beyond human appearance. At one time it was covered with vile spittle (Matthew 26:67), but now it beams with an uncreated glory, more brilliant than the midday tropical sun. May the light of that blessed countenance always be upon us! (See Numbers 6:25–26; Psalm 42:11; 43:5.)

What was John's response to this blinding vision of Christ? "When I saw him, I fell at his feet as though dead" (1:17). The Scriptures record the overpowering effects of the glorious vision of the Lord in the experience of other saints. Moses, Joshua, Job, Isaiah, Daniel, and Peter all knew what it was to behold His glory; and in beholding it they saw their own sin and weakness, and fell prostrate at His feet. Isaiah said, "I am a man of unclean lips, . . . my eyes have seen the King, the LORD Almighty" (Isaiah 6:5). John had often pillowed his head on his Master's bosom, but now he falls at His feet as though dead. Although John was the most loving and loved of the disciples, nothing avails now—not even the strength of human affection—in the light of the magnificent, resplendent glory of his Master. Many things have to die in our lives when we are bathed in such glory.

After John had fallen as dead at Christ's feet, Jesus reassured him with the words, "Do not be afraid. I am the First and the Last. I am the Living One; I was dead, and behold I am alive for ever and ever! And I hold the keys of death and Hades" (1:17–18).

That gracious right hand of Jesus raised John from his prostrate position, and the voice like the sound of many waters was heard in its consoling tones. The Master's reassuring "do not be afraid," so often repeated by Him, again fell on the ears of the apostle John, comforting him with the fact that His Lord was unchanged—that the heart that beat tenderly in Galilee still throbs with love toward His own—though He is in the glory.

Having calmed John's fears, Christ then announces a message rich with hope. As "the First and the Last," He reaffirms His deity, eternity, and absolute supremacy. He is the beginning and the end, and everything in between (1:8). As "the Living One," He proclaims Himself to be the source of life. Life did not commence for Christ at Bethlehem; His birth only revealed what had been His from eternity.

As the One who became dead, Jesus indicated the voluntary aspect of His death, for His life was not *taken* but *given.* Having power to lay down His life, He dismissed His spirit (Matthew 27:50).

As the One who is alive forevermore, Jesus proclaimed that He would never again feel the sting of death: "Behold I am alive for ever and ever" (Revelation 1:18).

As the One who holds "the keys of death and Hades," Christ expressed His complete mastery over the bodies and souls of all people and His absolute authority to open and shut (Revelation 3:7–8). Walter Scott says:

> This intimates His absolute authority over death and Hades, the respective jailers of the dead, and is exercised at His sovereign pleasure. Satan has not now the power of death (Hebrews 2:14). (For the force of *key* as a symbol of undisputed authority, see Isaiah 22:22 and Matthew 16:19.)

Having conquered death, the foe that humans have ever dreaded, and having proved Himself the Master of the clouded region into which humans are ushered by death, Jesus offers Himself to us as the Lord of life and liberty. Through faith in Him we live on, and always will, because as the great Lifegiver He can never again be bound by death. Whether we enter heaven by the way of the grave or the air makes little difference, for we know that through Christ's grace we are to share His changeless years with Him forever.

The Seven Churches

3

Seven Letters to
the Seven Churches

Revelation 2–3

*The seven stars are the angels of the seven churches, and the seven lampstands
are the seven churches.* (Revelation 1:20)

The letters that Christ dictated from heaven to the seven churches
have been written about more than any other part of Revelation. Special
mention should be made of the monumental classic by Sir William
Ramsay, *The Seven Churches.* Thomas Cosmades's background book
Nothing Beside Remains is also worth noting. Excellent expositors who
have dealt specifically with Revelation include Abraham Kuyper, Walter
Scott, William Newell, A. Rice, and Christina Rosetti.

The letters have several characteristic features. First, the various aspects of Christ's portrait in the first chapter are parceled out among the
churches, with a specific designation being adapted to each church.
Christ spoke of "my church" in Matthew 16:18, and His seven letters to
her prove that He is her Head, and as such He is concerned about her
spiritual welfare.

A second noticeable trait is the use of the number seven. Not only
do we have seven churches, but declarations and exhortations addressed to them are repeated seven times. We find a sevenfold "I
know" and a sevenfold "the Spirit said." There are also seven messages
"to him who overcomes." The general and personal applications of
each letter are indicated by the two phrases "to the church" and "he
who has an ear."

These letters were sent to actual churches in John's day. While they represent the pilgrim church universal, the separate assemblies are also viewed as each resting on its own base and sufficiently distinct for the Lord to walk in its midst. These churches were not seven in one; instead, each church was independently responsible to the Lord, who governs and controls the church as a whole. Each church was obligated to walk in the light because Christ is in the light and is the Light. All of Revelation was sent not only to the seven churches mentioned by name but to *all* the churches existing at that time (2:23) and to all that remain until the rapture.

The immediate readers of Revelation were the members of the seven churches in Asia Minor, from which the gospel had spread both east and west. It is not likely that the members of the churches knew anything about the successive stages of church history, as we do. These letters were addressed to *them* and must have had a humiliating effect.

Why were these churches chosen? Only two of them are mentioned in the epistles of Paul (Ephesus and Laodicea). Excluded are the prominent churches in Rome, Galatia, Colosse, Philippi, Corinth, and Thessalonica. Because seven is the number of completion, perhaps we are to understand that these particular seven churches represent the complete church of God during the church age.

The cities where these churches were located were all on the great Roman post road. The Roman emperors often addressed letters to the cities in the empire, but in John's time only Ephesus, Smyrna, and Sardis were mighty cities of the world. Therefore these seven churches were chosen not so much because they were the greatest or most important churches of that period, but because each one was a *representative* church.

Geographically, these seven churches formed a rough circle, which was in keeping with the vision of their Lord walking in their midst. But the Revelation was for the church as whole (22:16), just as Paul addressed his epistles to particular churches, but what he wrote was for all churches in all ages.

As lampstands, the seven churches gave off a dim and uncertain light. The Lord, who is justified in His utterances and vindicated when He judges, deals with these churches in judgment. Seven churches were enough to exhibit such judgment, for this number indicates the sevenfold or perfect expression of the church. Some of the seven were found by Christ's evaluation to be in better condition than others. But one was not judged by the other; each was responsible for itself. While some churches maintained their purity of life and doctrine longer than others, the whole tone of this church section of Revelation carries a notice of what the end was to be.

Why were these seven churches selected? One answer, suggested by Walter Scott, is worthy of consideration: "The seven selected assemblies form a symbol of the church in its universality in successive periods of its history, as also at any given moment till its final rejection as an unfaithful witness to Christ." The seven letters can be taken, then, as a kind of survey of church history. The particular churches formed a circle, and it may be that they represent the entire circle of church history.

However, we must never lose sight of the original significance of these seven letters. They were addressed to actual churches within the specific geographical areas cited by John, and therefore they had a local application. But their breadth of instruction rules out a merely local, narrow, or restricted use. The truths and principles embodied in these letters are intended for all churches and church members of succeeding ages.

The letters may also have a prophetic significance. Some interpreters see the final fulfillment of the letters in the synagogues or assemblies to be found in Asia Minor after the true church has been raptured to heaven. This idea may help to explain Jewish references in the letters. The commendations and condemnations cited in the letters have proved prophetic down through the church age. There have always been churches leaving their first love (Ephesus), churches enduring persecution and trial (Smyrna), churches worldly in practice (Pergamum), churches guilty of false teaching (Thyatira), churches allowing gross sin (Sardis), churches with only a little power (Philadelphia), churches denying the deity of Christ (Laodicea).

Satanic opposition as mentioned in John's record of the seven churches has never ceased. Satan is named eight times in Revelation, five of them in connection with the churches (six if we include the name "Devil" in 2:10). The professing church all through its history has been tempted by Satan in various clever ways.

A remarkable and impressive feature of these seven letters is their similarity of format. Addressed from heaven by Christ to His church, the form of each letter is the same, although certain details vary to fit each church. The headings of all the letters correspond. In each letter appears a description of Christ, His intimate insight into the life and labor of each assembly, His commendation of virtues, His condemnation of failures, His exhortation to repentance, and His promise of reward to those overcome.

For our enlightenment and edification, let us now examine, first, the location and history of each of the seven cities and, second, the letter to the "angel" of the church in each of those cities.

First Letter: Ephesus—First Love (Revelation 2:1–7)

The name "Ephesus" means "desirable" or "first love" and fittingly describes the first century of church history, which was generally characterized by deep love and ardent zeal for Christ, and by unflinching opposition to false teachers and doctrines. Ephesus was the center of a large Christian population. Through the efforts of John, the main body of pastors in the area had stood solidly against all heresy, firmly excluding false teachers from the church. But the church John knew and dearly loved had left her early zeal. The first light had faded to gloom (see Acts 20:17–31).

Ephesus, the renowned capital of the Ionian state, was known as "the light of Asia" and was famous for its wealth, wisdom, and wickedness. Its worship of Diana (see Acts 19) had spread over the then-known world. But the Ephesian church (mother of the Asian churches) stands out as the most spiritual in the sacred record. Campbell Morgan noted that the beginning of the church in Ephesus is described in Acts 18–20, the eloquent but partial ministry of Apollos being supplemented and amplified by that of Paul. The letter to Ephesus (Revelation 2:1–7) describes the condition of the church thirty-five years later.

When the Apostle Paul preached in this city, he came with signs of healing that would appeal to such a people. Even handkerchiefs and aprons that had touched him had a miraculous healing power imparted to them (Acts 19:12). The Ephesians were intrigued by these wonders. They acknowledged a supernatural power greater than their own magic, and those who accepted the gospel burned their books of magic in the marketplace.

At Paul's first brief visit he found a ready ear among the Jews in the synagogue who were subsequently instructed by Apollos, Aquila, and Priscilla (Acts 18). At a second visit, however, opposition drove him from the synagogue, and for two years he preached daily in the school of Tyrannus, with great blessing to Jews and Greeks (Acts 19). Ultimately Paul left for Macedonia after the uproar caused by Demetrius, the silversmith, and other followers of Diana. One of the most touching incidents in the life of the apostle was his farewell message at Miletus to the Ephesian elders, and their consequent sorrow as they realized that they would never see him again (Acts 20).

Ephesus was now given over to idolatry and to a prevailing heresy that Christians could freely participate in the immoralities of heathen festivals. Many Christians left their first love. Are we as ardent for Christ today as we were in the early days of our witness, when our all was on the altar? Though perhaps still theologically sound, can it be that our hearts no longer pulsate with the love of Jesus that we manifested in the first years of our Christian life?

To the angel of the church in Ephesus write:

These are the words of him who holds the seven stars in his right hand and walks among the seven golden lampstands: I know your deeds, your hard work and your perseverance. I know that you cannot tolerate wicked men, that you have tested those who claim to be apostles but are not, and have found them false. You have persevered and have endured hardships for my name, and have not grown weary.

Yet I hold this against you: You have forsaken your first love. Remember the height from which you have fallen! Repent and do the things you did at first. If you do not repent, I will come to you and remove your lampstand from its place. But you have this in your favor: You hate the practices of the Nicolaitans, which I also hate. He who has an ear, let him hear what the Spirit says to the churches. To him who overcomes, I will give the right to eat from the tree of life, which is in the paradise of God.

The angel, we understand, is the moral or spiritual representative of each church. Walter Scott regards "the angel of the church" as "symbolically representative of the assembly in its actual moral state. *Representation* is the thought . . . We could emphasize the remark that not official but *moral representation* is the idea conveyed in the word 'angel' as used in connection with the seven churches."

In each of the letters the speaker is the risen Lord, and the revelation of Himself is adapted to the need of each church. As we have indicated, Christ introduces Himself in symbolic terms taken from chapter 1. Thus we connect verse 1 here with verses 12, 13, and 20 of chapter 1. Christ is seen walking judicially among the churches. Every act is witnessed by Him who never slumbers or sleeps. And as the One holding the seven golden lampstands, He is able to remove any one of them from its place. Surely it is sobering to realize that the Lord knows exactly what each of us is doing. He knew that the Ephesians could not bear those who were evil. Can *we* bear them? Do we abhor that which is evil?

There was much to commend in this almost flawless church. Perseverance was highly commended: perseverance in service (verse 2) and perseverance in suffering (verse 3). Altogether our Lord had a sevenfold commendation for this Ephesian church: (1) hard work, (2) perseverance, (3) intolerance toward wickedness, (4) testing false claims, (5) persevering, (6) enduring hardship, (7) not growing weary.

But there is a sad "yet I hold this against you" in Christ's message to this church. The first love of betrothal to Christ had been forsaken. There was pure doctrine and perfect church order, but a lamentable lack of love. Love of Christ is the motive of all acceptable service (John 21:15–17). Did not Paul affirm in 1 Corinthians 13 that the very best in service is of little value if love is lacking? Other loves had crept in, and the Ephesian church was in danger of slipping. Christ calls the church to remember the height from which it had fallen and to return to its first works. With the first love went the first works. Love yearns for love, for where there is true love, there is also true labor.

Regarding the sect of the Nicolaitans, Irenaeus said it had been founded by Nicolas of Antioch, one of the deacons (Acts 6:5). This sect apparently plunged into every kind of excess and licentiousness, professing Christianity but practicing all the filthy impurities of the heathen around them. It abused grace to the disregard of plain morality.

The exhortation "he who has an ear, let him hear" ends each letter. In the first three churches the call comes before Christ's message to the overcomer. In the last four churches, it comes after.

The Holy Spirit is the Administrator of church affairs throughout this age, as indicated by the sevenfold repetition of "the Spirit says." To the overcomer in this church Christ promises the provision of the tree of life, which can mean exemption from bodily deterioration. The tree was significant to the Greeks as a symbol of life-giving divine power. "Paradise" means "a pleasure garden" and represents the sum of all spiritual enjoyment. In Eden "the life of innocence was dependent on obedience," says Walter Scott, but for the New Testament overcomer, "eternal life becomes an everlasting feast in the Paradise of God."

Second Letter: Smyrna—Persecuted Church (Revelation 2:8–11)

This last stronghold of Christianity before the Muslim conquest was a serious rival of Ephesus, some forty miles to the north. Attractively built in John's day, it was called "the beautiful." Smyrna is also famous as the birthplace of the Greek poet Homer. Its bishop, Polycarp, was martyred there in A.D. 168, when he was ninety years old. Because Smyrna is not mentioned elsewhere in the New Testament, nothing is known of the founding of the church there. Idolatry was rife in the city, and the fierce persecution raging at that time against Christianity had its center in Smyrna.

The name "Smyrna" means "myrrh," a word used three times in the Gospels (Matthew 2:11; Mark 15:23; John 19:39). Myrrh was one of the ingredients of the holy ointment (Exodus 30:23–25) and was used in embalming the dead. As Seiss remarks in his valuable commentary on the Revelation, "The name well describes a church persecuted unto death and lying embalmed in the previous spices of its sufferings, such as the church of Smyrna was. It was the church of myrrh or bitterness, and yet was agreeable and precious unto the Lord."

As myrrh must be crushed to release its fragrance, so the testimony of the church crushed by persecution produced a sweet fragrance that was well pleasing to God. The blood of martyrs in this period became the seed of succeeding churches. The "ten days" (2:10) may represent the ten attempts by imperial edicts to destroy the infant church or it may indicate that the last persecution was just ten years long. "Ten" can also signify that God will see to it that even suffering has its limit.

To the angel of the church in Smyrna write:

These are the words of him who is the First and the Last, who died and came to life again. I know your afflictions and your poverty—yet you are rich! I know the slander of those who say they are Jews and are not, but are a synagogue of Satan. Do not be afraid of what you are about to suffer. I tell you, the devil will put some of you in prison to test you, and you will suffer persecution for ten days. Be faithful, even to the point of death, and I will give you the crown of life.

He who has an ear, let him hear what the Spirit says to the churches. He who overcomes will not be hurt at all by the second death. (Revelation 2:8–11)

This letter shares the distinction (along with the letter to Philadelphia) of containing no blame. These two churches shared the experience of tribulation at the hands of those who claimed falsely to be Jews but belonged to "a synagogue of Satan" (see 3:9). Likewise, many say they are Christians, but are not!

This shortest of the seven letters has interesting features. First of all, how fitting it is that Christ is referred to as the one who died and came to life again. Many in this church were to die for their Lord, but as the One who had conquered death, Christ could promise them a glorious resurrection.

Then there is that brief but rewarding assurance, "yet you are rich." Heartless persecutors had reduced the saints to beggary, but they were rich in faith.

Amid gathering darkness there was the gracious and strengthening, "Do not be afraid." They needed to be courageous, for tribulation would have its limits, and the one binding them would ultimately be bound (20:1–3).

For this heroic church there was no condemnation, no word of censure or reproach. Persecution has a way of keeping saints close to the heart of God. Having remained true, the people of Smyrna receive no call to repent and no judgment is recorded against them.

Cicero described Smyrna as "the city of our most faithful ally." Only in this letter does Christ use the term "faithful." As Smyrna was loyal to its monarch, so the church there was loyal to her Lord in spite of intense suffering. Smyrna was also called "the gateway of the martyrs" because many of them passed through the ports there on the way to Rome—and martyrdom.

For their reward they would receive a "crown of life," the emblem of royalty and victory. Escape from "the second death" (implying a death beyond physical death) might have contained a message to those in Smyrna who were bent on destroying the saints. Perhaps they were warned so they would take heed and repent. It also reminds the sufferers that there is something more terrible than physical death. But it would not be theirs because they had earned the crown of life.

"He who overcomes will not be hurt at all by the second death." Being an overcomer in Smyrna meant being ready for martyrdom. Reputation, possessions, even life itself might be taken. Says Scott: "The overcomer may die under tortures prolonged and gloated over by the almost fiendish malice of man who delight in blood, but he is assured that he shall not be hurt of the second death." True life lies beyond. The very expression, "second death," emphasizes the certainty of that truer and fuller life.

The need for this assurance becomes clear when we look at the list of persecutions for the "ten days":

1. Under Nero	A.D. 64–68
2. Under Domitian	A.D. 90–95
3. Under Trajan	A.D. 104–17
4. Under Aurelius	A.D. 161–80
5. Under Severus	A.D. 200–211
6. Under Maximus	A.D. 235–37
7. Under Decius	A.D. 250–53
8. Under Valerian	A.D. 257–60
9. Under Aurelian	A.D. 270–75
10. Under Diocletian	A.D. 303–12

Third Letter: Pergamum—State Church (Revelation 2:12–17)

The city of Pergamum, or Pergamos, was the ancient political capital of Asia. Famous for its learning, culture, and science, it had a two-hundred-thousand-volume library, second only to that of Alexandria, Egypt.

The city has been described as a combination of a pagan cathedral city, a university town, and a royal residence. The art of preparing skins of animals for writing upon was perfected in Pergamum.

The city was the seat of emperor worship and was preeminent in idolatry—hence the designation "where Satan has his throne" (2:13). Pergamum is now an insignificant town of imposing ruins. Like many another historic city, its glory has departed. Because it was given up to emperor worship, which always leads to corruption and extinction, it no longer exists as a viable city.

The New Testament does not record the founding of the church here. By the third century the church had passed the martyr stage and was receiving imperial favors. Emperor Constantine united church and state by making Christianity the state religion.

Pergamum means "twice married," a fit description of the disastrous union between the church and the world. Since this fatal marriage, the church and the state system have never been separated. Decreasing spirituality has led to increasing worldly favor. This type of unholy union can cripple the spiritual effectiveness of the church.

To the angel of the church in Pergamum write:

These are the words of him who has the sharp, double-edged sword. I know where you live—where Satan has his throne. Yet you remain true to my name. You did not renounce your faith in me, even in the days of Antipas, my faithful witness, who was put to death in your city—where Satan lives.

Nevertheless, I have a few things against you: You have people there who hold to the teaching of Balaam, who taught Balak to entice the Israelites to sin by eating food sacrificed to idols and by committing sexual immorality. Likewise you also have those who hold to the teaching of the Nicolaitans. Repent therefore! Otherwise, I will soon come to you and will fight against them with the sword of my mouth.

He who has an ear, let him hear what the Spirit says to the churches. To him who overcomes, I will give some of the hidden manna. I will also give him a white stone with a new name written on it, known only to him who receives it. (Revelation 2:12–17)

Christ is introduced to the church at Pergamum as having a sharp sword with double edges, the symbol of judgment and execution. Comparing verse 12 with verse 16 clearly shows how applicable this title was to the Pergamum church. The sharp sword of the Word of God penetrates, divides, separates, commands, lays bare, searches out, and conquers. How apt is Isaiah's prophecy of Christ at this point: "He made my mouth like a sharpened sword" (Isaiah 49:2). The Roman envoy in Pergamum wore the sword as a symbol of office, of military power; and he had "the power of the sword"—the authority to pronounce the death sentence. But the sword of the Lord was greater than all the swords of the Caesars, and when He ultimately wields it (Revelation 19:15), He will dominate the empires of the earth.

Evidently Satan had his base of operations in this city, a fact that would make the position of believers somewhat perilous. The actual "throne" of Satan is in the air, while his center of activity can change from time to time.

In *Light from the Ancient East,* Adolf Deissman makes the suggestion that the huge altar of Zeus, which stood upon a base one hundred feet square and was elevated eight hundred feet above the plain, is the object of the seer's reference. "Actual inspection of the place," he says, "suggests that 'Satan's throne' can only have been the altar of Zeus; no other shrine of the hill-city was visible to such a great distance and could therefore rank so typically as the representative of Satanic heathendom."

In spite of satanic antagonism, the saints at Pergamum are commended for their loyalty to "my name," which signifies the person of Christ, and to the "faith," which signifies the teachings and work of Christ. The fidelity of these saints, even with martyrdom before them, is illustrated in faithful Antipas, who died for the Lord whom he dearly loved. Pergamum was one of the great centers of emperor worship, and the temptation to compromise by misdirecting the worship that belongs to God alone was particularly great. When the Christians compromised, Satan triumphed. When they were firm, often martyrdom was the price they paid for their loyalty to Christ.

In an intimacy of love and a blaze of glory unique even for Revelation, Christ draws out the name of Antipas. It means "one against many," and this courageous Christian dared to stand alone and seal his witness with his life's blood.

Unfortunately, while the Pergamum church in general was sound, it had tolerated error among its members. "I have a few things against you." This sad complaint is given three times (2:4, 14, 20). Has the Lord anything against you?

A lack of discipline is clearly evident as we think of those who followed Balaam and the Nicolaitans. Balaamism and Nicolaitanism seem to describe what came to be known as antinomianism, the teaching that God's covenant purposes are sure of realization and that therefore it does not matter how the subjects of the covenants conduct themselves.

Balaam was the hireling who loved the wages of unrighteousness. He represents the union of the church and the world, which is tantamount to spiritual unchastity. The doctrine of the Nicolaitans recalls those who tried to dominate the laity and the beginning of priestcraft. Priestly importance is abhorrent to Him who is the Great High Priest.

In the call to repentance we have Christ's "blitzkrieg"—"I will soon come to you." And when He comes, His Word will be the basis of judgment. For the overcomers there will be the manna of divine supply and the white stone of acquittal or victory.

Many interpretations of the white stone have been given. It is said that a white stone indicating distinctions and privileges was awarded to a conqueror in the Olympic games. Such a stone was also an evidence of acquittal and bore the name of the one acquitted. A. J. Robertson says that the pebblestones were used in courts of justice—a black pebble for condemning and a white pebble for acquitting. The white stone also suggested friendship: the stone was broken in two, and each of two friends retained the half with the other's name in token of abiding union and communion.

The message to the Pergamum church is sorely needed today. The carelessness and compromise in belief, and therefore in conduct, called for discipline back then—as it calls for discipline in the present-day church as well.

Fourth Letter: Thyatira—Roman Church (Revelation 2:18–29)

Travelers have asserted that the road from Thyatira to Pergamum is one of the most beautiful in the world. This military post of Pergamum was famed for dyeing the brilliant scarlet cloth used extensively throughout Asia and Europe. Within the city was a magnificent temple of Diana. It was also the home of Jezebel, the notorious and influential woman teacher who openly and militantly endorsed immoral living.

G. Campbell Morgan suggests that the history of the church at Thyatira might be traced back to the riverside prayer meeting described in Acts 16, since Lydia was a native of Thyatira. She was probably instrumental in founding the church on her return home.

F. R. Tatford says, "The city's titular deity was Tyrimnas, a sun-god, who was generally depicted as a warrior riding forth to battle, armed with a double-edged battle-axe—the symbol of smashing military power. Such a deity might presumably be deemed most appropriate for a pagan military town.

"It is, therefore, most significant that the character in which Christ is introduced to the church of Thyatira is that of One *'whose eyes are like blazing fire and whose feet are like burnished bronze'* (2:18), whilst the promise to the overcomer is that he shall be rewarded with irresistible power among the nations—that smashing power which the city's own deity pretended to wield with his battle-axe."

To the angel of the church in Thyatira write:

These are the words of the Son of God, whose eyes are like blazing fire and whose feet are like burnished bronze. I know your deeds, your love and faith, your service and perseverance, and that you are now doing more than you did at first.

Nevertheless, I have this against you: You tolerate that woman Jezebel, who calls herself a prophetess. By her teaching she misleads my servants into sexual immorality and the eating of food sacrificed to idols. I have given her time to repent of her immorality, but she is unwilling. So I will cast her on a bed of suffering, and I will make those who commit adultery with her suffer intensely, unless they repent of her ways. I will strike her children dead. Then all the churches will know that I am he who searches hearts and minds, and I will repay each of you according to your deeds. Now I say to the rest of you in Thyatira, to you who do not hold to her teaching and have not learned Satan's so-called deep secrets (I will not impose any other burden on you): Only hold on to what you have until I come.

To him who overcomes and does my will to the end, I will give authority over the nations—

'He will rule them with an iron scepter;
he will dash them to pieces like pottery'—

just as I have received authority from my Father. I will also give him the morning star. He who has an ear, let him hear what the Spirit says to the churches. (Revelation 2:18–28)

In Revelation 1, John saw Christ as the Son of Man but as invested with all the attributes and activities of deity. Here the divine Speaker introduces Himself as the Son of God, and as such He reveals His omniscience and authority. The description of His eyes and feet, taken from 1:14–15, illustrates the terrible aspect of judgment He assumes toward this church. Christ's most searching, crushing powers are before us in 2:23, 27, which are a development of verse 18.

Graciously this One who "knows" puts things of excellence *first*. If only those who misjudge us would follow such a divine example, how different the world would be! Service, love, faith, and patience are justly praised.

Then comes the complaint regarding evil permitted in the church— evil personified in a specific woman. (The Old Testament Jezebel is named as her prototype in sin.) This is the only letter that mentions a woman. "Jezebel" means "chaste," but how untrue she was to her own name! The Old Testament Jezebel was a brilliant, daring, and unscrupulous woman, recognizing God but actually serving Baal. In the previous letter our Lord compared false teachers to Balaam, who taught the Israelites to join in idolatrous festivals. Now He compares them to Jezebel, the heathen wife of King Ahab, who established idolatry in Israel. Thyatira's evil was spiritism—the woman Jezebel claimed divine revelation about occult activities. And her evil influence was multiplied because she taught and seduced the servants of Christ to follow her.

In this longest letter of the seven, a solemn warning is given to those who persistently indulge in spiritual harlotry. If they refuse to repent, they must share the condemnation of Jezebel. But the Lord is gracious even to the worst of evildoers—"I gave her time to repent." Repentance is always God's way out.

To those in Thyatira not influenced by Jezebel and her fornications a share in the rule of Christ was promised. Deeds based on love play a prominent part in this letter (2:19, 26). The Morning Star is Christ Himself (see 22:16), and all overcomers are to possess Him fully. What a future awaits those who have Christ in their hearts as the Harbinger of the coming glorious day! If we are faithful, we shall know the heights of sharing in the reign of our Lord.

Ephesians 2:6 reminds us that because of Christ we share even now in the power of His ascended reign. Psalm 2:9, quoted here by the risen Lord, has yet to be fulfilled; Christ's rising heralds God's dawn as His people rise with Him. The readers of this message, tempted to sink to the depths of Satan, might remember how Satan is spoken of in Isaiah 14:12 as the morning star fallen from heaven. We too must choose between the heights and the depths.

Authority over nations is reserved for all true overcomers, who will share Christ's reign. Those whose lives are molded according to Christ's pattern will be granted participation with Him in His dominion.

Fifth Letter: Sardis—Reformed Church (Revelation 3:1–6)

Ramsay's description of this city uses its physical surroundings to reveal its inner character.

Looked at from a little distance to the north in the open plain, Sardis wore an imposing, commanding, impregnable aspect, as it dominated that magnificent broad valley of the Hermus from its robber stronghold on a steep spur that stands out boldly from the great mountains on the south. But, close at hand, the hill is seen to be but mud, slightly compacted, never trustworthy or lasting, crumbling under the influences of the weather, ready to yield even to the blow of a spade. It was an appearance without reality, promise without performance, outward show of strength betrayed by want of watchfulness and careless confidence.

In the sixth century Sardis was one of the most powerful cities in the world. It was the capital of the kingdom of Lydia. The present name of this once-proud and wealthy capital is Sart. Its site is now deserted.

"Sardis" means "precious stone" or "things remaining." "Sardius," a beautiful diamond, is the same word. In the Sardis church the majority of its members were completely given over to heathen practices. They appeared to be alive, but they were dead. A few, however, remained true to the Lord and His Word.

To the angel of the church in Sardis write:

These are the words of him who holds the seven spirits of God and the seven stars. I know your deeds; you have a reputation of being alive, but you are dead. Wake up! Strengthen what remains and is about to die, for I have not found your deeds complete in the sight of my God. Remember, therefore, what you have received and heard; obey it, and repent. But if you do not wake up, I will come like a thief, and you will not know at what time I will come to you.

Yet you have a few people in Sardis who have not soiled their clothes. They will walk with me, dressed in white, for they are worthy. He who overcomes will, like them, be dressed in white. I will never blot out his name from the book of life, but will acknowledge his name before my Father and his angels. He who has an ear, let him hear what the Spirit says to the churches. (Revelation 3:1–6)

With this fifth letter Christ seems to make a new beginning. Indeed, Sardis does mark a change in the series. In the previous letters good was the rule and evil the exception. But here in Sardis the reverse is true—

only a small remnant can be commended by Christ, whose "I know" is one of searching and condemnation.

Both the Spirit and spiritual leaders are under Christ's control and are avenues of His operation. All the plenitude of power and wisdom that Sardis lacks are His. Though perfect before men, the church here is not perfect before God. It has a reputation for organization and orthodoxy but is destitute of life. It has labor without life!

"There was, in all probability," says G. Campbell Morgan, "conformity to the model of the church found in Acts 2:41, 42 so far as the ordinances and adherence to doctrine were concerned. The worship and giving were apparently beyond reproach. But in the eyes of the Lord all was a scaffolding to the structure, as a whited sepulchre, as flowers of wax."

In view of the Second Coming, the church is exhorted to repent. Like a thief, Christ will rob them of all they are if they fail to turn from their dead, barren orthodoxy. As a city, Sardis had been conquered twice because of failure to watch. Christ tells the church what its failure to watch for Him will mean.

A few in Sardis have not defiled their garments, however, and manifest victorious righteousness. The name "Sardis" comes from a Hebrew root implying "those that are escaping or escaped." In the church at Sardis a few believers can be found who have escaped the pollution surrounding them—who have a name that they lived courageously for Christ.

Are we numbered among the few who are separated unto the Lord and perfect in fidelity to Him? If so, then we too will share in the rewards the Lord has for those who are worthy. Note that "I will never blot out his name" does not contradict eternal security. The reference is to the book of profession, not the book of reality (compare with 13:8; 17:8; 20:15).

Sardis is a church of dead puppets, going through the actions of Christianity but producing works that are not animated by the life that flows from God. So the Lord speaks to them as the One in whom revival is to be found. He waits to pour out the Spirit in His sevenfold fullness, and the government of the churches is in His hand (1:20).

Sardis is given a command similar to the one given Ephesus in 2:5. She must go back to those things that were precious in the old days; in the light of what once was life she must stop the things she is now doing, lest the spark of life that remains should die out altogether. The condition of maintained life is watchfulness, or wakefulness. The alternative is the sleep of death and unexpected judgment from the Lord.

Every saint's name is in the book of life and can never be erased from such a sacred scroll (Luke 10:20). But those who tamper with the authority and veracity of Revelation will lose their "share in the tree of life" (22:19). Here "share" means "inheritance." All have an inheritance or reward that can be lost.

The wonder of wonders is that Christ is going to confess His victorious saints before the Father and His angels. And what a day that will be for us if we are found among those "dressed in white, for they are worthy"!

Sixth Letter: Philadelphia—Missionary Church (Revelation 3:7–13)

Situated at the mouth of a long narrow pass on the main road from the coast to Phrygia, Philadelphia was the gateway to the high central plateau of Asia Minor. It was founded as a center of Greek civilization and a means of spreading Greek language and manners in the eastern parts of Lydia and Phrygia. By A.D. 19 the Lydian tongue had ceased to be spoken in Lydia, and Greek was the only language of the country.

British historian Edward Gibbon remarked that among the Greek colonies and churches of Asia, Philadelphia shows that the "paths of honor and safety may sometimes be the same." The city derived its name from its founder, Attalus Philadelphus, king of Pergamum. Its modern name is Allah Shehr, or "the City of God." The Turks, however, do not regard the city with any degree of veneration.

In John's day, the church in Philadelphia was faithful, constantly taking advantage of opportunities. It endured longer than the churches in the other six cities. Here we have a true church within the professing church.

The name "Philadelphia" means "brotherly love," and is so used in the Greek of Hebrews 13:1: "Let your brotherly love continue" (KJV). In Philadelphia we see the evangelizing, missionary church of the nineteenth century. Out of the great Wesley revivals came the foreign missions movement, followed by the appearance of powerful evangelistic agencies.

To the angel of the church in Philadelphia write:

These are the words of him who is holy and true, who holds the key of David. What he opens no one can shut, and what he shuts no one can open. I know your deeds. See, I have placed before you an open door that no one can shut. I know that you have little strength, yet you have kept my word and have not denied my name. I will make those who are of the synagogue of Satan, who claim to be Jews though they are not, but are liars—I will make them come and fall down at your feet and acknowledge that I have loved you. Since you have kept my command to endure patiently, I will also keep you from the hour of trial that is going to come upon the whole world to test those who live on the earth.

I am coming soon. Hold on to what you have, so that no one will take your crown. Him who overcomes I will make a pillar in the temple of my God. Never again will he leave it. I will write on him the name of my God and the name of the city of my God, the new Jerusalem, which is coming down out of heaven from my God; and I will also write on him my new name. He who has an ear, let him hear what the Spirit says to the churches. (Revelation 3:7–13)

The church in Philadelphia (like the church in Smyrna) is not charged with any blame. Here the divine Speaker, who reveals Himself as "holy and true," is described as having the key of David. Anyone given the key to a city receives it with freedom and privileges. Here the key is the symbol of the undisputed right to enter and exercise all needful authority. Because Revelation as a whole looks toward the kingdom, Christ emphasizes His royal claims as the Lord and Head of David's house. All Davidic promises will be fulfilled by Him.

The church of Philadelphia is commended for its faithfulness according to its ability. It has been loyal with little. Although its obedience and faith are unimportant in the eyes of the world, the divine Administrator, who opens and shuts doors, is unstinted in His praise for the way the Philadelphia church entered the door of opportunity He had opened.

Philadelphia is one of the two churches that receive only praise and encouragement. Because its members have been faithful, they are given fresh work to do. While we are on earth, the reward of faithfulness is not idleness but greater responsibility. Those who are already idle must be brought back to devotion to God before they can be used by Him. So the Lord speaks to Philadelphia as the One who opens doors of opportunity.

It is in no condemnatory sense that Christ speaks of their "little strength." Humanly speaking, their strength is little because they are a tiny minority among Jews and pagans. Yet because their strength is based on naming the name of Christ, they can go forward through the open door. The text does not say what this door is, and consequently this verse has been precious to many generations of Christians in all spheres of service in which a new door has been opened.

Exemption was promised from a special trial, which can mean deliverance from the great Tribulation. The word "from" signifies "out of" and carries with it the idea of being kept away from tribulation (not merely kept through it, as some assert). Only when this trial overtakes the earth will the full importance of the message of preservation be fully understood or experienced.

In this letter also, Christ's Second Coming is used as an incentive to hold fast. May we be determined to retain our crown! Overcomers are to be made a pillar in God's temple. Though of little strength on earth, they are to be fashioned into massive, glorious pillars in heaven and will share Christ's ultimate victory. Then identification with the king will be complete. Even if they have no name here, they are to have a new, secret name in heaven. All who are truly saved by grace are in the register of the living because they have eternal life.

Seventh Letter: Laodicea—Today's Church (Revelation 3:14–22)

Laodicea received its name from Laodice, wife of Antiochus II, the Syrian monarch. Laodicea was near Colosse, where the Christians received a letter from Paul. Four references in Colossians (2:1; 4:13, 15, 16) prove that the Apostle Paul was familiar with the church at Laodicea. The city itself was a great banking center and a producer of black, glossy wool garments; its medical school was famous for a powder that cured ophthalmia (see 3:18). But the fame and splendor of Laodicea have been laid in the dust, for the city is now the scene of ruin and desolation.

To the angel of the church in Laodicea write:

These are the words of the Amen, the faithful and true witness, the ruler of God's creation. I know your deeds, that you are neither cold nor hot. I wish you were either one or the other! So, because you are lukewarm—neither hot nor cold—I am about to spit you out of my mouth. You say, "I am rich; I have acquired wealth and do not need a thing." But you do not realize that you are wretched, pitiful, poor, blind and naked. I counsel you to buy from me gold refined in the fire, so you can become rich; and white clothes to wear, so you can cover your shameful nakedness; and salve to put on your eyes, so you can see.

Those whom I love I rebuke and discipline. So be earnest, and repent. Here I am! I stand at the door and knock. If anyone hears my voice and opens the door, I will come in and eat with him, and he with me.

To him who overcomes, I will give the right to sit with me on my throne, just as I overcame and sat down with my Father on his throne. He who has an ear, let him hear what the Spirit says to the churches. (Revelation 3:14–22)

This last letter is the saddest of the seven. Communicating Christ's disapproval to an apostate church, it nonetheless reveals the heart of the Lord in a way that the other letters do not. Christ does not use a symbol to describe Himself. He declared Himself to be "the Amen," a title as expressive of His glory as "the Truth." As "the faithful and true witness," He is revealed as being in harmony with Himself. "The ruler of God's creation" indicates Christ's authoritative message, which is interpreted in Colossians 1:15 as "the image of the invisible God, the firstborn [preeminent One] over all creation." Everything implied by these titles was denied by the Laodiceans, who thereby earned His displeasure and condemnation.

The name "Laodicea" is from two Greek words meaning "people" and "judgment" or "custom." The name implies that the church there is governed by the decisions, judgments, and customs of the people instead of the Word of God.

The condition of this church is completely unfavorable, and so there is no commendation of any virtue. How tragic it is when there are no good works to commend in a church! Of course the Laodiceans have plenty of good things to say about themselves. They are self-confident, proud, and satisfied. But to their Lord they are spiritually lukewarm and therefore nauseating. The church in Ephesus left its love, but the church in Laodicea is lukewarm.

The Laodicean church has abundant material wealth, yet Christ declares it to be pitiable and bankrupt. We have the "you are" of lukewarmness, the "you say" of self-complacency (the church was without passion or emotion), and the "you are" of the Lord's infallible and terrible indictment. Like many a modern church, Laodicea is correct but conscienceless. Christ's contempt for such a condition is seen in His drastic treatment of the church: "I am about to spit you out of my mouth." Such a travesty of His church is loathsome to Christ.

Summary

Even to the most casual reader of Revelation it must be obvious that the basic theme is the Second Coming of Christ:

Ephesus: "I will come to you and remove your lampstand" (2:5)
Smyrna: "I will give you the crown of life" (2:10)
Pergamum: "I will soon come to you" (2:16)
Thyatira: "Hold on to what you have until I come" (2:25)
Sardis: "I will come like a thief, and you will not know at what time I will come to you" (3:3)
Philadelphia: "I am coming soon" (3:11)
Laodicea: "I stand at the door and knock" (3:20)

But grace also shines forth in the judgment, for judgment is the result of Christ's love. As He urges the church to a new zeal, He looks for someone who is willing to welcome the Lord. For such a person there is the great reward of sharing Christ's provision and throne. The divine guest becomes the divine host and lavishes glorious gifts upon those who willingly entertain Him (3:2).

In the gold, the white raiment, and the eye salve that Christ coun-seled the church to secure from Him, we have illustrations or symbols that would appeal to the Laodiceans, whose city was famous for such commodities.

At the close of chapter 3 we the saints are caught up and the sinners are spewed out. While John does not record the actual rapture, he takes it for granted, since he does not mention the word *church* again until he finishes the revelation and comes to the closing exhortations (22:16–17). In these letters to the seven churches the Lord divides the members into two classes—those who are overcomers and those who are not. In each letter there is an appeal, a warning, and a promise: an *appeal* to come back to the Lord as He represents Himself to each church, a *warning* if the appeal passes unheeded, and a *promise* if it is obeyed.

Only in 22:6–21 does John resume what he dwelt upon in the first three chapters of the book. After chapter 3, Christ is no longer among the lampstands but is the Priest-Judge, operating from His heavenly throne until He returns to earth.

Here is a summary of the broader meaning of the seven churches:
- *Ephesus* indicates ecclesiastical pretension and departure from first love, characterizing the close of the apostolic period (first love church, first century).
- *Smyrna* brings us to the period of the martyrs, concluding with the last persecution under Dioletian (persecuted church, A.D. 92–315).
- *Pergamum* reveals the decreasing spirituality and increasing worldliness common to the reign of Constantine and stem-ming from his public patronage of the church (state church, 315–500).
- *Thyatira* covers the Middle Ages with their cruel persecution of the saints of God (Roman church, 500–1500).
- *Sardis* represents God's intervention by means of the Reforma-tion, the light of which is still burning (Reformation church, 1500–1700).
- *Philadelphia* is related to the nineteenth century with its vast expansion of missionary activities (missionary church, 1700–1900).

- *Laodicea* portrays the present general state of the professing church (lukewarm church, 1900–).

It has been suggested that the histories of the first three churches are consecutive while the histories of the remaining four overlap, running concurrently to the rapture of the church (see 1 Corinthians 15:51–52; 1 Thessalonians 4:16–18).

SECTION TWO:
WHAT WILL TAKE PLACE LATER

■   ■   ■

Revelation 4–20

Period of Tribulation, Rapture, Second Coming, Armageddon, Great Tribulation, Millennium, Great White Throne

4

Seven Seals

Revelation 4:1–8:1

A scroll with writing on both sides and sealed with seven seals.
(Revelation 5:1)

The Throneroom (Revelation 4:1–11)

Understanding the seven seals involves considering the atmosphere and unfolding of truth in chapters 4 and 5. With the completion of the judgments of the sixth seal, the terrified multitudes cry out in 6:16 to be hid from "the face of him who sits on the throne" (the "Lord God Almighty" of chapter 4) and from "the wrath of the Lamb" (the One vividly portrayed in chapter 5).

Revelation is one of the most dramatic parts of the Bible. As symbolic literature and as a demonstration of the ultimate triumph of good over evil, the chapters of this book are unparalleled. At last we see Christ progressively overturning everything until He takes to Himself His rightful power and reigns supreme over all.

Chapter 4 opens with John being raptured to heaven—"Come up here" (4:1)—to receive God's blueprint for the future. At the end of chapter 3 people are invited to open a door for Christ; now a door is opened in heaven for people to enter. With this open door the truly prophetic part of the book commences, even though definite prophetic action does not begin until chapter 6. Chapters 4 and 5, with their heavenly scenes, appear to be introductory to the first series of judgments detailed in chapter 6.

The opening phrase, "I will show you what must take place after this" (4:1), refers to what has just been considered in chapters 2 and 3. Now we have a new beginning. John passes from church matters to an entirely different subject. The scene is also different, for now John is in heaven. From the heights he is made to understand what is to transpire below.

When standing on the ground we cannot see very far, but what a panorama is spread out before us when we climb some lofty height! This is also true with the things of God. Prophecy has its source in heaven, above the mists and clouds. Even when they concern the earth, heavenly matters can only be understood from the heavenly standpoint.

Twelve times in this chapter the word "throne" is mentioned. Altogether it occurs thirty-eight times throughout Revelation, making this book "the throneroom of the Bible." And the "thrones" of Revelation make a profitable Bible study. The book opens and closes with a throne (1:4; 22:3). The throne of 4:2 is preparatory to the judgments beginning in chapter 6 and ending in chapter 20. So we travel from the judgment of the wicked living to the judgment of the wicked dead. The throne before us is "in heaven" (4:2), speaking judgments that are righteous and holy. "The Lord has established His throne in heaven" (Psalm 103:19). Nothing but perfect, unbiased judgment emanates from this throneroom.

By "the voice I had first heard" (4:1) we understand the voice of the Lord (1:10). It now speaks from heaven, trumpetlike. Revelation has six references to trumpets associated with thrones and judgments. In the Old Testament, trumpets were used to call assemblies. Here in Revelation they seem to prepare the way for judgment. The divine Occupant of the throne, without shape or form and unseen at any time, is named "Lord God Almighty" (4:8). Two precious stones, the jasper and the carnelian, are used to describe the qualities of the awesome Throne Sitter. Taken together, the stones are emblematic of the various excellencies of God's character and perfection. The jasper, or diamond, is translucent and is the emblem of *light*, while the carnelian, or ruby, a carnation color, is the emblem of *love*. Thus the One on the throne is characterized by both principle and passion.

"A rainbow, resembling an emerald, encircled the throne" (4:3), reminding us that God will be true to His covenants and that a gathering storm is about to break. We have here a circular rainbow, not the customary half-circular one. And instead of the manifold colors of the rainbow, this perfect one carries the beautiful green of the emerald. Green never tires the eye and can symbolize our never-tiring gaze upon the manifested glory of God. The complete rainbow is the symbol of *hope.*

Twenty-Four Elders (4:4)

Surrounding the throne were twenty-four other thrones, and seated on them were twenty-four elders. (Revelation 4:4)

The identification of the "twenty-four elders" (4:4) is a matter of dispute among theologians. Some assert that these elders are the heads of an angelic priesthood. Having crowns and white raiment, they must be kingly and priestly beings of a governmental order. Other writers identify the elders as Old Testament and New Testament saints, the twenty-four being made up of the twelve tribes and the twelve apostles.

Walter Scott says that it is incongruous to "imagine *spirits* sitting, clothed and crowned, and therefore they must represent the general body of the redeemed there in heaven" (see 5:9). Notice that the "seats" or "thrones" are subordinate to *the* throne of verse 2. The number twenty-four is associated with heavenly government and worship. Twelve is the governmental number of earth. If the elders are the redeemed—and John says they are (5:9)—then the golden crowns intimate the royal dignity and authority that every saint is to share.

A throne is the center of action and interest; it intimates the unleashing of natural forces as the precursors of coming judgment. The perfect, searching ministry of the Spirit is symbolized by the seven blazing lamps (4:5). As the seven Spirits of God, the Holy Spirit is brought before us in the perfection of His being, intelligence, and activity. Identified with the righteous judgment of the throne, the Spirit will expose all that is alien to the absolute purity of the throne. "A sea of glass, clear as crystal" (4:6) declares the eternal holiness and purity of the divine Occupant of the throne.

Four Living Creatures (4:6)

Around the throne ... were four living creatures. (Revelation 4:6)

The "four living creatures" (4:6) are equivalent to the Old Testament cherubim. These living ones symbolize the judicial attributes and authority of the Throne Sitter and are connected with Christ, the Living One. These "living ones" are also represented as having perfect wisdom and rendering unceasing worship and service. They likewise ascribe holiness and eternity to Him who sits upon the throne.

As representatives of this throne and as court attendants, they stand ready to do the will of the Judge. They are real, literal beings, vibrant with life. ("Four" is the number of man and creation, so the four living ones represent the animal creation of the world.) The "living creatures" have fullness of intelligence: "covered with eyes, in front and in back" (4:6), they have both *foresight* and *hindsight*—the past and future are open to them as a scroll. *Insight* ("eyes within") is also theirs.

In the symbolism of the faces Christ is presented as King, Servant, Human, and God (4:7). The lion face suggests omnipotence and majesty; the calf face, patient labor; the human face, intelligence and sympathy; the eagle face, remarkable vision and rapidity of action. These wonderful creatures also render unceasing service and undying praise. In activity and adoration they do not rest day or night.

This throne chapter closes with the anthem of the elders (4:10–11). Praise ascends to the Lord as the Creator of all things. In the next chapter, as the Redeemer, He receives His due. In casting their crowns before the throne, the elders indicate that the Lord alone is worthy to reign. "You are worthy, our Lord and God, to receive glory and honor and power, for you created all things" (4:11).

The Scroll with Seven Seals (Revelation 5:1–14)

> I saw in the right hand of him who sat on the throne a scroll with writing on both sides and sealed with seven seals. (Revelation 5:1)

In chapter 5 we have the unfolding of the earthly administration of heavenly government. The unopened scroll contains the divine program and is "sealed." This does not mean that it cannot be read, but simply that no one has been found yet to carry out the heavenly order.

Regarding this seven-sealed scroll, it is first of all in the right hand of Him who sits on the throne (5:1). The Bible has much to say about that "right hand"—the position of authority and power. Also, the scroll is sealed (5:1). Why is it sealed? A seal implies finality and privacy. It also requires lawful authority to be broken. The "seven seals" imply the perfect purpose of God in respect to the world. Each portion was individually sealed, with the seventh seal fastening the outside of the entire scroll.

Who could possibly be authorized to open this scroll? Must the drama of history fail at this crucial point? There is something very human in the reference to John's tears (5:4). His sorrow is overwhelming as he realizes creation's utter inability to even look upon the scroll (5:3). No one above or below can break the seals and set in motion those forces liberating the long-awaited kingdom. So John bursts into tears of anguish, for it seems that Satan and sin will continue their control of world affairs.

John's tears are quickly dried, for one of the elders calls, "Do not weep!" (5:5).With unbounded joy, John looks upon One who can and will open the scroll (5:5–6). The seals of divine judgment, which no one could break, *can* be broken by Him in whose pierced hands rest the title deeds of world dominion. The breaking of the seals is the Lamb's prerogative, and nothing can happen apart from His governmental will.

In response to the summons, John turned to behold the Lion described by the elder, but instead saw a Lamb (5:6). The Lion and the Lamb! Christ was both. As to His humanity, He is the Lion of the tribe of Judah, the Root of David. The Lamb is His dominant designation in Revelation, occurring over twenty times. John uses a word meaning "the little lamb"; it suggests Christ's innocence and gentleness, in contrast to the malevolent "beast." Notice also that he emphasizes the Lamb slain and standing (5:6). So Christ is portrayed as living and risen. The Lion overcomes in the Lamb slain. Sovereignty is based upon sacrifice. From the Cross comes the crown. The centrality of Christ reappears in the phrase "standing in the center" (5:6). The seven horns and seven eyes recall the perfect power and intelligence attributed to the Lamb and the Holy Spirit.

A dramatic scene accompanied the taking of the scroll from the hand of God (5:7). It recalls Daniel's prophecy regarding governmental power: "In my vision at night I looked, and there before me was one like a son of man, coming with the clouds of heaven. He approached the Ancient of Days and was led into his presence. He was given authority, glory and sovereign power; all peoples, nations and men of every language worshiped him. His dominion is an everlasting dominion that will not pass away, and his kingdom is one that will never be destroyed" (Daniel

7:13–14). As we shall soon see, the breaking of each seal reveals the accomplishment of a divine purpose in and through Christ.

With the taking of the scroll came worship by the twenty-four elders, each with a harp of thanksgiving, holding golden bowls of intercession (5:8). The worship by the elders is based upon redemption (5:5, 9, 12). Christ is the only One who could die as Savior because He needed no Savior Himself. The harps evoke a victory celebration (5:8). Used some forty-three times in the Old Testament, the harp is always connected with song. The harps on the willows meant captivity, and therefore no song (Psalm 137:2–4). The prayers of the saints (5:8) are referred to by John because they helped bring about Jesus' investiture as Judge and Lord of all. Think of the millions of prayers stored up, all centering around the prayer that multitudes have prayed—Thy kingdom come!

The redemption song is called new (5:9) because there has never been anything like it before. The whole group of worshipers rendered homage to the Lamb and blessed His sacred name. What a hallelujah chorus!

This song of the glorified (5:9–10) has three themes in it: redemption ("with your blood you purchased men for God"), royalty ("you have made them to be a kingdom"), and consecration ("priests to serve our God"). The saints are to reign over and on the earth (5:10), but the Lamb is the center, as emphasized in the sevenfold note of triumph (5:12).

Here in this chapter we have the divine setting for judgment. All judgments now begin with this universal anthem. The patience of God is exhausted, and the punishment of the seals is about to begin. Thus chapters 4 and 5 form an impressive approach to the seals. Tremendous events are about to take place. The chapter concludes with the singing of the new song, myriads of angels joining in the adoring ascription of praise. The whole creation also unites to adore the Lamb, this being the consummation of her groaning and anguish.

The Lamb Opens the Scroll (Revelation 6:1)

I watched as the Lamb opened the first of the seven seals. (Revelation 6:1)

As we enter this strictly prophetic part of Revelation, we find what has been called "procedure preceding victory." In chapter 6, John writes as an intensely observant eyewitness. "I saw" and "I heard" express personal experiences that we cannot overlook as we study the book as a whole. In chapters 4 and 5 everything is in heaven, where we are privileged to glance into the secret of God's presence and witness the preparation of the coming Judge. But from chapter 6 onward our attention is directed to earth, with the commencement of its judgments. Christ, as the Lamb by right of purchase and power of redemption, now takes full control. Sovereignty based on sacrifice is about to be manifested.

Because the judgment period stretches from chapter 6 to chapter 20, we need to note the connection between the seals, the trumpets, and the bowls. The judgments of the seals and trumpets are not contemporaneous but successive. The seals cover a larger area than the trumpets, but the trumpets are more severe and searching. The Lamb opens the seals, the angels blow the trumpets, and God empties out the bowls. The seven seals, then, include the entire judgment period. The trumpets and the bowls display in detail what the seals express in general.

Think of a telescope with three sections: the middle section is drawn out from the first section, and the third section from the middle section. Out of the seals the trumpets issue, and out of the trumpets the bowls issue.

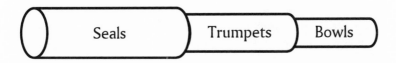

The seventh seal holds the seven trumpets; the seventh trumpet holds the seven bowls.

As previously indicated, some expositors take a "historical" view of chapters 6 to 20 (that the judgments cover the opening of the Christian era down to the present time). But our position is that the church is not on earth during these apocalyptic judgments, which are related to the Jews as a nation and to the Gentiles as nations. Because the church is neither Jew nor Gentile, but "a new person" (and therefore not the object of judgment), she is away from the earth as its divine visitation begins. With this sixth chapter, the divine ministration of the Lamb commences, and it will not end until He has made all His enemies His footstool (Psalm 2).

A common question today is, Why does God not intervene and do something about the sinful, chaotic condition of the world? If only the people who talk this way would read the book of Revelation, their questions would quickly be answered and their problems of divine nonintervention would be solved. Here the Lord is about to show His hand.

And what action there is! In chapters 4 and 5 the throne is set. In chapter 6 Daniel's last week begins (Daniel 9:26–27). Daniel had not been invited to heaven, as John was. Daniel saw everything in night visions, but the full understanding of his visions was withheld. Thus Revelation complements the book of Daniel. Right now a usurper controls the world, but Christ's day is coming. This corrupt earth is ready and ripe for judgment. The evil forces that have for so long gone unchallenged are about to meet their Master. Human and material instruments of vengeance are about to execute their divinely appointed task.

God may appear to be slow in settling accounts, but He always pays at last! If to us His mills appear to grind slowly, we are assured that they do grind surely. In this age He extends grace to the inhabitants of earth. He is slow to chide; but once the rod falls, woe to the hordes of earth!

First Seal: The White Horse—Conquest (Revelation 6:1–2)

I watched as the Lamb opened the first of seven seals. . . . and before me was a white horse. (Revelation 6:1–2)

In the loud summons introducing the seals, a significant point is made. John heard "a voice like thunder." The word "like" indicates that John is using symbolic language. What he heard was a loud, thunderous voice calling attention to the opening of the seals. "Come!" summons the horsemen (the human instruments employed in these earthly chastisements) to appear and to act. And the imperative command of the living creature is instantly obeyed.

The four horsemen symbolize divine power in judgment. Revelation hardly ever alludes to something not biblical, and horses are used figuratively in Zechariah 1 and 6. In fact, almost every symbol in this book is interpreted for us in some other part of Scripture. We should keep in mind a golden principle enunciated by Walter Scott: "On no account seek the interpretation of any part of the Apocalypse outside the covers of your Bible. The meaning of every symbol must be sought for in the Word itself." Comparing Scripture with Scripture, we are led to the conclusion that horses are prophetic of the final phases of world dominion by humans, and of human instruments used by God in His providential judgment of earth.

Two other thoughts are important as we approach the seals. First, the Lamb opens the seals while He is still in heaven in the midst of the throne. Officially and governmentally, Christ is about to exercise the dominion that His death, resurrection, and ascension gave Him. The breaking of the seals is the Lamb's prerogative, for nothing can happen outside His governmental will. Second, the four beasts (or living creatures) are here found connected with the execution of divine judgment. Because of their full knowledge of the divine will, they are qualified to assist in this judgment.

The identity of the rider of the white horse is a matter of contradictory exposition. Some say we have here a vision of the armies of heaven, with the rider symbolizing the heavenly host antagonistic to a godless earth. Others see the riders as impersonal agencies going forth to their tasks. Anti-Christian ideologies express themselves in various forces and movements. So the first rider symbolizes spiritual war, the second rider bloody war itself. But a figure usually heads up a force, and behind all powers there is a dominant personality. Other writers affirm that the rider is Christ Himself, and link verses 1 and 2 with 19:11.

We believe that the rider in this first seal is not the same person who appears as Kings of Kings and Lord of Lords in 19:11–16. These two riders have nothing in common beyond a white horse—no more proof that they are symbolic of Christ than are the white horses in Zechariah 1:8 and 6:3–6.

The rider in chapter 6 is not named and has no title, but the rider in chapter 19 is named "Faithful and True" and "the Word of God" and bears the title "King of Kings and Lord of Lords." Christ as the Lamb is the One opening the seals, and therefore He cannot be the rider in any of the first four seals. The white horse rider has a crown *given* him (by whom we are not told). Christ is not *given* any crown; many diadems adorn His brow by divine right and conquest (Revelation 19:12).

Other contrasts to note: the rider in the first seal comes out of the earth, but Christ descends from the opened heavens (13:1; 19:11). The first rider causes, and is followed by, war, famine, pestilence, death, and hell—horrors accompanying the rule of an ambitious conqueror as cruel as he is cultured. But Christ is followed by the armies of heaven, clothed in fine linen, white and pure. We also read that the first rider is to go forth to conquer, just as dictators conquer and acquire territory and possession by wars of conquest. But Christ is not coming to conquer. When He appears, He will take to Himself His rightful power and reign. He will not ride *to* victory but *from* victory, which He accomplished at Calvary when He cried, "It is finished!" His judicial authority and reign, set forth in Revelation, are the fruits of His finished work at the cross.

We have no hesitation in affirming that the rider of the white horse is the antichrist (the first beast of 13:1–10). Throughout the ages, the spirit of antichrist has manifested itself in an individual with tremendous and terrible power. Now the persistent conflict comes to a climax. Christ and Satan's masterpiece meet. In this rider we have the first manifestation of the man of sin, the accepted head of the ten confederated nations. In the crown given him, we have his acknowledgment as head of the revived empire. Passages to compare are Psalm 110:6; Daniel 7:8; Isaiah 14:16–17; Revelation 13:1–10.

White, the color of the horse, denotes the victorious power of the rider. Sacred white horses accompanied every Persian army. The antichrist, a great political leader and military strategist, will produce a series of successive bloodless conflicts. With his genius for conflict and conquest, this universal dictator will have wisdom to settle all national and international unrest and disorder. Then people will cry, "Peace and safety!" But terrible destruction will be just around the corner, as the second rider indicates: "He will be succeeded by a contemptible person who has not been given the honor of royalty. He will invade the kingdom when its people feel secure, and he will seize it through intrigue" (Daniel 11:21). False authority characterizes all that is related to this white horse rider.

Halfway through the seven years this brilliant figure becomes the beast, who will be responsible for much that is bestial in character. Then the sword will replace the bow, but the beast, taking the sword, will perish by it (13:10). Beasts are already with us, destroying the very foundations of human society. Increasing drunkenness, widespread drug addiction, legalized sodomy and abortions, sexual promiscuity, and fleshly indulgences are all precursors of the time when iniquity will burst forth uncontrolled.

Second Seal: The Red Horse—War (Revelation 6:3–4)

> The Lamb opened the second seal . . . another horse came out, a fiery red one. (Revelation 6:3–4)

The various horses symbolize the different agencies employed in the execution of divine judgment. The living creatures and horses are only related to the first four seals. Forfeiture of life is figuratively represented by the red, black, and pale colors.

As the white horse indicates bloodless victories, so the red horse brings about bloody victories. Red signifies judgment, blood, and vengeance (Jeremiah 25:15–33). With the second rider comes a global war of terrible carnage, a grim shadow of which was cast by World War II. Red, the color of blood, is a symbol of strife, violence, and war. The bow of the first rider gives way to a great sword. At present "the secret power of lawlessness" is being held in check (2 Thessalonians 2:7), but with this red horse comes unparalleled bloodshed. Now the sword is unsheathed for vengeance, not merely victory.

The phrase "was given power" brings us to the permissive will of God. This grim rider has a divine mandate to "take peace from the earth"—the false peace that he himself instituted. God promised peace to the Israelites if they were obedient, but a sword if disobedient. War ("the sword") is one of God's four sore judgments (Ezekiel 14:21; Joel 3:9–10). The devastation of modern wars is appalling, and if the world should experience a nuclear war, the destruction of life and property would be colossal. Treaties, pacts, and covenants will be torn up as scraps of paper. Life will be terribly cheap, for human beings will be but dung or manure for the earth, fit only for fertilizer (see Ezekiel 39).

Third Seal: The Black Horse—Famine (Revelation 6:5–6)

> The Lamb opened the third seal . . . before me was a black horse! (Revelation 6:5)

This black horse rider—with scales in his hand for measuring food—is a symbol of dread famine. In Lamentations 4:8 and 5:10 we discover that black is the Old Testament description of famine and destitution. Because war is no time for sowing, terrible attrition and desolation follow—thus the black horse follows the red.

Famine is the natural result of ambitious conquerors who take peace from the earth. The scorched-earth policy introduced by Gen. William Tecumseh Sherman and practiced by retreating armies during recent years is another forerunner of the ravages of famine yet to be experienced. This condition foreshadows the lamentation and mourning of those who will have to pay famine prices for bread in the great Tribulation, when a quart of wheat will be sold for one day's wage of a laborer or soldier.

Many of the rich, it would seem, are to be temporarily protected—though their sorrows come later (see James 5:1–5). Chastisement here is particularly for the majority, who will have just enough to live on (hence the mention of wheat, the bare necessity of the poor). The rank and file suffer first when revolution comes; the more affluent are the last to suffer: "Hurt not the oil and wine." (Oil and wine, as luxuries, are found on the tables of the rich.) Corn, wine, and oil are often grouped together to give the idea of plenty (Proverbs 21:17; Jeremiah 31:12; Psalm 104:15).

None are to escape the retribution they deserve. Prince and pauper alike must share in judgment (Matthew 24:6–7). God often used famine as an instrument of judgment. Thus we read of a famine in Egypt, and another when the Babylonians besieged Jerusalem, and yet another when Titus conquered Jerusalem, in A.D. 70. Ezekiel reminds us that famine is judgment upon flagrant sin (Ezekiel 14:13).

By way of contrast, note the difference in Ezekiel 36:29–30: "I will save you from all your uncleanness. I will call for the grain and make it plentiful and will not bring famine upon you. I will increase the fruit of the trees and the crops of the field, so that you will no longer suffer disgrace among the nations because of famine." (The church, we believe, will be away from the earth before these seals are broken.)

If coming events can cast their shadow before, then the terrible condition in famine-stricken areas of today's world, where thousands die daily for lack of food, portend the tragic Tribulation events, when the black horse will be conspicuous and vast multitudes will perish from hunger.

Fourth Seal: The Pale Horse—Death (Revelation 6:7–8)

When the Lamb opened the fourth seal, before me was a pale horse! (Revelation 5:6)

These initial judgments increase in severity, as the description of this new harbinger of judgment implies. Here for the first time the rider is named. And what a dreadful name it is—Death, with Hades acting as "death's hearse," as Bengel expresses it. We describe a face as being "deathly pale," an unearthly green-yellow color that implies a cadaverous hue, or a sickly looking, deathly, or corpselike aspect.

Death and hell, or Hades, are the respective custodians of bodies and souls. Death claims the body, while Hades takes the spirit. (See 1:18; 6:8; 20:13; also Isaiah 5:14.) Under this seal, all four sore judgments predicted in Ezekiel 14:21 are unleashed: "For this is what the Sovereign LORD says: How much worse will it be when I send against Jerusalem my four dreadful judgments—sword and famine and wild beasts and plague—to kill its men and their animals!" The days of Israel's greatest sorrow, long foretold, are now here.

Thus the corpselike color of the horse is in keeping with the rider. Death and Hades, inseparable companions, now act together in judgment and also provide the spoil. Hell as the consort and companion of death receives those whom death cuts off.

One of the horrors of the Tribulation will be the ghastly trail of death. War, famines, persecutions, pestilences, and earthquakes will all add their quota to the reign of the king of terrors. The pale horse and its rider will be an all-too-common sight as the shadows of final judgment gather in a condemned world. Every judgment sent upon Israel for disobedience (see Deuteronomy 28:21; Psalms 49:14; 91:6) will be repeated in the Tribulation and will be recognized as sent by God.

In this death seal, the wild beasts of the earth also become an instrument of death (see Jeremiah 5:6; 8:7). D. M. Panton would have us remember that:

Even in the day of grace, animals are only held in leash by the dread of man which God put upon them in the Noahic Covenant. What will happen in the Tribulation is obvious. Famine, with the scarcity of food for both man and beast, will drive beasts mad with hunger; depopulation will embolden them, for wherever men die out, savage beasts multiply; and God increasing their number and unchaining their ferocity, will seek to reason with carnal men by the only arguments the carnal understand. What the removal of animal dread of man will be, even from the ox or the dog, is unimaginable. God has foreshown, once for all in Israel's history, how He can use this sore weapon (Daniel 6:16–24).

The beasts of the earth (6:8) are the wild beasts who will complete the destruction. All such beasts have the culmination of their cruelty in the beast. In wrath God remembers mercy, so the rider's authority is limited. The rider of the pale horse, with Hades as his companion, is limited to "the fourth part of the earth"—that is, the political empire. The fourth world empire was the Roman Empire and covered a large area of the earth.

Sword, hunger, death, and beasts—what terrifying avenues of judgment! Would that those without Christ could be aroused to the terrible days awaiting them! Finally, Death and Hades are to be cast into the lake of fire forever, which is truly a fitting and deserved end for this horseman and his companion (20:14).

Fifth Seal: The Martyrs (Revelation 6:9–11)

When he opened the fifth seal, I saw under the altar the souls of those who had been slain. (Revelation 6:9)

Now we turn from horses to heroes, from steeds to saints. The scene darkens, and the public intervention of God in human affairs becomes more obvious. In the last three seals we have the full expression of God's wrath on guilty Christendom.

Who are these martyred saints? Some say they are two classes, Jews and Christians. But the church can hardly be included, since all believers are with the Lord by this time, having received their new bodies at the rapture. These martyrs are mainly Jews, although there are many Gentile martyrs as well. In the "How long, O Lord?" of verse 10 we have the cry of the Tribulation martyrs for the avenging of their blood—an attitude in harmony with the imprecatory psalms (see Psalms 13; 74:9, 10; 79:5; 89:46; 94:1–3; also Deuteronomy 32:40–43).

This plea for judgment upon murderers proves that the martyred were recently slain and their murderers are still alive. Cries for vengeance that are not proper now, in an age of grace, will be proper then. We have here the remnant pleading for vengeance. The martyrs are told to await restfully the right time of judgment, as many other martyrs will be added to their number. God accepts and approves their attitude.

The slain souls are "under the altar," the place of sacrifice, indicating that they are covered by the sacrifice. The ancient cry, How long shall the wicked triumph? remained unanswered until John was given the vision of those under the altar. The answer is in the white robes. In days of military triumph, Roman citizens walked through the streets dressed in white following a victorious general who had returned with trophies from battle. Did not Christ promise that His overcomers should walk with Him in white? "White robes" takes us back to the Old Testament, in which we find robes associated with honor and reward.

The fifth seal closes the first three and a half years of the Tribulation. There still remain the most severe forms of tribulation, when multitudes more who refuse to worship the beast will be killed. With them the list of martyrs will be complete.

Sixth Seal: Earthquake—Tribulation (Revelation 6:12–17)

> I watched as he opened the sixth seal. There was a great earthquake. (Revelation 6:12)

The scene now described is both terrible and exalted. As the sixth seal opens, we have the premonition of coming events: natural convulsions and human consternation. These verses are an unparalleled picture of social chaos in which nature shares the violent disruption, general catastrophe, and universal terror. Is the language literal or symbolic? Perhaps both are interwoven in John's description of governmental and moral collapse, of disasters and disturbances in social and material realms.

In this awful picture of the terrible results of apostasy, kings are found leading the agonizing hosts of earth. A disturbed heaven and earth bring about the destruction and complete overthrow of all civil and moral order. The whole structure falls. Thunder and earthquakes symbolize the upheaval within the social, ecclesiastical, and political spheres. Black represents the darkening power of Satan. The sun stands for the complete authority of government, while the moon symbolizes dependent authority and the stars picture still lesser authorities. How hearts will fail for fear!

The Great Tribulation

For the great day of their wrath has come, and who can stand? (Revelation 6:17)

Now the great Tribulation is about to begin. "The LORD takes vengeance on his foes and maintains his wrath against his enemies" (Nahum 1:2). These days of revolution and slaughter are the forerunner of the tragic time of the Tribulation. People will pray, but not to God, from whose face the horrified multitudes will flee. Instead, they will pray to the mountains (6:16). Their only safety is in hiding *in* the Lamb, not *from* Him. There is only one Refuge, the Rock of Ages, but He will offer no protection for the unrepentant, since the time of grace has now passed. No cry of repentance arises from these fear-driven multitudes, no entreaty to be delivered from their sin and from coming eternal woe—only an urgent plea for their physical safety.

The classes of people named in verse 15 include kings and princes (the rulers), chief captains (the military), rich and strong (the influential), bondslaves (the oppressed), and freemen (all the rest). They hide from God just as Adam tried to do in the Garden of Eden. As with Adam, so it will be with a guilty world when the Lord prepares to come in glory. (Note how this sixth seal corresponds to the prophecy of Isaiah 2:12, 17–22; 13:6–13; 24:1–6, as well as Psalm 2 and Nahum 1:6.)

Parenthesis—Sealing of 144,000 Jews (Revelation 7:1–17)

And God will wipe away every tear from their eyes. (Revelation 7:17)

Chapter 7 is a parenthesis of grace. In this chapter we have two separate visions: the first concerning Israel (7:1–8), and the second concerning the Gentiles (7:9–17). John gives us a deeply interesting episode of blessing for each group of redeemed saints. Just when this blessing takes place we are not told. But we do know that the return of Christ for His church will create a profound impression in the world. After the translation of the saints God will work in grace among His ancient people, the Jews, and also among the Gentiles. Many people will be saved after the rapture, and these people will incur the active and cruel hostility of the unsaved people around them. Many of these converts will be among the first group of witnesses preaching the gospel of the coming kingdom throughout the Roman world (Matthew 24:14). They will also be its first martyrs.

This break in God's judgments is provided for an outflow of God's grace. The four angels (7:1) are related to the four main directions of the compass (Isaiah 11:12; Revelation 20:8). They control the four winds, which implies that through them God controls or releases judgment. "Four" signifies the completeness and universality of judgment.

The fifth or sealing angel of verse 2 cannot be Christ, as some have suggested. The Angel-Priest of 8:3–5 and the strong Angel of 10:1–10 refer to Christ because the terms used and the actions described could not truthfully be applied to any created being, however exalted. The sealing angel is evidently a distinguished spiritual being who is authorized to seal the servants of God. He appears from the East, which is the direction from which God manifests Himself.

In Revelation 7:4–8 the sealed Jews (unlike the Gentile throng) are numbered, and the tribes are carefully distinguished. In precise figures there are 144,000 sealed Jews. These Jews are saved *before* the great Tribulation and are sealed to go *through* it. Any tampering of an official seal carries the liability of punishment. So the seal here speaks of freedom from molestation. Twelve is Israel's number, and we have in this sealing a complete yet limited number of Israel—the Jewish remnant preserved from martyrdom. This group of 144,000 is not identical with the same number of people mentioned Revelation 14. Here we have 144,000 of all Israel; in chapter 14 we have the 144,000 of Judah only.

We are not told when the sealing of the specific number out of the twelve tribes of Israel takes place. But because the seal is in the name of the Lamb and the name of the Father, the Jews who are described must have accepted the Lamb as their Messiah and are now protected because of the choice they made. Those Israelites who were faithful to God in spite of the abominations committed by others among their nation were protected by a mark on their foreheads (Ezekiel 9:4). So the 144,000 are among those whom Daniel refers to as "found written in the book" (Daniel 12:1; see also Malachi 3:16–17).

A seal represents official recognition and possession, so any tampering with it is subject to penalty. God will have a sealed people whom He will protect and deliver through the tragic time overtaking the whole earth. This seal will also shield those who possess it from the demons released from the pit (Revelation 9:4).

The vast, unnumbered multitude of Gentiles (7:9–17) is in sharp contrast to the more limited and exactly defined number of Jews. This palm-bearing Gentile multitude must not be confused with either the church or Israel. This is the mighty ingathering of souls that Joel predicted when he said that in the day of the Lord whoever called upon Him would be saved (Joel 2:30–32). The innumerable company represents the fruit of an extensive work of grace begun after the translation of the church and continued through the future prophetic week of seven years. Previously John had described the ascription of praise for those redeemed out of every nation (Revelation 5:9–10). This great multitude is clearly identified in verse 14 as having come out of "the tribulation, the great one."

Will the Holy Spirit Depart with the Church?

Some people teach that the Holy Spirit will be completely withdrawn from the earth once the church is caught up to meet the Lord in the air. But because the Spirit is always virtually connected with human salvation, He must be the active Agent in the great revival among those on the earth after the rapture. In 7:14 the word is "come," not "came." John is recording not a past act but a present action, and these who keep coming are blood washed, so the Spirit must be near, since He is always the One to apply the efficacious blood of the Lamb.

The phrase "in the blood of the Lamb" should read "*through* the blood of the Lamb," implying "because of." Nothing can ever be made white by washing it in blood. All who stand before the throne of God are eternally secure because of all Christ accomplished on their behalf, and their acceptance of Him as their Substitute.

This great saved multitude will not form part of the church but will have a place before the throne. C. I. Scofield remarks, "They are not of the priesthood, the church, to which they seem to stand somewhat in the relation of the Levites to the priests under the Mosaic Covenant." We cannot regard this saved company as a heavenly one, for what is presented is an earthly scene. All the people of earth who pass into the millennium must be those who acknowledge the Lamb as their Lord. Millennial blessings, however, are to be shared by this white-robed throng (7:15, 17).

For these Tribulation saints there are manifold rewards, as John clearly indicates (7:14–17; 14:13; 15:2–4; 20:4). The rewards include:

- to be before the throne of God;
- to serve God continually in His temple;
- to have God forever in their midst;
- to be delivered from future hunger and thirst;
- to be protected from sun or heat;
- to have the Lamb as their Shepherd to feed and lead them;
- to have God wipe away all their tears;
- to experience rest from their labors;
- to be commended for their faithful work;
- to have harps of God and sing upon the sea of glass;
- to reign with Christ forever.

Seventh Seal—Silence (Revelation 8:1)

There was silence in heaven for about half an hour. (Revelation 8:1)

Why does a whole chapter intervene between the sixth and seventh seals, breaking the orderly sequence of events? One answer is that the sixth seal (6:12–17) announced such appalling judgment that people will think this horror is the great day of the wrath of the Lamb. But it is not. So before the seventh seal is opened in preparation for further and more severe judgments, the veil is drawn aside to introduce two great groups of people redeemed by grace even while judgment is desolating the earth.

When this seventh seal is opened and all the contents of the previous six seals are completed, there will be silence in heaven, and not elsewhere.

This seal of silence is somewhat startling, since we have little silence in the book as a whole. Indeed, Revelation is a book of speech, thunder, voices, and fast-moving action.

What is the significance of this silence, the only content of the seal? It represents a brief pause during which the course of divine judgment is suspended. God is reluctant to smite, for He has no pleasure in the death of the wicked. The silence also indicates a pause between two series. This seventh seal is a unique conclusion to all the terrible judgments of the other seals and a fitting interlude between them and the terrible events of the seven trumpets to follow. It is a stillness before the storm, a calm before catastrophe. It is a solemn sign that the Lord is about to leave His holy place to punish the earth. It foreshadows the terrible nature of coming anguish.

This silence is in heaven, seeing that the source of earth judgments is the throne set in heaven. As to the "half an hour," it simply signifies a brief period during which judicial action is suspended. Half an hour will be long enough. It will seem like centuries to those who wait breathlessly for the Lord to smite! When the silence is over, His work of judgment will be a short one. "The LORD is slow to anger and great in power; the LORD will not leave the guilty unpunished. His way is in the whirlwind and the storm, and clouds are the dust of his feet" (Nahum 1:3).

5

The Seven Trumpets

Revelation 8:2–11:19

Then the seven angels who had the seven trumpets prepared to sound them.
(Revelation 8:6)

The Angels (Revelation 8:2–6)

The fact that the word "angel" occurs over seventy times in Revelation proves how prominent angel ministry is in the unfolding of God's final purposes for the world. His angels are the media of His manifold operations. In this church age we are not dependent upon angels, since the Holy Spirit is the Administrator of the affairs of the church and acts as the Executor of the Godhead, the true Vicar of Christ. But after the rapture of the church the angels are again conspicuous in the execution of divine edicts. "Things they desire to look into" will be fully understood by them as they come to carry out their heaven-given mission. The more we read Revelation, the more we are impressed by the obedience, dignity, and authority of these angelic beings, who are mentioned more often in Revelation than in any other book of the Bible.

The Greek word for "angel" means simply messenger and is used for human as well as heavenly heralds. The "angels of the seven churches" (1:20) are the spiritual rulers in the churches who were responsible for maintaining the light of the glorious gospel during the dark night of church history.

The context where the word "angel" is used determines its application to human or heavenly beings. In such passages as Luke 7:24, 9:52,

2 Corinthians 12:7, and James 2:25, the word "messenger"— the same word in the original as "angel"—is used of those sent on messages of various kinds. When the term is used specifically for heavenly beings, it also implies the great characteristic of service (Psalm 103:20–21; Hebrews 1:13–14). In other passages "angel" carries the idea of "representations" or "guardianship," as in our Lord's announcement about the little ones having their angels in heaven to represent them (Matthew 18:10). "His angel" in Revelation 1:1 was a heavenly being prominent in the hierarchy of heaven, who in his ministry represented the Lord of Angels.

In this gospel age the angels are ministering spirits, sent forth for those who shall be heirs of salvation (Hebrews 1:13–14). In the section of Revelation that deals with the preparation for and execution of Christ's judicial authority, almost every phrase has its angel or angels, as this brief summary shows:

- An angel is the intermediary between Christ and John in the conveyance of the book of Revelation (1:1–4).
- Angels are the moral representatives of the seven churches (1:20; chapters 2 and 3).
- An angel challenges the universe to bring forth One competent enough to fulfill the righteous counsels of God relating to the world (5:2).
- Angels are a numberless throng that worships and praises Christ as the slain Lamb (5:11–12).
- Angels are given power to control natural elements (7:1).
- Angels have authority to seal those who are true servants of God (7:2–3).
- Angels are trumpeters, each of the seven trumpets having its own angel (chapter 8).
- Angels are identified with the seven bowls of divine wrath (chapter 6).
- Angels are allies of God in the heavenly war against hellish forces (chapter 12).
- An angel proclaims the everlasting gospel (14:6).
- An angel announces the dread news of the fall of Babylon (14:8).
- An angel thunders forth the terrible doom of the worshipers of the beast (14:9).

- An angel comes out of the temple (14:15), and another angel comes out of the altar (14:18).
  An angel is the guardian of the waters—a symbol of the peoples of earth, who are controlled by the angel under the governing hand of God (17:15)—who acquiesces in divine judgment.

Two groups of seven angels are singled out. The first is associated with the trumpet judgments (chapters 8–14) and is called "*the* seven angels." The article "the" is emphasized in the original text, implying their high and honored position before God's throne. The second group is associated with the divine wrath, or the last plagues (15:1; 16:1). The plague angels are not given the definite article, so they are probably not of the same order as the angel trumpeters who have the honor of standing before God (8:2). Two other numbered groups of angels include four angels (7:1) and twelve angels (21:12).

While it is true that a numberless host of angels wait upon the throne of God (Daniel 7:10), it would seem as if these seven trumpet angels are *presence* angels, similar to Isaiah's "angel of his presence" (Isaiah 63:9), and are therefore of an exalted order. Gabriel describes his position as standing in the presence of God (see Luke 1:19). Can it be that all seven of these angels are archangels?

The number seven implies that these angels represent the complete power of God in judicial affairs and that they are the executors of His will in respect to judgment. Behind their pronouncements and actions is the authority of the throne before whose divine Occupant they stand. That there are distinctions among the angelic hosts is hinted at by Paul in Ephesians 6:12. But while various orders and ranks are distributed among the angels of God, they never usurp their position, but unitedly offer God unquestioning obedience and activity in service.

Seven Angels with Seven Trumpets (8:2)

Angels who had the seven trumpets prepared to sound them. (Revelation 8:6)

In Joshua 6, the seven trumpets of ram's horn that were sounded by the seven priests on seven successive days announced and achieved the overthrow of Jericho. The priests blew their trumpets together; the angels blow theirs one by one. Thus it would appear that one angel is the equivalent of seven priests, and therefore "greater in power and might," as Peter says.

Trumpets served many purposes in Old Testament times. They were used for journeys, alarms, public notices, and preparation of God's hosts against His enemies (Numbers 10:1–9; Jeremiah 1:14–18; 4:19; Joel 2:1; Matthew 24:31). Walter Scott remarks, "The *seven* trumpets signify a complete and full announcement. The *mystic* trumpets of Revelation are not to be confounded with the literal trumpets of Old Testament times." Once these trumpet blasts are heard, people will not be confused as to their significance and dread message. Is there not something majestic yet solemn about these angelic trumpeters as they prepare to sound? There they stand in rank, trumpet in hand, waiting to blast forth their respective judgments (8:6).

Out of the impressive silence of the seventh seal, the seven trumpets emerge with their increasingly severe judicial mission. The first four trumpets describe the civil and ecclesiastical condition of the revived western Roman Empire. The fifth trumpet or first woe is related to apostate Judaism. The sixth trumpet or second woe is associated with the guilty, godless inhabitants of the Roman world. The seventh trumpet or third woe suggests the universal effects of God's judgments.

As to the seven seals, the seven trumpets, and the seven bowls, these are not identical judgments executed concurrently. They present three *different* series of judgments experienced successively during the great tribulation, or Daniel's seventieth week.

Another Angel (8:3–5)

Another angel, who had a golden censer, came and stood at the altar. . . . took the censer, . . . and hurled it on the earth. (Revelation 8:3, 5)

Before we examine more closely the announcements of the seven angels, we must identify the separate angel—"another angel"—who appears in their company (8:3–5). Is this just another angel or is it someone in particular? Whenever the phrase "another angel" appears in Revelation, the Greek word *allos* is used—*another of the same kind.* Most expositors believe that the expression "the angel of the Lord," wherever it occurs, implies the presence of deity in angelic form and sometimes even in human form (Genesis 18:1–14, etc.). They call these the *theophanic appearances of Christ* before His incarnation. Christ is like angels in respect to His heavenly, spiritual being. But He is infinitely better than angels because He is the Son of God and the Lord of the Angels, who in order to save lost mankind was made a little lower than the angels.

Some expositors of Revelation affirm that the special angel functioning at the altar is one of the angelic host, not the Lord Jesus Christ. They maintain that He is the Lamb opening the seals and directing the processes of judgment and that His mission in the Tribulation is not one of intercession but of processed condemnation. They further explain that the incense mentioned is given to this prominent angel, whereas Christ would have needed no one to hand Him the censer.

But we are convinced that no angel, whatever its high rank, is qualified to stand at the celestial altar before God on behalf of humans, nor is an angel given priestly functions to exercise.

As there is only one Mediator between God and men, the Man Christ Jesus, who gave Himself a ransom for all, we are convinced that this Angel-Priest, whose action at the altars is of a mediatorial character, is Christ, our Great High Priest.

The glory of the descending Angel of Jehovah is seen in a threefold way: as the Angel-Priest, on behalf of His suffering remnant (chapter 8); as the Angel-Redeemer, taking possession of His inheritance (chapter 10); and as the Angel-Avenger of His people, taking vengeance on Babylon (chapter 18).

The Angel-Redeemer is not an ordinary angel because He refers to the two martyred prophets as "*my* two witnesses" (11:3), which could not be written of any angel. Further, the *rainbow* (10:1) is never used in the Bible apart from God. Therefore the angel here must be the Son of God. "He gave a shout like the roar of a lion" speaks of Him as "the lion of the tribe of Judah" (5:5).

This Angel-Priest must surely be the Mediator, Jesus Christ, for no other can add efficacy to the prayers of the saints. In the heavenly scene that John received and recorded, discernible features appear under Jewish imagery. For example, priests alone served at both the brazen and golden altars. The altar of burnt offering, standing in the court of the tabernacle, is recalled by the language John uses.

The Spirit-inspired prayers of saints are never forgotten. If these prayers are not answered in the lifetime of those offering them, they are often answered after the intercessors have gone to heaven. The Lord never forgets any of His own. They are always in remembrance before Him.

Incense represents the Savior's life and labors. His sweet savor is the incense, and His efficacious death and resurrection give God's acceptance to our Spirit-inspired prayers. The altar is the place of substitutionary atonement, while fire speaks of divine judgment upon sin (and judgment upon the earth is what the angel-trumpeters announce—8:5–6). It must be noted that the angels only announce judgment; they do not execute or dispense it. But the Angel-Priest hurled on earth the judgment (8:5).

First Trumpet: Third of the Earth Burns Up (Revelation 8:7)

The first angel sounded his trumpet, . . . A third of the earth was burned up. (Revelation 8:7)

Scripture is not silent as to the symbolic significance of the figures used. Symbols occur in the visions and all through Revelation. These symbols were understood by the first readers of the book, and we too can understand them, for Scripture interprets Scripture.

Hail, coming from above, proves God to be the Executor of severe judgment in a sudden, sharp and overwhelming calamity. (See Joshua 10:11; Isaiah 28:2, 17; 30:30; Ezekiel 13:13, etc.)

Fire, symbolically used of God, of Christ, and of the Holy Spirit, is often employed as an expression of God's wrath upon people because of their sins (see Deuteronomy 32:22; Isaiah 33:14; Matthew 25:41). It also indicates the purifying influence of the Word of God (see Jeremiah 23:29; Malachi 3:2).

Blood signifies dreadful slaughter, life forfeited by sin but claimed by a holy God, and complete apostasy from God and truth (see Leviticus 3:17; 17:10–14; Revelation 14:20; 16:3).

Hail and fire mingled with blood present a fearful combination. Such a trinity expresses a terrible manifestation of divine wrath upon the earth and its inhabitants. As for the seven trumpet judgments, the first four are upon places, material things, and the accessories of life. The last three are upon persons—upon people and life itself.

Under the first judgment, a third of the trees are burned up. Different parts of the world have experienced devastating forest fires, but history records no such event as a third of all the trees in the world being destroyed by fire. Therefore a historical interpretation can be ruled out. The twelvefold repetition of the phrase "third part" is impressive. As used by John, it is equivalent to the revived power of Rome. We must not forget that the shadow of Rome, past and future, is cast over this book of Revelation. The twelve third parts can represent God's vengeance upon Rome, since twelve is God's governmental number concerning the most guilty part of the earth.

Trees symbolize human greatness and pride (see Ezekiel 31; Daniel 4; Revelation 8:7). Our righteous God hates human pride and will overtake the high and mighty of the earth with judgment.

Grass, symbolic of temporary prosperity (and likewise of human frailty), here describes the desolation of so many people, even though they had the "green grass" of a highly prosperous condition (see Isaiah 40:6–7; James 1:10; 1 Peter 1:24; Revelation 8:7).

Second Trumpet: The Sea Turns to Blood (Revelation 8:8–9)

A third of the sea turned into blood. (Revelation 8:8)

Comparing Scripture with Scripture, we find that the sea is used of the restlessness of human nature and also of peoples in a state of anarchy and confusion (Isaiah 57:20; Revelation 8:8; 13:1). Ships represent travel and commerce (Genesis 49:13; Revelation 8:9; 18:19).

Phrases such as "something like" (8:8) occur often in the book of Revelation and indicate symbolic language (see Jeremiah 51:25, where "mountain" is the symbol of a kingdom; see also Psalm 46:2 and Zechariah 4:7). All the Gentile world is to suffer God's righteous vengeance.

The sea becoming blood corresponds to the plague that overtook the Nile River (Exodus 7:17–21). Just as the ever restless sea symbolizes the masses of earth in rebellion because of the absence of a strong hand to rule them, the bloodlike sea describes the fearful destruction that will overtake them. Make the sea impassable, and the world's main highway of trade is blighted. The uses and products of the sea—the "third of the living creatures" (8:9)—are indelibly stamped with the sign of death. The symbol of a burning mountain cast into the sea denotes that this destruction is not caused by anything within human power, but comes directly from God as a judgment warning.

The destruction of a third of the ships reveals how commerce and communication will also feel the weight of divine judgment. Exports and imports will be seriously curtailed. In World War II there was a colossal toll of sinkings; about a third of all the naval ships of the nations involved in the war went to the bottom of the sea! A tremendous ship-building program replaced this dreadful toll of sunken ships. In the Tribulation days, however, with men and materials destroyed, such replacement of losses will not be possible.

Third Trumpet: Water Becomes Bitter (Revelation 8:10–11)

A third of the waters turned bitter. (Revelation 8:11)

Rivers and fountains of waters suggest sources of profitable pleasure or of nations acting under turbulent influences (Revelation 16:4–5; 17:15; Jeremiah 2:13; Joel 3:18). But as the third angel sounds, the call goes out to earth's pleasure-producing sources to go to war against rebellious people. The meteor, with its gaseous vapors covering the fresh-water supply, will be absorbed by a third of the waters, rivers, and fountains, recalling what happened in the first Egyptian plague.

In this judgment of terrible severity there falls from heaven a great star, which symbolizes the instrument of God's power. This particular "star" is not to be confused with the falling star under the fifth trumpet (9:1). Still, both are spiritual rulers, fallen from their high position. Heaven is the center and source of divine authority ("The heavens do rule"—Daniel 4:26), and the apostate rulers are subject to such dominion. We are not told who the one of exalted rank is (but see Isaiah 14:12).

The term "wormwood" is not so much the name of the person referred to as it is descriptive of that person's evil influence. Some writers identify the great star as Satan or the antichrist. Wormwood is related to sagebrush and is the source of an essential oil obtained from the dried leaves and tops of the plant. As such it symbolizes bitterness (Deuteronomy 29:18; Jeremiah 23:15). The continuous use of this liquor produces mental deterioration and even death (Lamentations 3:15, 19).

Earth is to reap the bitter fruits of sin, as essential supplies are contaminated by this plant. In times of war, nations experience how detrimental it is to have their natural and communal supply of water polluted or cut off. Under these circumstances the wonder is not that many died but that any lived.

Every earthborn pleasure has bitter "wormwood" in it, and in the Tribulation judgment a third part of the earth, instead of finding life in fountains of water, finds death. Conversely, God is able to make bitter waters sweet (Exodus 15:25–27). The geographical area affected by the blight of bitterness is the third part, suggesting that the steps of God from mercy to judgment are always slow, reluctant, and measured.

Fourth Trumpet: The Sun, Moon, and Stars Are Darkened (Revelation 8:12–13)

And a third of the sun was struck . . . the moon . . . the stars . . . the day . . . and a third of the night. (Revelation 8:12)

The judgment of the fourth trumpet will be hard on those lovers of astrology who believe their life is regulated by the movement of the sun, the moon, and the stars. The declarations of horoscopes about the events of our present or future life are pure nonsense. Our times are not wrapped up in the stars but are in the hands of Him who made the stars! Astronomy is a most fascinating and legitimate study, but astrology is simply guesswork on the part of money-inspired necromancers.

People speak about the laws of nature being fixed, but God's command of the luminaries in the heavens declares Him to be the Lord of the universe. When it comes to light or darkness, He can do just as He pleases, as the Egyptians discovered when they suffered a terrible blackout but saw that the Israelites had light in their dwellings. When first created, sun, moon, and stars were commissioned to give light upon the earth, and their power for good has always been great. Now, however, the benefit received from them is diminished by one-third, for God's edict goes forth to destroy a third part of them.

During World War II the British people were accustomed to black-outs during disastrous air raids. But all they could do was to extinguish artificial lights. They could not stop the heavenly lights from shining. During a blackout it seemed ironic to hear an air warden shout to a house-holder, "Put out that light!" while above a most brilliant moon was send-ing out its light as usual, making visible so much for the raiders to see. But a divine blackout is coming, and when God withdraws the rays of sun, moon, and stars, the earth will experience a darkness it will dread.

The last verse of this chapter contains a loud and universal an-nouncement of three woes that usher in the three last trumpets. These solemn woes indicate the severity of further judgments, and their terri-fying effect. These last three trumpets will result in a new quality and de-gree of divine displeasure and consequent disaster. The woe is threefold because the three worst judgments are yet to come.

Fifth Trumpet: The Stars Fall to Earth (Revelation 9:1–11)

I saw a star that had fallen from the sky to the earth. (Revelation 9:1)

With the sounding of the last three trumpets we pass from the visi-ble to the invisible. The previous trumpets dealt with material sur-roundings, things seen by the human eye; this fifth trumpet deals with the spiritual realm. A sad sight is presented under this judgment, but worse is yet to come. In the verses before us we have one of the most fearsome descriptions of devastation ever penned, as the fifth angel goes forth to exercise a frightful mission.

Here again the star falling to earth has been variously identified. Some say it indicates Satan being cast out of heaven, or the antichrist, or the false prophet, or a religious or political system. We feel that the fallen star may be the antichrist, Satan's chosen instrument to inflict such scenes of cruelty and bloodshed depicted by John. To this expelled one is committed "the key to the shaft of the Abyss" (9:1)—the prison house of demons. Possession of "the key" means doleful power and authority to execute death. The smoke arising out of the abyss results in a most devas-tating army of locusts. By smoke we can understand the blinding and withering effect of satanic delusion. Paul's portrait of "the work of

Satan" in 2 Thessalonians 2:9 corresponds to the power that Satan makes possible for the locust army.

The locusts with power as scorpions symbolize those hordes of devilish agencies bringing vengeance upon the guilty, who are described as those "who did not have the seal of God on their foreheads" (9:4). As 144,000 of Israel are sealed, and therefore secure from judgment (7:3–4), it is the unsealed Gentile multitudes who must drink the cup of vengeance. As Israel escaped the plagues that punished Egypt, so the new Israel is exempted from the attack of the locusts of the abyss.

The description of these locusts is heavy with meaning. This locust plague is based upon similar plagues in Exodus and Joel, where we are reminded of the fearful havoc locusts wreaked upon plants. Under the fifth trumpet they are the symbol of the terrible nature of the judgment to overtake people.

The locusts are given power as scorpions (9:3). Travelers in the East, where scorpions are very common, are wary of this creature, which can sting sharply and severely when disturbed. Lobsterlike in appearance, scorpions secrete poison from their tails. This striking weapon is an instrument of excruciating pain, mental distress, and, sometimes, even death. Native peoples fear the sting of the scorpion because of the dreadful suffering it causes. Our Lord connected serpents and scorpions with the power of Satan (Luke 10:19).

The locusts are commanded not to hurt the grass (9:4). Why this specific prohibition? God as the Creator breaks in upon natural law again and suspends the natural food habits of locusts, which normally feed on grass, other plants, and trees. This sparing of the vegetable world suggests a temporary preservation of the most necessary commodities. Under the eighth Egyptian plague the locusts destroyed every green thing (Exodus 10:12–15). But now their consumption of green things is in abeyance, and they hurt only humans who do not belong to God.

The locusts are given the power to torment for five months (9:5). Why only five months? Such a limited time implies that this trumpet judgment will not separate the guilty from God forever and is permitted mainly to warn sinners of the final doom awaiting them unless they repent. The specified months are likewise related to the locusts themselves because the natural lifespan of the locust is from May to September. Thus their entire lifespan is taken up with inflicting anguish. Here we have a brief but determinate period of woe for those marked for torture. How relieved the tormented will be that the locusts do not live longer than five months! During the activity of these creatures, the human anguish will be both indescribable and unrelievable, a gnawing and horrible plague that is dreadful in the extreme.

In these days people will seek death and not find it (9:6). Sin produces torment, takes away all pleasure of living, and often causes the sinner to long for death. But the permitted powers of physical distress are not allowed to kill, and therein lies the warning to repent. Death would be a welcome relief to those so grievously afflicted, but death eludes them. Suicide will not be possible, and the power to kill is withheld from the locusts themselves, for the commission is only to torture. What despair will possess those who desire to end their anguish by taking their life, but are not able to die!

The locusts are shaped like warhorses (9:7). Sin brings its own punishment, and there are forces always ready to assail the sinner, as is emphasized by this further description of the locusts. Like warhorses, the locust army stands arrayed and ready to carry out the command of its king. Hostile armies, especially cavalry, are symbolized by a locust invasion in Jeremiah 51:27 and Joel 2. In Italy and other countries where locusts abound, they are called little horses because their heads resemble horses' heads. "They have the appearance of horses; they gallop along like cavalry" (Joel 2:4).

The locusts wear "something like crowns of gold" (9:7). The characteristic phrase "something like" suggests a make-believe sovereignty. "Crowns" represent victory and dominion, and "gold" denotes deity. A divinely conferred crown of gold rests upon the head of Christ (Revelation 14:14), but here the dignity and pretension of royal authority is spurious. Satan has always been an imitator of the real.

The locusts have faces that resemble human faces (9:7). They do not have real human faces, but imitation ones. Underlining this description is the thought that the pain of the locusts is not inflicted indiscriminately, but is intelligently regulated according to the sin committed. The faces of these demonic hordes, suggesting human intelligence and capacity, will give them added terror. But, lacking human intelligence, they cannot heed an appeal to human reason. They act mechanically as commanded.

The locusts have teeth like lions' teeth (9:8). What is more suggestive of destruction than the teeth of lions! Sin, when eagerly pursued, ultimately destroys the sinner as if his head were literally crushed between the massive teeth of a lion's jaw. The implication of this symbolism is that the smoke-borne, fearsome locusts will be cruel, savage, and relentless in the torment they cause.

The locusts have, as it were, breastplates of iron (9:9). These hellish agents of torture are immune from personal destruction. Destitute of all feeling, on they come, showing no pity. Humans are helpless to pierce their defense. Any effort to drive them back will be useless. No human weapon will be strong enough to keep them back. But for the child of God there is always protection against all the forces of darkness. Paul calls it "the breastplate of righteousness" (Ephesians 6:14).

The locusts' wings make a sound like chariots in battle (9:9). How vivid is the symbol at this point! "The sound of their wings was like the thundering of many horses and chariots rushing into the battle." Humans will not be able to overcome or force back their deserved judgment by the might of their own armaments nor will they be able to evade or escape the judgment, for the armies of terror will march down upon them from all sides. Joel employs a similar description of the utter hopelessness of resistance against the oncoming armies of destruction (Joel 2:5).

The locusts have stings in their tails (9:10). Naturalists tell us that the scorpion constantly shakes his tail to strike, and that the torment caused by his sting is severe. Another reading of Revelation 9:10 is, "There were stings, and their authority was in their tail to hurt." Charmed into sin, only to be destroyed by its lionlike teeth, the sinner who follows after sin is sure to receive its scorpionlike sting.

The locusts have a king (9:11). Solomon, one of the greatest naturalists of the past, tells us that ordinary locusts have no king (Proverbs 30:37). But the horrible scorpions that John describes have a cruel leader. From Joel we learn that the invading host does not wander aimlessly around but that each one walks in its designated route. The destructive forces that John depicts are under the devil, who is the king of the infernal powers of hell. While the antichrist will be the personification of Satan's malignant influence, the commander of the locust army is Satan himself.

John gives Satan the names Abaddon and Apollyon. Abaddon means "perdition" and is a name given to the place of destruction. Job tells us that before God, "Destruction [Hebrew *'abaddon*] lies uncovered" (Job 26:6; see also Proverbs 15:11). Apollyon is the Greek form of the Hebrew name and means "Destroyer." Satan is not just the king but is also the spirit of destruction that inspires these dreadful hosts. This vivid picture reveals Satan as "a destroyer of nations" (Jeremiah 4:7)—not only of corrupt Christendom but also of apostate Judaism.

Sixth Trumpet: An Army of Two-Hundred Million
(Revelation 9:12–21)

The number of the mounted troops was two hundred million. (Revelation 9:16)

The judgment of this second woe trumpet, while resembling the judgment of the previous trumpet, is more grievous. To the vast hosts— to the powers of the horse, the lion, and the scorpion—are added new desolating forces. The multitudes are more numerous and the horses' heads are more lionlike. As the sixth trumpet sounds, John hears "a voice coming from the horns of the golden altar that is before God" (9:13). The golden altar stood in the immediate presence of God and received the offered incense, symbolizing the accepted prayers and worship of God's people. Here the golden altar reminds us that the judgments to follow come in response to the cry of persecuted and martyred saints, "How long, O Lord?"

The separate quartet of angels has an ominous mission to perform, and their united authoritative voice carries God's answer to the cries of His suffering children. Now they are to avenged. The number four is significant, for it is the number of earth and suggests universality. We have four seasons of the year and the four quarters of the earth. The four metals and the four beasts of Daniel 2 and 7 represent the four universal empires—Babylon, Medo-Persia, Greece, and Rome. The four divisions of the human race are "nation, tribe, people, and language" (Revelation 7:9).

"Horn" symbolizes strength and power (Psalm 132:17) and "golden altar" speaks of the privilege of worship and communion made possible by the blood that was shed at the brazen altar. Chained in loving obedience to the altar until needed, the four angels (God's love slaves) are liberated to accomplish their deadly task. This angelic quartet is different from the four restraining angels of 7:1–3, whose mission is to hold in check evil forces. Here the four angels liberate destructive powers and operate in the circumscribed region of the Euphrates River.

The Euphrates River is worthy of being called great because it is some 1,780 miles in length, the longest and most important river in Western Asia. On the northeast boundary of Palestine this famous river formed a line of defense against the powerful enemies of Israel, the Assyrians. Sometimes its waters overflowed, sweeping everything before them. This is why Isaiah used the river as a symbol of the destructive onrush of the Assyrians to execute divine judgments upon Israel (Isaiah 8:5–8). As used by John, this same river is the site of God's judgment on the unsaved world, although the destructive element is limited to "the third part." The Euphrates was where human sin began and where Satan held dominion for so long. Now it endures the divine scourge (Revelation 9:14; 16:12).

The angelic ministers of retribution cannot act without God's signal. They are held in check until "this very hour and day and month and year." These periods of time refer to the restraint of the angels, not to the duration of the ministry of destruction. Why they were held in check so long we are not told. All we know is that they could not strike until the set hour on God's clock. They were always ready to perform their task, but were not let loose until the exact moment appointed in the counsels of God had arrived (9:15). God's judgments are held in His divine limitations.

This sixth judgment will be sharp and overwhelming: "a third of mankind" will be slain. Under the third seal a fourth part was slain (6:8), and now a third of the remaining three-fourths are slain. What a bloodbath awaits the inhabitants of all the territory associated with the Euphrates!

In 9:16–19 John describes 200 million horsemen. For the terrible slaughter of the godless, God orders out His reserves, who are not human beings, but demon incarnations. (Global wars have accustomed us to seeing millions die; think of the millions upon millions of deaths associated with World War II!) The vast and overwhelming army is to rid the earth of those who have long held God in contempt. One out of every three humans will succumb to these horsemen of hell, whose defensive armor is a combination of fire, smoke, and sulfur—symbols of everlasting torment. As J. Stafford Wright expresses it:

> John now sees all the horrors of war. In his day armed cavalry were some of the most terrible forces, and he sees these first. But as he looks, he is aware that these are no ordinary horses, but strange monsters that destroy with smoke that comes from their mouths, and from other mouths at the end of serpent-like tails. There is no doubt that John was allowed to see the destroying instruments in the form of artillery. Under the inspiration of Satan, man turns everything to his own destruction, and war succeeds war.

Scripture references to the qualities of the horse are numerous, but little is said of its use as a beast of burden or for agricultural purposes. The Jews were forbidden to have many horses because acquiring them involved returning to Egypt (Deuteronomy 17:16), which was most famous for its cavalry horses. In Scripture a horse is regarded as a symbol of war, just as a donkey is a symbol of peace. Successful power in war and conquest is associated with the horses that John describes (Revelation 6:1–8; Zechariah 6:1–8). Under this sixth trumpet the locusts, with their destruction and agony, give way to horses—fearful and hideous, the aggressive and military agents of rapine and slaughter.

They have heads like lions' heads (9:17). Have you ever paused to study the head of a lion in a zoo or in a photograph? What majesty, courage, strength, and fearlessness its features portray! No wonder the lion is spoken of as the king of beasts. These judgment horses, with lionlike heads, are invested with all the fearsome qualities of lions.

They have mouths of smoke (9:17). Satan is to arm his four-legged host with a trinity of offensive destructive forces: fire, smoke, and sulfur. These elements out of the mouths of the horses will give the godless a foretaste of the agony of the lake of fire. Belching forth hellish fumes, the horses will manifest diabolical pleasure in their task. Further references to these symbols of anguish can be found in 2:18, 14:10, and 19:20.

They have tails like serpents (9:19). In Scripture, the tail symbolizes false prophets and false teaching (Isaiah 9:14–15). As used in Revelation, it expresses Satan's malignant influence, falsehood, and mischief (12:4).

"Heads with which they inflict injury" (9:19) shows that Satan's craftiness is intelligently directed. Head is emblematic of the seat of moral government, and intelligence, and power (Isaiah 7:8–9; Zechariah 6:11; 1 Corinthians 11:3–10). What hope has a single sinner against such a combination of satanic subtlety and misdirected wisdom!

The fact that the third part of humanity is killed by the fire, smoke, and sulfur has no sobering effect on the survivors. The limit of divine forbearance has been reached, and so God permits those deserving of His wrath to reap what they have sown. Persistent forgetfulness or defiance of God ends in abandonment to merited fate. The spared apostates persist in their hardness of heart in spite of the fearful terrors of the horsemen of hell. Twice, we read, they "did not repent." Because of this, sin is allowed to work out its inevitable doom.

Describing the end-time period of the Gentile age, Jesus declared that "iniquity shall abound." Here we have summarized some of the gross forms of iniquity during those last days.

- *They worship demons.* Demonism, Satan worship, and black magic are widespread today. We live in a demonized world. John predicts the time when the demon host will be worshipped openly and universally.
- *They worship idols.* The rest of the people have lifeless idols, according to their station in life. The rich have gods of gold and silver. The middle class have idols of brass and stone. The poor have idols of wood. Satanism and idol worship give rise to evil deeds.
- *They are murderers.* "Nor did they repent of their murders." Our Lord said that Satan was a murderer from the beginning; he was the instigator of Cain's murder of his brother, Abel. Since that first murder in the world, countless millions of people have been murdered, including a vast host of believers as martyrs for their faith. In our time the daily toll of murders is frightening, but in the time that John describes, when murderers are satanically energized, the practice will be even more habitual.
- *They are sorcerers.* Witchcraft and illicit dealings with spirits (which is an integral part of spiritism or spiritualism) have made rapid strides over the last fifty years and cast a grim shadow on the future. Strongly condemned in Scripture, sorcery

meets its doom when judgment descends upon all who traffic with "familiar spirits." Interestingly, our English word "sorcerer" is *pharmakos* in the original, from which we get *pharmacy*. From a root meaning "enchantment" the word came to signify "drug." We have certainly come to a drugged age, when various drugs are warping the minds of multitudes, especially many of the youth of our time. Repentance will be far from the narcotic addicts of the Tribulation era.

- *They are fornicators.* When God and justice are rejected, and when general wickedness prevails, what else can be expected but indulgence in the wildest forms of unbridled lust? Easy divorces make a mockery of the safeguard and bulwark of the marriage tie. Unions are broken almost as quickly as they are made. Our low moral standards are a shadow of the corrupt condition of the world when the sixth trumpet is to sound.

- *They are thieves.* Never before in the history of the world has thieving been as widespread as it is today. Thefts from stores, banks, and other business concerns have reached an appalling number. The mass of people not killed by hell's horsemen will have little respect for each other's rights. The gospel of the day will be, "Each for himself, and the devil take the rest." People will live to enrich themselves at the expense of their neighbors. International gangsters, who have no regard for the property of others, will become more common as the age deteriorates. But their doom is sure.

Before we approach the parenthesis between the six and seventh trumpets, let us review the meaning of the first six trumpets.

The first *four trumpets* show us humans as citizens of a sin-blighted world; everything above and around them tells of the curse brought by their fall.

The *fifth trumpet* presents humans as the actual sinners and shows us the whole world "lying in the wicked one." Humans sin and are therefore of the devil, and their sins bring hell-sent torments.

The *sixth trumpet* makes it clear that judgments come upon sinners by virtue of the fixed law that sin must inevitably bring suffering. The divinely inflicted judgments remind us that God is angry with the wicked every day. Under the sounding of this trumpet the positive infliction of

God's judgments upon humanity is symbolized. Because humans are left without excuse, their escape from punishment is impossible.

Interlude (Revelation 10:1–11:14)

> I saw another mighty angel . . . He was holding a little scroll, which lay open in his hand. (Revelation 10:1–2)

Between the sixth and seventh trumpets we have an impressive and significant parenthesis, containing one of the most profound yet simple sections of Revelation. In it, John sees the mighty angel, the little book, the measuring rod, the two witnesses, and the earthquake.

Things are now drawing to a close. The first half of Daniel's seventieth week is nearly spent; its last days show the world in open rebellion against God and His people, upon whom the beast and the antichrist pour out their fury. But before the last dregs of the Lord's vengeance are drunk by the Gentile and Jewish apostates and their followers, this consoling vision breaks through the dark clouds of judgment. It is a stern reminder to the world that, in spite of the raging of the wicked, the government of the earth is the just claim of the Creator—a claim that will now be made good in power. The vision is also designed to strengthen and console believers, and especially suffering believers, for the same power that will crush the enemy will exalt the sufferers to honor.

The Mighty Angel (10:1–7)

> Then the angel I had seen standing on the sea . . . said, "There will be no more delay." (Revelation 10:6)

Who is this glorious angel who occupies heaven, earth, and the sea? God's chariot is in the clouds (Psalm 104:3) and sends forth this angel who comes with glory. Some versions speak of him as a "*strong* angel." Some writers see in him the herald angel announcing the solemn crisis under the third woe or seventh trumpet (11:15–19). Because the word "angel" does not necessarily mean an individual member of the angelic race, but often denotes a thing or person in active service, can it be that this "mighty angel" is *Christ Himself*, coming forth to act on behalf of

His faithful people? Let us look at the separate features of this awesome being who dominates the universe.

Christ not only leaves heaven as a place of departure, He also comes "down from heaven" as His native home (10:1). Providential dealings with earth are about to cease, so the Lord leaves His abode to establish His worldwide kingdom once His judgment work is finished. How the angelic and redeemed hosts in heaven will praise Him as He leaves their presence to take to Himself His power to reign!

Christ is "robed in a cloud" (10:1). The cloud is a symbol that requires little interpretation, for clouds figure largely in Scripture as an indication of the presence and majesty of Jehovah. How dependent Israel was upon the cloud of Shekinah glory! The cloud garment, then, is the visible, public sign of our Lord's majesty.

Christ has a rainbow on His head (10:1). The rainbow that surrounded the throne (4:3) now encircles the head of the mighty angel. The rainbow symbolizes the fact of a kept covenant, and by it God's faithful remnant is assured that even amidst the fiercest conflict they are secure and need feel no fear. Christ is coming as the Messenger of the covenant-keeping God, and He will call the earth to witness that. But He is about to break His covenant because the world has rejected it. What a glorious sight He will present with His head diademed with a magnificent rainbow!

Christ's face is as the sun, and His feet are as fire (10:1). Here we have a repetition of what we saw in the Patmos vision (1:15–16). The double metaphor of sun and fire speaks of the supreme, searching, and fixed character of the message about to be given. Taken together, the sunlike face and feet as pillars of fire can suggest Christ's supreme majesty and His eternal stability as earth experiences the unbending holiness of His judicial mission.

Christ has a little book in His hand (10:2). The word for "book" comes from *biblos*, from which we get Bible. Here is a "little bible," a larger version of which is the seven-sealed book of chapter 5. The "little" book is open, but the larger book was sealed, then opened by the Lamb. It is open for all who read its unmistakable message.

Christ's right foot is on the sea, and His left foot is on the earth (10:2). In this bold and graphic picture, the mighty Angel is presented as a colossal figure standing astride both land and sea. As the Lord of creation, He dominates the scene entirely.

It has been asked whether there is any special significance in the position of the feet. There certainly is! The sea—turbulent, agitated and restless—represents the chaotic, revolutionary condition of the nations. The earth, which humans have partially harnessed, symbolizes the orderly government of civilized and educated people. Three times over the Angel is depicted as standing on sea and earth (10:2, 5, 8), and this repetition denotes divine emphasis. The strong and sure tread of Christ's feet of fine brass signifies the complete subjugation of all people and forces in the world to Him. Human and natural forces everywhere will acknowledge His dominion as He exercises both His right and His might.

Christ's voice is like a lion's roar (10:3). Here we have another feature of "the voice of many waters." No voice is more feared by people and beasts in the jungle than the roar of the lion. Loud, roaring voices are not always intelligible, but there will be no mistaking the meaning of the roar of the Lion of Judah as it causes intense terror and despair (Psalm 68:33; Hosea 11:10; Joel 3:16). In the wonderful voice psalm (Psalm 29) we are given a sevenfold description of the Lord's majestic voice.

If the lion's roar suggests irresistible power, the seven thunders (10:3) speak of the terror of the Lord in all its completeness as He comes in judgment. Just what the nature of this judgment is we are not told, as John was commanded not to write what the thunders said (10:4). Ten times over thunder occurs in Revelation, and because the thunderings proceed out of the throne they have a divine message and mission. Job speaks of "the thunder of His power" (Job 26:14), and while Jesus was here on earth the voice of God seemed like thunder to some who heard it (John 12:28–29). Thunder is God's voice in judgment, the expression of His authority therein.

Like Daniel's visions, the contents of the seven thunders had to be closed and sealed. John understood them and knew that they were the perfection of God's intervention in judgment, but the divine command as to their nature was, "Do not write it down." Much of the prophetic section of Revelation will be fully understood only as the predicted events actually take place.

When Jesus ascended to heaven, He lifted up His hands in priestly benediction on His own people. Now, as He descends, His hand is lifted up to heaven (10:5) as if through an oath He will fulfill the righteous judgment of God's holy throne. A hand lifted up to heaven was a customary gesture in taking an oath (Genesis 14:22; Deuteronomy 32:40; Daniel 12:7). We have here one of the most sublime visions in Revelation. Try to visualize the scene: the mighty Angel of Jehovah, with the sea and earth under His feet; the book of closing prophecy in His left hand, and His right hand lifted up to heaven, swearing by the ever living God and Creator that judgment upon the godless will be immediate.

How are we to understand the phrase "there will be no more delay" or, as some versions put it, "no longer delay" or "time no longer"? Can it be that the age-old cry for retribution, "How long, O Lord?" (Psalm 13:1–2; Revelation 6:10) is about to be answered, and humanity's day will now end in sharp and severe judgment? As we have seen, "seven" suggests perfection, and the seven trumpets and seven thunders signify the perfect completeness of God's warning judgments. No space is left for anything else to transpire before the final judgment, of which all previous judgments have been previews. In virtue of His native right and His redemptive work, Christ returns to consummate the judgment committed to Him by the Father (John 5:22, 27).

The word "revelation" implies an unveiling of a mystery; here, the mystery of God (10:7) that was foretold by the prophets and apostles is about to be finished (Romans 16:25–26; Ephesians 1:9–10, etc.). Now we see so many things in a glass darkly—for example, the mystery of God's apparent silence when His saints are crushed and cruelly persecuted. As a God of justice, why does He allow terrible sins to go unpunished, and why does He not intervene to right the wrongs of earth?

The mystery John speaks about may be the brutal martyrdom of the Tribulation saints and the silence of heaven about this terrible wrong. But the mystery is about to end. Christ appears to wrest world government from the grasp of Satan, to expel him as the usurper, and to end his tyranny on earth. The mystery of divine patience for over six millennia is now about to cease. The judgment hour has come for God to fully and finally avenge His own elect who have cried out to Him day and night.

How moving is Hervey's eloquent tribute to John's unrivaled description of the "mighty Angel" (from Hervey's *Meditations*):

Observe the aspect of this august Personage. All the brightness of the sun shines in His countenance, and all the rage of fire burns in

His feet. See His *apparel!* The clouds compose His robe, and the drapery of the sky floats upon His shoulders; the rainbow forms His diadem, and that which compasses heaven with a glorious circle is the ornament of His head. Behold His *attitude!* One foot stands on the ocean, and the other rests on the land. The wide extended earth and the world of waters serve as pedestals of those mighty columns. Consider His *action!* His hand is lifted up to the height of the stars; He speaks, and the regions of the firmament echo with the mighty accents as the midnight desert resounds with the lion's roar. The artillery of the skies is discharged as a signal; a peal of sevenfold thunder spreads the alarm and prepares the universe to receive His orders. To finish all, and give the highest grandeur, as well as the utmost solemnity, to the representation, He swears by Him who lives forever and ever.

The Bittersweet Book (10:8–11)

It tasted sweet as honey in my mouth, but when I had eaten it, my stomach turned sour. (Revelation 10:10)

John is now commanded to take and eat the little book that he saw in the hand of the mighty Angel. We can safely assume that the contents of this volume were the counsels and prophecies of the rest of Scripture, from Genesis to Jude. The time has now come to declare the divine counsel to peoples, nations, tongues, and rulers. John must mentally digest the message of the book and then declare it.

Several times in Scripture, God's Word is compared to food that must be assimilated. Ezekiel, like John, experienced the sweet taste of prophecy (Ezekiel 2:8; 3:1–3). Jeremiah likewise had to consume the divine word (Jeremiah 15:16). The first effect of the prophetic communication was an unbounded delight as John saw how past predictions were about to be fulfilled. It was sweet to his taste to realize that at last earth's rule was to pass from Satan to Christ, that an evil age was about to end and a new era begin.

But then the apostle meditated on the effect of judgment upon the multitudes without God, and he thought of the final wrath under the seven vials and the terrors of the Lord about to overtake the godless. As he pondered the final doom of the lost, anguish gripped John's heart.

What was sweet to his taste would have a bitter effect upon rebellious earth dwellers. His commission was renewed, and out John had to go, prophesying to the multitudes about judgment to come.

For all preachers in this age of grace, the same principle holds. They must receive a God-given message and absorb it into their own being. Secondhand, unexperienced truth is never dynamic. Both the sweetness and the bitterness of a God-revealed gospel must be part of the spiritual training of heralds. Truth that they delight to receive demands the death of the self-life and a taste of the bitterness that comes from the hardships and disappointments of true witness bearing.

The Measuring Reed (11:1–2)

I was given a reed like a measuring rod and was told, "Go and measure the temple of God and the altar." (Revelation 11:1)

The reed, a measuring instrument about ten feet in length, is frequently mentioned by the prophets of the Old Testament. Ezekiel speaks of the measuring rod being applied to the temple (Ezekiel 40:3; 42:16–20). In the New Jerusalem an angel measures the glorified church with a golden reed (21:15); here John uses a wooden reed to measure the temple. Such a measuring suggests the appropriation, preservation, and acceptance by God of temple, altar, and worshiper.

Mention of the court and the temple reveals that we are approaching Jewish ground. In fact, the whole chapter is anticipative. The Jews are to be back in their own land, and the temple is to be rebuilt. As a whole, the trumpets section deals with the devastation of Gentile, Christianized lands and peoples, but now judgment is about to be transferred from the Gentile to the Jew.

God's dealings with the apostate part of the Gentile world are about to conclude. The times of the Gentiles have run their course. We now approach the second half of Daniel's seventieth week, which is the last half of the Tribulation era. The man of sin makes a covenant with the Jews for seven years, but turns traitor halfway through the period. The agony of Israel's closing hour of unbelief during this time is here depicted.

This period covering the trampling of the Gentiles is given in different forms. Forty-two months, each thirty days long, correspond to the 1,260 days of the two witnesses. These forty-two months, or 1,260 days, make three and one-half years, which are equivalent to a "time" (one year), "times" (two years), and "half time" (one-half year), as stated in Daniel 12:7 (see also Revelation 11:3; 12:6, 14; 13:5). This period is the duration of the blasphemy and power of the beast. Such a denomination of time is also referred to as "the midst of the week" (Daniel 9:27). Jerusalem's coming agony, then, is limited to forty-two months. And this will be long enough as she drinks the cup of the Lord's fury.

The Two Witnesses (11:3–14)

And I will give power to my two witnesses, and they will prophesy for 1,260 days. (Revelation 11:3)

In our chapter on the seven Spirits of God we briefly referred to these martyred prophets as being raised by the Spirit of life. We now look at them in more detail, noting that we have passed from worshipers in the sanctuary to witnesses in the city, and that worshipers and witnesses both testify to the priesthood and royalty of the One of whom it was predicted, "he will be a priest on his throne" (Zechariah 6:13).

As to the identity of the two witnesses, the language points to two well-known characters. The article is emphatic—"*the* two witness of me." Therefore they must have been known at least to John.

What else do we know about these two inspired witnesses who are to be raised up to minister encouragement to the afflicted? John does not give us any clue to their identity, but simply describes them as witnesses, olive trees, lampstands, prophets. (One witness may be John himself. See 10:11.) "The two olive trees" takes us back to Joshua and Zerubbabel (Zechariah 3–4), who ministered to the Jewish people, just as the two olive trees emptied the oil out of themselves into the bowl of the lampstand (Zechariah 4:11–14). The "two witnesses" in the Tribulation period are to be channels of the oil feeding the remnant, and symbols of coming peace. The Holy Spirit will be the oil in them, making their ministry of encouragement possible.

As "lampstands," these witnesses are to give a sure and clear testimony. Their ministry will be exercised in the clear light of God because they stand before the Lord of the earth. As representative light bearers, they will testify that the One who was so widely disowned on earth is now about to be recognized openly as the rightful King over all. As "prophets" (11:10), they will preach in such a faithful way as to make people conscience stricken. Sin with its tragic consequences is a tormenting subject to even the most hardened and scarred conscience. Thus these witnesses are to have a tormenting ministry by the plagues they have power to inflict, and also by their testimony against their human environment.

The two witnesses are to prophesy clothed in sackcloth, that is, in a dress suited to their message. Sackcloth was the garment of prophets when they called the people to repentance. Their exterior appearance accorded with their words (Joel 1:13; 1 Kings 20:31). Perhaps *sackcloth* is a catchword, linking this episode under the sixth trumpet with the one under the sixth seal where "the sun turned black like sackcloth" (6:12) in righteous retribution on the apostates who rejected God's righteousness.

The days of their prophecy, or preaching, under the inspiration of the Spirit (a message of judgment against apostates) are to be 1,260. They are not to give an intermittent testimony. Daily they will testify until the allotted period is exhausted—a period that covers the last half of Daniel's week, or the great Tribulation proper.

Unlimited, delegated power is to be granted these witnesses. They will perform miracles "as often as they want" (11:6), repeating those that Moses and Elijah performed against slavery and apostasy: turning water into blood (Exodus 7:17) and withholding rain (1 Kings 17:1).

But the two preachers in sackcloth are "immortal till their work is done." The immediate certainty of the accomplishment of their mission is indicated by the phrases "if anyone tries to harm them" (two times in 11:5) and "they have finished their testimony" (11:7). Prophesying in Jerusalem, the center of prophetic and political interest during the three and one-half years of the Tribulation, they are invincible until their dynamic and spectacular task is over.

The conclusion of the prophecy of the two witnesses is to be marked by a violent death. "The beast [or "the wild beast," as the original has it] . . . comes up from the Abyss." Nothing less than the antichrist, who is here mentioned for the first time in Revelation, will satisfy the picture here. The beast is fully described in Daniel 7:8, 11 and Revelation 13:1, a sure proof of the unity of Scripture. The triumph of this beast, who exceeds in cruelty and blasphemy any previous wickedness that has appeared upon the earth, is evidently complete, for the witnesses are silenced and slain. Martyrdom and massacres of the saints in all ages find their climax here. With the killing of divinely empowered witnesses, brute force appears to triumph over truth and righteousness.

To add to the humiliation and scornful treatment of the two witnesses, their bodies are allowed to remain in the street for the same number of days as the years of their ministry. For three and one-half days the spectators gloat over the dead bodies with a delight that is both fiendish and childish.

"Sodom and Egypt," as applied to Jerusalem (11:8), stand as a symbol of oppression and slavery. "Sodom" represents filthiness and wickedness (Genesis 18:20, 21; Jude 7; 2 Peter 2:6–8). "Egypt" represents oppression.

The jubilant celebration over the death of the two prophets is universal; "people, tribe, language and nation" indicates the fourfold distribution of the human family. Gifts are distributed as at a joyous festival. The death of truth was the cause of public rejoicing, but divine vindication was just around the corner. Remorse was about to replace rejoicing.

Public vilification now gives way to public vindication. The Spirit of life from God causes the dead bones of the witnesses to live, and the spectators are panic stricken. Similarities can be drawn between Israel's dry bones (Ezekiel 37:10–11; Hosea 6:2) and our Lord's resurrection after three days. Christ's ascension was in the presence of His friends (Acts 1:9), as was Elijah's (2 Kings 2:11). But the ascension of these two raised witnesses (compare 11:12 with 4:1) is in full view of their enemies.

Now retributive justice quickly falls on the people and the city. An earthquake, called "severe" because of its appalling destruction, causes a tenth of the city to fall and seven thousand people to perish. In the "tenth" we have complete judgment, for "ten" signifies perfection of divine order. In the seven thousand slain we have God's blacklist. These were marked out as deserving of God's righteous judgments. By contrast, we have the seven thousand people in Israel whom God reserved for Himself (1 Kings 19:18). In this fixed number of people who are doomed to death we have the two perfect and comprehensive numbers seven and thousand, implying the full and complete destruction of the impenitent.

Summarizing the courageous ministry of the two witnesses, we have them declaring Christ, the rejected One, as the Lord of the whole earth. They testify unsparingly of human wickedness, thereby incurring the hatred of the godless. They proclaim the just character of the Judge, warning the people of righteous retribution in the days to come, decrying the blasphemous claims of the wild beast, and preaching against Jerusalem (which, although holy in God's purpose, had become corrupt and was destroyed).

Of "the survivors" (that is, the spared Israelite inhabitants) it is said that they were filled with godly fear and gave glory to the God of heaven, where the two witnesses had gone. At long last the God of heaven is also acknowledged as the God of the earth.

Seventh Trumpet: Christ Will Reign Forever (Revelation 11:15–19)

> The seventh angel sounded his trumpet, and there were loud voices in heaven, which said, "The kingdom of the world has become the kingdom of our Lord and of his Christ, and he will reign for ever and ever." (Revelation 11:15)

We now reach the third woe, which is the seventh trumpet. Six is close to seven, but does not reach it. World judgments are complete in six, but by the fulfillment of seven the world kingdoms become Christ's. Six is the number of the world given over to judgment. It is half of twelve, the number of the tribes and apostles, even as three and one-half is half of seven, the divine number for completeness.

The beast had ascended up out of the Abyss to perform his deadly work, and now Christ descends out of heaven to take to Himself His great power as the blessed and only Potentate. What a dramatic scene is presented of God's panorama of future and final events!

In the seventh trumpet angel, some writers see Gabriel, whose name is a compound of *El* ("God") and *Geber* ("mighty man") and who appropriately announced to Mary the advent of the mighty God-man. It would be fitting for this archangel to announce the final triumph of the Christ of God.

The loud voices in heaven are in contrast to the silence in heaven of 8:1. Exultant praises abound over the setting up of heaven's sovereignty over the earth visibly—when it was invisibly exercised, the earthly rulers rejected it. The anticipation of the kingdom (rather than its actual establishment) causes the heavenly joy in this passage.

This seventh trumpet is akin to the seventh seal in that no immediate judgment is announced. Nothing is recorded as immediately resulting from the trumpet's being blown. We are simply given a summary of the final phases that bring us to the portal of the new creation. The setting up of the world kingdom is treated as a fact: "The kingdom of the world has become the kingdom of our Lord and of his Christ."

Of course, this is the crowning lesson of the Apocalypse. Christ's absolute sovereignty is the sure and glorious outcome of an age-old struggle. He scorned partnership with Satan in ruling the world, and now He is about to exercise His sovereign rights, and to reign as world emperor. Earth is to enter its last throes of agony. Its millennial morning will dawn with Christ as King over all. His beneficent rule will provide a happy contrast to past and present governmental rule! One universal kingdom will cover the globe, with Christ as the sole reigning Monarch.

Such a sublime prospect demands the adoration of the elders. Profound worship is their response to the heavenly voices. A doxology follows, in which the elders magnify God and Christ for uniting in taking the kingdom. There are seven doxologies in the course of these apocalyptic visions, of which this is one. These are introduced only on occasions of deep interest: 5:12–14; 7:12; 11:15; 12:10–12; 14:2–3; 15:2–4; 19:1–3.

Heaven's wrath will match that of earth (11:18). There is fearful progress in these words, for the unbounded anger of the nations will be destroyed by the divine anger. How petty the nations' impotent anger, standing here side by side with that of omnipotent God! (See Exodus 15:9–16; Psalm 2 for allusions to this double anger.)

The judgment of 11:18 is the judgment of the unbelieving. We are now brought to the conclusion of the kingdom, with the great white throne. Among the many judgments, these four must be kept distinct: the judgment of the earth during its whole course of history (Acts 17:31); the judgment of believers at the "bema" (1 Corinthians 3:12–15); the judgment of the nations at the beginning of Christ's reign (Matthew 25:32); and the judgment of the wicked dead at the end of Christ's reign (Revelation 20:11–12).

Rewards are to be bestowed on all God's saints who deserve them. In the kingdom there will be varying degrees and positions of honor. While rest and glory will be for all saints, special crowns will be awarded only to those who have earned them. The faithful believers of every era of church history are to be graciously recompensed.

But retribution awaits all destroyers. Satan, the beast, the false prophet, and all who have followed them are to be recompensed for their wickedness (Daniel 7:14–18; Luke 19:27; Revelation 16:5–7). Destruction overtakes all destroyers.

"Then God's temple in heaven was opened, and within his temple was seen the ark of his covenant" (11:19). This temple is the sign that God is taking up the cause and interests of Israel, and it is in heaven that God is occupied with His people rather than on earth. The ark of His covenant is the token of Jehovah's presence with His earthly people and His unchanging faithfulness toward them. God will remember His covenant with Israel. (This is one of the seven great "openings" in Revelation; the other six are a door is opened in heaven [4:1]; seals are opened [6:1–9]; the abyss is opened [9:2]; the tabernacle of the testimony is opened [15:5]; heaven is opened [19:11]; and books are opened [20:12].)

The trumpet judgments close with judgment action over the whole earth. Here is the storm of divine wrath that has its origin in heaven. Short, sharp, and decisive judgments are indicated by the combination of destructive elements. Natural forces are unleashed by their Creator to mete out His righteous wrath upon all who persist in resisting His claims. God now operates in terrible might and majesty.

By the seventh trumpet we learn that the warnings of God are perfect and complete, leaving humans without excuse when final and irreversible doom falls upon them.

6

Seven Persons

Revelation 12–13

A great and wondrous sign appeared in heaven. (Revelation 12:1)

The close of Revelation 11 left us with the tragedy and triumph of the two faithful witnesses. Chapters 12 and 13 bring us to the rise and reign of the two foul beasts. The unity of these two dramatic chapters is reflected in the fact that almost every verse of the original text begins with the conjunction "and" (31 in all). Chapters 12 and 13 form one connected prophecy.

We now come to the heart of Revelation. The stage is set and the drama of the ages is about to begin. We are to witness the clash of heavenly, human, and hellish forces. Christ receives authority and adoration in chapters 4 and 5, where we have the *divine* setting for judgment. Here, in chapters 12 and 13, Satan receives man's adoration, and we have the *devilish* setting of judgment.

Twice the word "sign" appears (12:1, 3), a word that also indicates "wonder" and "momentous truths and events." It appears again in 13:13 ("He performed great and miraculous signs"). This word is associated with the significance and nature of the work wrought; the element of wonder is in the thing itself (see Matthew 24:3, 24; John 4:48; Acts 2:22; 5:12). John was given these signs from heaven (1:1; 11:19), implying that all of God's purposes are known there. The adjective "great," a characteristic word of Revelation, is used six times in chapter 13 and reveals it as a chapter of great subjects.

First Person: The Sun Woman—Israel (Revelation 12:1–2)

A woman clothed with the sun, with the moon under her feet and a crown of twelve stars on her head. (Revelation 12:1)

The earliest appearance of a female figure in Revelation is in 2:20. Altogether we have four representative women, each of whom is the expression of a corporate body of persons in a system.

1. Jezebel (2:20)—the past corrupt church

2. The woman invested with the fullness of governmental authority (12:1)—Israel

3. The great harlot (17:1)—the future corrupt church

4. The bride, the Lamb's wife (19:7)—the church glorified in heaven

There are different identifications of "the woman clothed with the sun." Some say it is the Virgin Mary. (Mary was indeed the Jewish woman who brought forth the Man-child, Jesus.) Others identify the sun-clothed woman as the church, the mother of us all. Still others say that Christendom is meant.

We believe that the woman is Israel. National Israel is often referred to as a married woman (Isaiah 54:1–6; Jeremiah 3:1–11; Hosea 2:14–23). Jesus came out of the tribe of Judah. It is true that both Israel and the church stand closely related to Christ—Israel as the mother and the church as the wife. It was Israel, however, who became the mother of the Messiah (Isaiah 9:6; Micah 5:2; Romans 9:5, etc.) A passage like Isaiah 54:1 is very expressive: " 'Sing, O barren woman, you who never bore a child; burst into song, shout for joy, you who were never in labor; because more are the children of the desolate woman than of her who has a husband,' says the LORD." To hold that the woman is the church would mean that she brought forth Christ. But it was *His* anguish that produced the church.

The symbolism of the sun, moon, and stars suggests a summary of Israel's history, as given in Genesis 37:9, where the whole family is represented in similar manner. In the celestial luminaries we have the presentation of a complete system of government. These luminaries, then, symbolize the twelve tribal heads as seen in national restoration.

Clothed with the sun

Here we have Israel depicted as the bearer of divine, supernatural light and authority. Or the sun can stand for Christ, whom Israel will yet recognize as the Sun of Righteousness.

The moon under her feet

As the moon is subordinate to the sun and derives its light from the sun, all Israel's glory and influence are derived from the One who brought her into being. The moon shines at night; Israel is to give her light, her bright witness, amid the world's gathering darkness in the Tribulation era.

A crown of twelve stars on her head

By the twelve stars we understand the twelve tribes of Israel. In Joseph's dream (Genesis 37:9) the future glory of these tribes is symbolized in the same way. Israel's future glory and rule, therefore, are portrayed here. She is yet to be invested with the splendor and fullness of governmental authority on earth. Twelve, as we know, is the number of government.

Crying out in pain

The metaphor of childbirth is common in Scripture (John 16:21; Galatians 4:19; etc.). The woman's travail may refer to Israel's coming hour of trial. But *before* the great Tribulation, the Messiah, the Manchild is born. The prophet Micah confirms this in a clear and unmistakable passage. After referring to the birth of the Messiah (5:2), he adds, "Therefore Israel will be abandoned until the time when she who is in labor gives birth and the rest of his brothers return to join the Israelites" (v. 3). The travail of the woman is at least two thousand years after the birth of the Messiah and refers to her sorrow in the coming Tribulation.

Why then is the travail of the woman linked in this special way with the birth of the Messiah?

First, notice that the present lengthened period of Israel's rejection, coming as it does between the birth and the travail, is passed over in silence in the chapter before us. It is a parenthesis whose history is not given in prophecy but is found elsewhere.

Second, it shows the deep interest the Messiah takes in His people. He prepared the Tribulation and made provision as to enlightening it many centuries ago (Matthew 24:15–22).

Third, at the time in which our chapter will take place, the Jewish nation will undergo its awful sorrow, and the reason for going back to the birth of Christ is to connect Him with them in it. The travail, then, indicates Israel's sufferings during the Tribulation. The Jews have been and are being cruelly persecuted, but still darker days are ahead for God's chosen people after the man of sin breaks the seven-year covenant guaranteeing her protection.

Second Person: The Red Dragon—Satan (Revelation 12:3–4)

An enormous red dragon with seven heads and ten horns and seven crowns on his heads. (Revelation 12:3)

Without doubt this great red dragon represents Satan in his worst character. John expressly identifies the devil as the dragon in 20:2. Both Pharaoh and Nebuchadnezzar are spoken of as great dragons because of their cruelty and haughty independence (Ezekiel 29:3; Jeremiah 51:34)—perhaps recalling the Old Testament crocodile or leviathan. "Dragon" appears ten times in Revelation and is a fitting symbol of God's chief adversary in his role as the relentless persecutor and murderer of multitudes of saints and sinners. Job gives us a most remarkable description of a dragon, "he is king over all that are proud" (Job 41:1–34; see also Isaiah 27:1). The term is used of Satan only in the book of Revelation. It suggests the hideousness and horror of his rule, the insatiable violence represented by the dragon.

Red, being a blood color, indicates the devil's murderous nature, for he has been a murderer from the beginning (John 8:44). Red can also represent pseudosanctity—"Why are your garments red?" (Isaiah 63:2). Once the most beautiful of angelic beings, Satan is now the object of abhorrence. Copying Christ, who as the Conqueror will wear many diadems, Satan is adorned with his crowns or diadems. The seven crowned heads signify the cruel and despotic exercise of earthly power and authority, while the ten uncrowned horns can stand for the future limits of the empire as distributed into ten kingdoms. (The rule of Satan is in a ten-kingdom form.) Satan delegates power and authority to the first beast, who is similarly described 13:1.

The tail represents the most dangerous part of a dragon. As a lying prophet is likened to a tail by Isaiah (9:15), Satan's malignant power and influence as a liar and a deceiver are similarly described. With power and wisdom combined, Satan will bring about the utter moral ruin of a third part of the stars of heaven, which can mean eminent rulers in places of authority. There may be in John's words a veiled reference to all those angels who rebelled with Satan before creation.

As a dog on a leash, the devil is permitted certain operations. He can only produce moral collapse at this time among those in the third part, identified by some writers as the western part of the Roman Empire. His dragging down the stars with his tail (12:4), lashed back and forth in his fury, implies Satan's eagerness to cause apostasy.

The terrible spectacle of the dragon standing before the woman, waiting to devour her newborn child, is easily interpreted. It was not the woman but her child whom the monster was bent on destroying, just as Pharaoh tried to murder all the male children of Israel (Exodus 1:15–22). What a fascinating study it is to trace Satan's efforts to destroy Israel, the royal seed that was to produce Christ, and then to destroy Christ Himself! As soon as Jesus was born, there was a satanic effort to destroy Him during the slaughter of the innocents (Matthew 2:16).

Third Person: The Son of the Woman—Christ (Revelation 12:5–6)

> She gave birth to a son, a male child, who will rule the nations with an iron scepter. (Revelation 12:5)

The male child, ("a son, a male," as the original expresses it) *surely represents Christ,* who was born to rule (Genesis 3:15; Psalm 2:9; Revelation 12:5; 19:15; Psalm 110:1, 5). Yet there are teachers who see in the child a group out of Israel, the firstfruits to God from Israel out of the Tribulation. The 144,000 sealed Jews, for example, are identified with

Christ in a special way, and because of their relation to persecution they are sometimes thought to be the child here.

But the following prophecy of universal rule nullifies such an interpretation. It was the virgin who brought forth the promised male child, born of the flesh of Israel (Romans 9:4–5; Galatians 4:4–5) and threatened by Herod with death while He was under two years of age. The persistent enemies of Christ—the scribes and Pharisees—also tried to destroy Him. Born as a King (Matthew 2:2), Christ came into the world having universal dominion, which He will yet exercise (Psalm 8:1).

The iron rule of the nations will be broken by Him who comes to shepherd them with an iron rod. Here the word "rule" means "to tend as a shepherd," and in this role Christ will break up the consolidated powers of the earth gathered against Himself and His people. With irresistible might He will mete out judgment to the guilty kings and peoples. Further, this ruling with a rod (for long continued obstinacy, until submission results in obedience) reveals the nature of Christ's reign. The revolt at the end of the millennium manifests what reluctant submission characterized large numbers of the people of the earth during His reign.

The ascension of Christ is expressed in "her child was snatched up to God and to his throne" (12:5; see also Mark 16:19; Luke 24:50–51; Acts 1:9; 7:56). Nothing is here said of the death of the child, seeing that He is connected with Israel and the rule of all nations, both of which are dependent upon His birth and His ascension to His throne. And yet in that Shepherd hand grasping the rod will be the marks of the nails. It is as the slain Lamb that He reigns.

We reject the interpretation that sees in this verse the rapture of those who are sufficiently holy when Jesus comes. Those who hold the "partial rapture" theory sometimes employ the last part of this fifth verse to teach the erroneous doctrine of a selected rapture. *All* who are Christ's, irrespective of their state, will be caught up to meet the Lord. If unfit, they will suffer loss in respect to their reward. Between verses 5 and 6 we have the whole stretch of history from Christ's ascension to the Tribulation (the time of Jacob's trouble).

By the determined counsel and foreknowledge of God, a place of safety and sustenance is provided for the remnant. There are those who suggest that this place of refuge is Petra, at Mount Seir, in the land of Edom and Moab. Petra or Sela means "rock" or "stronghold" and as such can accommodate thousands of people. The rapid flight and journey of the persecuted woman is likewise aided by God.

Between the interrupted statement of 12:6 and its resumption in 12:14 we have the episode of the war in heaven and the heavenly rejoicing upon its success. The careful numbering of days, 1,260 in all, testifies to the Lord's tender interest in His afflicted people. This last half of Israel's week of prophetic sorrow will elicit constant care and provision on the Lord's part. The desert is sometimes used to indicate a condition that is destitute of natural resources, a place of isolation. In Ezekiel 20:35–36 we find the desert employed not literally and locally but spiritually, as a state of discipline and trial among the Gentile peoples. It was in a desert that our Lord was tempted by the devil (Mark 1:12–13).

Fourth Person: Michael (Revelation 12:7–12)

And there was war in heaven. (Revelation 12:7)

After the complete picture of the first six verses given under the two signs, we come to the climax of age-old antagonisms. The book of Revelation is a book of wars, and here in the war in heaven we have one of the most dramatic battles. At last the prophetic word of Isaiah is about to be fulfilled—"In that day the LORD will punish the powers in the heavens above and the kings on the earth below" (Isaiah 24:21).

The most significant battle in all of world history is now to be staged. What a spectacle! Forces heavenly and hellish are to clash in the grim conflict. Opposing ideologies are grouped together: the Allies (Michael and his angels) and the Axis (Satan and his angels). Of the outcome there is no doubt. The declaration of final victory against Satan was given by Christ in Luke 10:18 and John 12:31. Surely such a hope should impel us to soul-saving activity!

The phrase "war in heaven" (12:7) is somewhat startling, especially after "silence in heaven" (8:1). By "heaven" we are not to understand the immediate presence of God, but the sphere that Satan has occupied since he was cast out of God's dwelling place because of his rebellion. He is the prince of power of the *air*, and the atmospheric heavens are peopled with multitudes of beings both heavenly and hellish. There Satan has his seat of operation, and there the battle is to rage. The result will be his expulsion to earth, from which he will be consigned to the bottomless pit for a thousand years and ultimately to the lake of fire.

Michael and His Angels (12:7–8)

Michael and his angels fought against the dragon. (Revelation 12:7)

Michael is peculiarly the prince or presiding angel of the Jewish nation. This grand leader of the unfallen angel warriors, who is to force the usurper from the heavens, is mentioned five times in Scripture (Daniel 10:13, 21; 12:1; Jude 9; Revelation 12:7). This leader of the angelic hierarchy is always related to Old Testament saints. His name signifies "who is like God?" To Michael is assigned the safety of God's people, and in the grim conflict described in this chapter of Revelation, he will see to it that Israel shall not perish. Michael and his angels, who excel in strength, overcome the dragon and his angels only by ferocious battle.

The Dragon and His Angels (12:7–9)

The dragon and his angels . . . lost their place in heaven. (Revelation 12:7–8)

Our Lord refers to Satan and the rebellious angels under his command in Matthew 25:41, while Paul reminds us of Satan's ability to appear as an angel of light (2 Corinthians 11:14). He is the archangel of the fallen angels. If the movements of nations—their wars, politics, and social policy—are shaped and dictated by higher and spiritual powers, then these powers are the good and bad angels, as Daniel 10 demonstrates. Wars and strife on earth are merely the reflex of opposing spiritual powers in the lower heavens. Because these heavens are the abode of Satan as "the prince of the power of the air," God must declare that "the stars are not pure in His sight."

The invisible struggles between the powers of light and the forces of darkness are real and earnest (1 Samuel 16:13–15; 1 Kings 22:19–23), and by the influence of these spiritual beings the world is providentially governed. With this "war in heaven" the climax is reached in the struggle between invisible and visible forces, and the outcome of this battle is the overthrow of the dragon and his angels. Satan suffers an ignominious defeat and is expelled from the heavens with the suddenness of a flash of lightning. Baffled and beaten, the dragon will then roam this doomed scene and vomit his wrath against the Jewish remnant.

The sixfold description given of Satan and his work is worthy of our special notice. He is called at least six prominent names.

The great dragon: This diabolical fiend has always been conspicuous for his remorseless cruelty. Legend paints the dragon as a monster in form and appearance outside the limits of the animal kingdom, a combination of superhuman craft and cruelty. What a sad day it will be for the inhabitants of earth when this hellish foe roams abroad unchecked!

The ancient serpent: The allusion here is to Genesis 3:1, 4, where we have the record of Satan's first and successful attempt to destroy God's purposes and mar human happiness. "Ancient" refers to Satan's first historical connection with the human race. The title "serpent" speaks of our enemy's subtlety, deceit, cunning, and craft (2 Corinthians 11:3). The degradation of the serpent even in millennial days is hinted in Isaiah 65:25.

The devil: This personal name is from *diabolos,* a Greek word meaning "one who throws down, slanders, tempts." Such a name represents all that the devil stands for. The devil throws down, debauches, and destroys, but Christ elevates from the dunghill to a position among princes.

Satan: "Satan" is the Hebrew term for "adversary," especially in a court of justice. This twofold designation, Greek and Hebrew, marks the twofold objects of his accusation, which include the elect Gentiles and the elect Jews. Both names prove Satan to be an actual, historical being.

The deceiver: The special work of Satan is stated. With the accumulated wisdom and cunning of millennia, he is able to deceive the inhabited earth. To act as the master deceiver is the devil's aim and occupation. Artful in his beguiling, he often succeeds in getting us to deceive ourselves (1 John 1:8). In Tribulation days he will attempt to deceive the elect by miraculous signs (Matthew 24:24; 2 Thessalonians 2:7–12). The last glimpse of Satan in the Bible is as the deceiver (Revelation 20:8, 10).

The accuser: In some mysterious way Satan is able to present his accusations against the saints before God (Job 1:6–12; 2:1–6). Often he accuses us to our own conscience, but we have the efficacious blood to plead (1 John 2:1–2).

I hear the accuser roar
Of ills that I have done;
I know them well, and thousands more;
Jehovah findeth none!

Our solemn obligation is to live in such a way that we shall never give Satan any cause for lodging a complaint or any ground for making an accusation.

In the scene described in 12:9, Satan is completely vanquished and overthrown. Never again will his accusations, just or unjust, be listened to in the courts of heaven. The three elements in victory over Satan are emphasized in 12:11—the blood of the Lamb, the word of testimony, and the willingness to sacrifice. The precious blood of Christ is the ground and means of victory. Through His blood we have boldness before God, which in turn produces boldness before men. The testimony is *prophetic*. The willingness to die challenges the devil to do his worst, since a glorious resurrection awaits all who hazard their lives for Christ's sake.

All the redeemed in heaven and all the saints on earth now unite to rejoice over the complete expulsion of Satan. "Now have come the salvation and the power and the kingdom of our God, and the authority of his Christ." The Greek emphasizes "*the* salvation." Fullest hallelujahs arise because the defeat of the devil has been accomplished fully and finally.

While the doxology of 12:10–12 announces that the kingdom has come, it is only in an anticipatory sense. A necessary and preliminary step in the setting up of Christ's millennial kingdom is the casting out of Satan from the heavenlies as the prince of the power of the air. Now that the power of the kingdom has been so gloriously vindicated in heaven, all is announced *there* as already come. With the imprisonment of Satan in the abyss, the kingdom will actually be set up on earth. Postmillennialists (who say that we Christians will bring in the kingdom) should remember that there can be no kingdom without the King and that the kingdom will not be inaugurated until the King appears in all His power and glory and takes His kingdom by force. At present, He is completing His church, which is His mystical body.

The contrast in Satan's defeat is striking: music versus misery; "Rejoice, you heavens" versus "woe to the earth and the sea" (12:12).

Knowing that his time on earth is short, Satan manifests great rage, exceeding even the wrath of the nations that he himself inspired (11:18). "Wrath" here means "boiling rage." Great anger is Satan's because he was exiled from the heavenly realm and because his permitted time for doing harm on earth is now severely limited. No wonder the devil hates this book of Revelation that we are considering, since his doom is written prominently in its pages!

Fifth Person: The Male Child (Revelation 12:13–17)

The dragon ... pursued the woman who had given birth to the male child. (Revelation 12:13)

After the episode of 12:7–12 we resume the discourse from 12:6. With his sphere of operation now restricted to earth, Satan gives himself to the destruction of the woman, the line of Judah from which the male child came. The bitter persecution of the last half of Daniel's future prophetic week now begins (Daniel 7:25). Now that the dragon is confined to the earth, he seeks to work vengeance on Judah, which is restored to the land and represents the whole nation of Israel before God. (Ephraim, the long lost ten tribes, are not yet in view.)

Fiercely persecuted, the woman is forced to flee (12:6, 14) but is wonderfully assisted in her flight. She receives "the two wings of a great eagle." We cannot agree with those who interpret these eagle's wings as the world powers of Babylon and Egypt. The eagle symbolizes God's protection of His own people. His past care and deliverance from impending danger are indicated in this way in Exodus 19:4 and Deuteronomy 32:10–12. "You yourselves have seen what I did to Egypt, and how I carried you on eagles' wings and brought you to myself." "[The Lord] guarded him as the apple of his eye, like an eagle that stirs up its nest and hovers over its young, that spreads its wings to catch them and carries them on pinions. The Lord alone led him; no foreign god was with him."

The wings convey the idea of rapid motion and guaranteed protection, and we attribute these to God. The two wings can mean help and safety. To suggest that "wings" refer to the remote parts of the earth and that the *two* wings symbolize the east and west divisions of the Roman Empire is to destroy the providential aspect of this part of the chapter.

Divine protection is afforded for 1,260 days (12:6) or "a time, and times, and half a times" (12:14), which expresses the same length of time as forty-two months (or three and one-half years). All these expressions cover the last half of a week of anguish, the time of Jacob's sorrow.

Regarding the desert (the place prepared by God where He will exercise His care of the woman and her seed), scholars present differing views. The sanest interpretation is that the remnant, having an earthly destiny, is provided with an earthly refuge. Petra—the rock city located southwest of the Dead Sea—is a possible hiding place. With its accommodation for a quarter of a million people, such a marvelous cavern would afford an excellent protection.

The image of the woman fleeing "out of the serpent's reach" (12:14) offers a strong contrast to earth and heaven fleeing from the face of Him who sits on the great white throne (20:11). The crafty nature of Satan is emphasized in the effort of the serpent to destroy the woman by a flood. The earth swallowing the flood may represent those friendly nations willing to befriend the Jews, thereby neutralizing and circumventing Satan's wily method of energizing other nations against them. These nations sheltering the Jewish remnant will be the "sheep nations" in the judgment of the living nations (Matthew 25:31–46).

Such overruling will stir up the anger of the dragon, causing him in his frustrated rage to make war with the godly remnant in Palestine (12:17). The phrase "to make war" can imply every form of attack upon the saints, whether by persecution or by battle. Physical harm and every evil the devil is capable of are included under this technical expression (see 11:7; 16:14; 17:14; 19:19). But both the male child and the God-fearing Jews will be delivered from the murderous hate of the devil.

Sixth Person: The Sea Beast—Dictator (Revelation 13:1–10)

I saw a beast coming out of the sea. (Revelation 13:1)

The whole of Revelation 13 is devoted to a description of the nature and activities of two fearsome and awe-inspiring beasts. The earth is now the scene of satanic operations, and God-fearing Jews and Gentiles become the objects of the devil's murderous intentions. His principle ministers of deceit and cruelty are two beasts, actual men who use their delegated power efficiently on behalf of their hellish master.

The first beast—the sea beast—is apparently a Gentile and exercises a rule characterized by brute force. The second beast—the earth beast (13:11–18)—is probably an apostate Jew and will be conspicuous because of his subtle religious influence. Later on, these blind dupes will stand in battle array against Christ and His heavenly hosts (19:11, 19).

Because the word "beast" is used of a power or kingdom (or the personal head of a power or kingdom), the term is sometimes used interchangeably for an empire or its personal head. In Scripture, "beast" seems to carry a double significance: first, the folly of acting without a feeling of responsibility toward God (Daniel 4:16; 1 Corinthians 15:32); second, the error of imperial power acting without reference to God (Daniel 7). The word for "beast" in this chapter is *thērion*, "wild beast," indicating the demonic, vengeful reign of terror on the part of the two beasts.

With the appearance of the first beast we have Satan's masterpiece and the most awesome personage ever to appear on the earth. He will be the composite of all beasts who have gone before, the embodiment of all misrule and anarchy, the personification of iniquity. Every feature of his portrait is pictured in Psalm 10 and Daniel 7:3–7. With the appearance of this wild, fierce beast comes the ultimate struggle for world dominion, the final clash of opposite ideologies. Let us try to understand the person and prestige of this satanically inspired superman as John sees him from his vantage point on the sand of the sea.

This beast emerges from the sea, which can represent the unsettled human condition. John uses the sea as a symbol of the chaotic, revolutionary forces that are at work as the beast appears and that he will command in the interest of brute force. Out of the general collapse of all governing authority (under the sixth seal, 6:12–17) the beast will emerge. One writer suggests that this sea may be the Mediterranean Sea, since the four great empires of the world came from around this body of water (Daniel 7:1–3). Gentile nations or peoples are symbolized by the great waters of the sea (Revelation 17:15).

We must not lose sight of the fact that this beast is an actual person, not a mere principle or force, as demonstrated by his presence in the lake of fire (19:20; 20:10). This beast is as definite a personality as Jesus, whom he seems to counterfeit. Satanically inspired and energized, he is also satanically sustained and controlled and will be the last Gentile ruler or the last Gentile form of government.

Among the beast's identifying titles are "the little horn," "the blasphemer," "the king of the North, of Syria," "the great Assyrian," and "the man of sin," in whom the sin of humankind will reach its climax. Revealed after the rapture of the church, this beast is "the ruler who will come" (Daniel 9:26).

He will be the last Gentile world ruler before Christ and will oppress Israel. Arising from the province of Syria (of the ancient Greek Empire, including ancient Assyria, even Babylon) with Jewish assistance, he will displace three rules of the League of Ten, and will revive ancient Greece.

Concerning the symbolism of the heads and horns of the beast (13:1), the seven heads represent seven Gentile nations that have ruled or will rule the Bible world and Israel. Additional help comes from 17:8–18, especially verse 10: "five have fallen, one is, the other has not yet come." From Abraham to Christ, five emperors fell: Egypt, Assyria, Babylon, Medo-Persia, and Greece. "One is" refers to Rome, the empire ruling when John wrote. The "other" who has yet to come is the ten-nation league, symbolized by the "ten horns" (13:1). The "seven heads" signify pseudosupremacy; the "ten horns" signify pseudostrength. The expression, "The beast . . . is an eighth king. He belongs to the seven" (17:11) refers to the revival of one of the seven and also the final gentile government. That he is an eighth king implies that he usurps authority and forms a government distinct from the ten kings.

The form of the first beast is likened to a leopard, a bear, and a lion (13:2; reversed in order from Daniel 7:4–6). Daniel looks *forward* down the ages, whereas John looks *back*. The antichrist will unite in himself the God-opposed characteristics of three preceding kingdoms, resembling respectively the leopard, the bear, and the lion. Shepherds in Palestine are familiar with the speed of the leopard, the slow, crushing power of the bear, and the fearsome ravenousness of the lion.

Combined in this dread creature are the infamy and ferocity of past empires: Macedonian swiftness and brilliancy of conquest; Persian tenacity of purpose and massiveness of power; Babylonian voracity and autocratic dominion. All civil and legal power will be vested in this despotic head, whose throne will be one of corruption (Psalm 94:20).

Names of blasphemy upon his heads speak of his utter defiance of God. Blasphemous titles assumed by the Roman emperors of the first and second centuries (and of certain succeeding Roman leaders) are the forerunners of names that the beast will proudly display. Nero, for example, was saluted as "the eternal one." In the beast's blasphemous conduct we see defiant and flagrant opposition to God and to His Christ.

Delegated, constitutional rule is committed to the beast by the dragon. Embodying all the strength and brutality of the Babylonian, Median, and Persian empires, the beast is a fitting agent for Satan to use. The sovereignty of the world that was offered to Christ by the prince of the world (John 12:31) was refused by our Lord (Luke 4:5, 8). Here it is offered to, and accepted by, the beast.

Death and resurrection are here, and they result in universal adoration for the beast. He received a "fatal wound," but it healed. (The Greek implies being "slain to death." In seven other places Revelation uses "as though slain.") Having been brought back from the realm of death and bearing the apparent marks of resurrection, the beast proves how tremendous the power of Satan will be and how easily the world will be deceived.

Some writers see in the healing of the deadly head wound the political death and resurrection of the beast. Imperialism, as represented by the worldwide dominion of the Caesars, has lain in the iron grip of political death since A.D. 476. But God will permit an empire to rise out of revolutionary passion and conflict. The healing of the deadly wound has been explained as the revival of the Napoleonic dynasty, after its overthrow at Waterloo. But because the bulk of Revelation is prophetic, the historical interpretation must be ruled out (except by way of illustration). John here views as an accomplished fact a revived imperial form of the Roman Empire. Present-day events and the movements of today's nations are preparing the world for the beast's universal, commanding influence. The lack of ability on the part of today's rulers to govern adequately is preparing the way for this satanically inspired dictator.

In the worship of the dragon and of the beast we see another aspect of imitation. Satan wanted Christ to fall down and worship him, but the Master bowed the knee to no one but God. Contrasted with Who is like Thee, o Lord?" we have Who is like the beast? (13:4). Michael and his angels make war with the devil and his angels and overcome them, but here a deluded people throw down the gauntlet: "Who can make war against him [the beast]?" This beast with his deadly wound healed is surely immune to further destruction! Although he will reign over only one of the ten kingdoms during the first half of the prophetic week, he will reign over all ten kingdoms through the last three and one-half years.

This beast, this "king [who] will do as he pleases" (Daniel 11:36), will be cruelly anti-Semitic and will act in the superhuman power of the dragon. He will manifest a warlike prowess that is devoid of pity. The presence of such a terrible dictator, with the destiny of millions in his hands, will be the sign of hastening judgment for all who bear his mark.

Finis Jennings Drake has this summary of the beast's character and characteristics:

> He will be a man who will possess the talent and leadership of all previously gifted conquerors and leaders. In addition to these natural gifts, he will possess the miraculous power of attracting people of every class, fascinating them with his marvelous personality, successes, superhuman wisdom, administrative and executive ability, and bringing them under his control through well-directed flattery and masterly diplomacy. He will be endued with the power of Satan in the exercise of these gifts until the world will wonder after him and worship him as God.

What follows in 13:5–7 is an extension of what is implied in "a blasphemous name" and "a mouth like that of a lion" (13:1–2). The old Roman Empire was guilty of blasphemy in that it assumed divine names in public documents. The contempt and mockery of anything divine will be openly practiced when devil worship is widely recognized. Boasting and blasphemy will come from the loud lion mouth of the beast, "a mouth that spoke boastfully" (Daniel 7:8). God Himself, including His name and His dwelling place with all its inhabitants, will be cursed by the beast. We can understand the blasphemy against those in heaven, since they rejoiced over the dragon's expulsion from heaven (12:10).

The faithful saints on earth are to be given over to the power of the beast, who will be allowed to wreak his vengeance upon them and overcome them. His authority to kill or spare will be unlimited in range and extent, as seen in the mention of the four divisions of the human race

(13:7). The dragon, enraged over his defeat in the war in heaven, now pours out this rage upon the saints on earth.

Beast worshipers are clearly defined as those whose names are not in the divine register belonging to the slain Lamb. The elect "live in heaven" (13:6) and are heavenly; the worshipers of the beast are "all inhabitants of the earth" (13:8) and are earthy. The widely proclaimed humanism today is simply self-worship and is just one step away from devil worship. For a consideration of "the book of life belonging to the Lamb" (13:8), see the discussion at 20:11–15. In the personal exhortation "he who has an ear, let him hear" we have Christ's own words of admonition used both in the Gospels and in Revelation. As employed here it is a call to a full understanding of the apocalyptic judgments about to break loose.

Punishment with retribution in kind is the principle indicated for friends and foes alike. Whether saints or sinners, we reap what we sow. Saints crushed under the rule of the beast are not to resist. Here is the patience or endurance of the saints. They must bear their appointed sufferings and thereby triumph. As those whose names are written in heaven and as those who dwell there, the weapons they wield are not carnal but spiritual. No hellish or human power can rob them of moral victories. Trusting in the vengeance of God, the saints of the Tribulation use their captivity as a means of grace, knowing that an eternal captivity in the lake of fire is to be the portion of the beast. All who cause God's people to suffer must face retributive justice. With what they measure they use it shall be measured to them again (Matthew 7:2; Jeremiah 15:2).

Consider the following contrasts:

Christ	Antichrist
Son of Man	Son of sin
Son of God	Son of Satan
Son of Righteousness	Son of perdition
Superhuman	Superman
Very God	Claims to be God
Redeemer	Destroyer
King of Kings	World dictator
Agent of God	Agent of Satan
Humble	Proud
Sacrificing	Tyrannical

Seventh Person: The Earth Beast—False Prophet (Revelation 13:11–18)

> Then I saw another beast, coming out of the earth. He had two horns like a lamb, but he spoke like a dragon. (Revelation 13:11)

As we approach our study of this second beast, the lamblike monster (or the pretender lamb), let us contrast and compare the two beasts of Revelation 13:

Contrasts

First Beast	*Second Beast*
Out of sea (unsettled state)	Out of earth (ordered government)
Tool of Satan	Tool of first beast
Satan's vice-regent	Beast's vicar
Secular power	Spiritual power
Has ten horns	Has two horns
A Gentile?	A Jew?
Paramount in authority	Subordinate to first beast
Glorifies himself	Defies the first beast
Appears first	Appears second
Rules from Rome	Rules from Palestine
Noted for brutal power	Noted for cunning wisdom
Political head	Ecclesiastical head
False deity	False prophet

Comparisons

Both beasts are from below, not from above.
Both beasts are faithful allies; they act as one.
Both beasts are to suffer the same doom.
Both beasts are mimics of the Lamb.
Both beasts are actual persons.

Let us summarize the teaching of Scripture on this second beast, who, because he is a religious beast, is more dangerous than the first beast. Though this second beast is mentioned after the beast out of the sea, it does not follow that he will come into existence after the sea beast. The way the earth beast works to enforce the worship of the sea beast proves that they appear together and exercise similar powers concurrently. Once the sea beast takes the stage, his companion beast quickly follows.

The Origin of the Earth Beast

The second beast that John saw comes out of chaos and revolution but quickly produces a civilized, consolidated, and ordered condition in society. Troubled agitations are speedily overcome by the rider of the white horse, who is able to achieve bloodless victories among the various peoples. Out of this established order of civil and political government emerges this more dangerous executive agent of the devil.

With his appearance the arrogant imitation of the Holy Trinity is complete, for opposing God, Christ, and the Holy Spirit we have the dragon, the antichrist, and the false prophet. The Greek word used of the false prophet is *pseudoprophetes* (16:13; 19:20; 20:10). Both beasts are false prophets, the second being the executor of the first. "Earth" or "world" is symbolic of peoples on the earth; if the part of the earth that this second beast arises from is the land of Israel, he will probably be an apostate Jew.

"Coming out of the earth" (13:11), he will seem akin to ordinary people. The second beast's rise coincides with the healing of the first beast's deadly wound and his resurrection. With the appearance of the lamblike beast, Christ's three offices are perverted. The first beast is the false kingship; the harlot represents false priesthood; the second beast is the false prophet. The beast may be identified as the bodily power of antichristianity, the false prophet, its intellectual power, and the harlot, its spiritual power.

The Characteristics of the Earth Beast

"Two horns like a lamb" mark this beast as the false Messiah. Both beasts imitate God's Lamb—the first beast was wounded to death and revived; the second beast has two lamblike horns (differing from God's Lamb who has seven horns, 5:6). Fullness of power belongs to the true Prophet, but limited power belongs to the false prophet. A writer of the sixth century remarked that the false messiah feigns to be a lamb that he may assail the Lamb—the body of Christ. His activities, however, are confined to the followers of the Lamb on earth, for before his appearance the church will have been caught up to heaven.

The horn is the symbol of physical, moral, or kingly power, and the earth beast's two horns represent the combination of king and prophet. These two horns can also speak of the combined power of natural and miracle-working religions. This counterfeit messiah has only two horns, in contrast to the ten horns of the first beast. His authority covers two realms, religious and miraculous, and in both we see his lamblike yet satanically deceiving speech. The horns will also give the false prophet a strong religious appeal, and he will be able to unite all conflicting religious bodies into one universal church.

Specifically mentioned as a "false prophet" (16:13), the earth beast fills a role as servant. A prophet is one who comes in the name of another and who speaks for another. Thus Satan's counterfeit "Christ" will have a counterfeit "Elijah." The false prophet will be the Elijah of the antichrist. Malachi predicted that Elijah would appear before the day of the Lord (Malachi 4:5). (More on this when we come to the beast's miracles.)

The manifold character of this false prophet is hinted at by our Lord in His description of the last days: "Many false prophets will appear" (Matthew 24:11, 24). Under this title, the false prophet (16:13; 19:20; 20:10), he exercises great spiritual authority among the Jews and the people of Christendom generally.

As the false prophet, he is found only with the antichrist. The unholy two are unseparable. The dragon gives his external power to the first beast (13:2) and his spirit to the second beast, for he speaks as a dragon (13:11). He is to employ the same subtlety and deceit that Satan used when he deceived Eve and that he currently uses to deceive an ungodly world. Lamblike in appearance, he is betrayed by his speech as Satan's minister. Because the dragon's goal is physical and moral ruin, he uses the beast for political and civil purposes and the false prophet for spiritual and moral purposes. Thus the two beasts will be Satan's two chief lieutenants as the end approaches.

The Activities of the Earth Beast

Comparing Scripture with Scripture, we find these features of the works of the earth beast:

- He exercises all the authority of the first beast.
- He carries out the will of the first beast.
- He empowers an image of the first beast.
- He demands absolute worship of the first beast.
- He shares the doom of the first beast.

He exercises all the authority of the first beast: Here is a statement as dreadful as it is specific: "He exercised all the authority of the first beast on his behalf" (13:12). The phrase "on his behalf" implies "in his presence," as ministering to and upholding him. He is the active minister of the first beast, exercising a subordinate power. The wording here does not imply that the first beast is a mere passive head. The first beast is the titular and powerful head of a mighty federation of nations (17:9–13) and, as the imperial ruler, remains bold and blaspheming until his defeat by Christ, the mightier One.

The false prophet will exercise the power of the first beast by using the force and prestige of the beast's authority to bring people everywhere into worship of the beast. Of the two, the false prophet is the worse, since he influences people religiously. A wolf in sheep's clothing, his deceptive activities win him great victories. In his description of "the little horn," Daniel speaks of him as having "the eyes of a man" as well as the mouth of blasphemy (Daniel 7:8). The phrase "the eyes of a man" symbolizes cunning and intellectual culture, the very characteristics of the false prophet.

With all persuasiveness he will succeed in claiming exclusive worship for himself in the land of Israel, where he will be blasphemously deified. He will arrogate to himself divine worship and will sit in the temple built by the unbelieving nation. He will set himself above all authority, whether divine or human, and will take God's place as much as he can. Outside the Holy Land the false prophet will also exercise authority, forcing upon the nations the worship of his great confederate, the first beast.

He carries out the will of the first beast: Raised up to represent the beast and receiving his commission from this dragon-inspired creature, the false prophet will live, move, and have his being in the will of the beast. He will play the role of a devoted servant. Later on, as we shall see, he will inspire the nations to have one mind and to give their power and strength to the beast (17:13). And in this he will imitate Christ, who delighted to do the will of His Father. The false prophet will have supreme delight in carrying out the wishes of the beast and forcing those wishes upon the world at large.

Christ's devotion to the will of God was rewarded in many ways. His miraculous ministry, for example, attested to His identification of aims and wishes: "No one could perform the miraculous signs you are doing if God were not with him" (John 3:2). And here is the false prophet doing great wonders in the sight of all—demonic miracles, not merely tricks. By demonic aid, wonders of "signs" are worked that are designed to deceive the earthly minded, though not the elect at this time. Followers of the true Lamb will know that a miracle is not enough to warrant belief in a professed revelation unless that revelation is in harmony with God's already revealed will.

Publicly, "in full view of men" (13:13), he produces fire from heaven to deceive them. Other miracles performed "on behalf of the first beast" or "before the beast" produce the same delusion. Because of such usurping of divine prerogatives, retributive judgment should and will begin to descend on those already given up by God. Handed over to the working of error and thus believing a lie (2 Thessalonians 2:11), those guilty of devil worship in a triune form are ripe for judgment.

He empowers an image of the first beast: In the creation of a remarkable image of the first beast we have the setting up of an actual, literal representation by which he will be worshiped. This image will be as real as the one Nebuchadnezzar set upon the plans of Dura, when at the beginning of Gentile supremacy people were compelled under pain of death to worship an image representing the power and majesty of the first major world empire (Daniel 3). Now we see the end of Gentile dominion as the false prophet rejects image worship by giving life (or breath or spirit) to the image of the beast. True life can be given by no one but God, so the image is energized by a spurious vitality. Breath is given so that the image can speak, producing a ventriloquism similar to that in Acts 16:16–17.

He demands the absolute worship of the first beast: The three Hebrew youths were cast into the fiery furnace for refusing to worship the image of Nebuchadnezzar. Roman consul Pliny "The Younger" in his letter to Trajan states that he consigned to punishment those Christians who would not worship the emperor's image with incense and wine. These and other images set up to test secular and spiritual allegiance are merely forerunners of the worship of the beast's image that the false prophet will demand under pain of death. Even as the Holy Spirit presently directs our attention to Christ as the Object of worship and adoration, so the false prophet will direct the worship of multitudes to the beast, and all who refuse to bow the knee to the beast image will be murdered.

Universal subjection to the beast will also be forced by the most rigid control of commerce ever practiced. A stupendous boycott of food and trade will operate universally. Whether rich or poor, people will not be able to buy or sell unless they have the official ration mark—the emblem of the kingdom of the man of sin. The choice will be idolatry or starvation, and the false prophet will make sure there are no black markets or bootleggers. The most fearsome secret police force will be created to enforce the economic union for trading and living. The most abject submission to the vilest tyranny ever experienced will be evidenced by a mystic mark on the right hand or the forehead, even as animals and slaves have often been branded with their owners' name or mark.

Absence of the mark of the beast will mean relentless ostracism. Such a mark will be necessary for life and for all social business relations. In effect, it will be a diabolical trading license. It will be in plain sight, upon the hand, indicating that the branded person is the active slave of the beast. The raised open hand is a form of the Roman salute; when hands are raised to the image, it will be seen immediately whether those who salute the beast are beast worshipers and therefore qualified to buy and sell. The brand upon the forehead will be the public sign of abject submission to the beast.

The name of the beast is another phase of satanic mimicry. Christ has a name that is truly above every other name, but the false prophet will see to it that the beast's name is honored above every other name. A name, as we know, can mean an emblem of allegiance. Faithful believers, however, will refuse to wear such a name. In stern and solemn protest they will refuse to be branded with any symbol of submission to the beast. They will die rather than bow to the beast. Sealed by God, they will scorn any imitation. In those days Psalm 23 will be exceedingly precious, for despite imminent starvation, the Lord will prepare a table for His loyal servants in the presence of their enemies, and, passing through the valley of the shadow of death, they will fear no evil. The ideal shepherd will preserve His own from the cruel deceptions of the "idol shepherd" (Zechariah 11:15–17 KJV).

Spiritual wisdom will be needed to solve the *mystery* of iniquity, so as not to be deceived by it. The full meaning of the number of the beast will be granted to those saints who are on earth when the beast is here in person. Of this we are certain: no one at present has sufficient wisdom to understand the number of the beast. What is meant by the trinity of sixes has been the subject of much research and debate. Many Greek and Hebrew names have a numerical value of 666. Many ingenious interpretations have been given for this symbolic number.

Ellicott, in his most valuable commentary, devotes much space to the significance of this symbolic number, but wisely concludes his treatment of it by saying:

> I am disposed to interpret this six hundred and sixty-six as a symbolical number, expressing all that it is possible for human wisdom and human power when directed by an evil spirit to achieve, and indicating a state of marvelous earthy perfection when the beast-power has reached its highest development, when culture, civilization, art, song, science and reason have combined to produce an age so nearly resembling perfection—an age of gold, if not a golden age—that men will begin to say that faith in God is an impertinence, and the hope of a future life is a libel upon the happiness of the present. Then will the world-power have reached the zenith of his influence; then will only wisdom descended from above be able to detect the infinite difference between a world with faith and a world without faith, and the great gulf which the want of a little heaven-love can fix between an age and an age.

Expositors have brought skill, learning and, in some instances, great research to the question, What is meant by the number 666? There is divine wisdom wrapped up in this symbolic numeral (which also occurs in 1 Kings 10:14 and 2 Chronicles 9:13), and only spiritual understanding can unlock its mystery. No doubt its full, precise, and final solution will be apparent to the wise or godly during the Tribulation days, when the power of the beast will exhibit the highest human development in pride, impiety, and combined religious and political opposition to God and His anointed. In general this is the moral significance of 666. Its meaning, when finally known, will call for prompt repudiation of the beast, who is the political minister of Satan in blasphemous opposition to God.

The number 666 is man's number, the unit six being impressed upon him at his creation and in his subsequent history. Man was created on the sixth day. His appointed days of toil are six per week. The Hebrew slave was to serve six years. For six years the land was to be sown. Under the sixth seal in the sixth chapter of Revelation an appalling and universal breakdown of all governmental power and authority takes place in the coming days of Tribulation.

The numeral seven is God's number and usually denotes what is perfect or complete, but six falls short of that and signifies human imperfection and toil. In the growing development of man's history he goes from bad to worse, and six combined with six increases in moral significance until man openly and directly opposes God.

There is an obvious connection between the first and the last of the four major world powers. In character they are identical, except that the last is the worst of the four. The image of gold set up by Nebuchadnezzar for his own glorification was sixty cubits high and six cubits wide (Daniel 3:1, according to the Aramaic). No doubt this image was meant to consolidate and unify the numerous different religions of the Babylonian empire—under threat of awful death it had to be worshiped. Daniel 3 points forward to the even deeper and truly satanic evil of Revelation 13.

He shares the doom of the first beast: Both beasts share the same fate at the same time. Existing together in their terrible reign, they are consigned together to hell and ultimately to the lake of fire. Defeated together at Armageddon when Christ appears in power, they leave this earth to endure the torment that their crimes deserve (Revelation 17:13–14; 19:19–21). When we come to the seven dooms, we will have more to say about the final destination of the trinity of evil. What a purge this will be when Christ takes to Himself His power and reigns! If Christ's return for His own is not far away, then these very beasts may be alive on earth today. But before they are fully revealed to the world, we shall be caught up to meet the Lord in the air. Praise God, the church will not witness the beast worship and agony of the great Tribulation! Our present obligation is to seek and save the lost around us in order to spare them from the horrors of the age to come and from a more terrible fate forever.

7

Seven Words

Revelation 14:1–20

I looked, and there before me was the Lamb. (Revelation 14:1)

This parenthetical chapter in Revelation is largely anticipative. Chapters 14–16 describe preparations for messianic judgment and offer a mingling of songs and sobs, music and misery, joy and judgment, glory and gloom, heaven and hell. Chapter 14 contains a sevenfold divine intervention in grace and judgment. It constitutes an answer to the cry of the remnant, "Why, O LORD, do you stand far off? Why do you hide yourself in times of trouble?" (Psalm 10:1). The oft-repeated cry, "How long, O Lord?" finds an answer, a responsive chord in our own hearts, as we think of the slaughter, misery, and anguish of our sin-laden, war-torn days. Will God never show His hand? Are the forces of iniquity to be forever victorious? Has God abandoned His saints to the will of the enemy? When will He intervene?

This chapter proves that God will have His day. The mills of God's justice may appear to grind slowly, but they grind exceedingly sure. This chapter is well placed, since it serves as a necessary prelude to the fearful providential judgments of God. Chapters 12–14 form an episode of dramatic interest—a single connected prophecy. Chapters 12–13 describe the doings of the dragon and the beasts. Truth has fallen upon the streets; the blood of the saints flows as freely as water; open defiance of God is the order of the day. Good is almost banished from the earth (Psalm 4:6) and faith has gone (Luke 18:8). The whole prophetic scene has become Satan's playground.

But we breathe more freely in chapter 14. The divine reaper is at hand. Earth's horrible iniquity is about to end. Coming between the trumpets and the bowls, this fourteenth chapter sounds the death knell of arrogant, blasphemous, cruel rulers and people. The accumulated load of anguish and distress will now vanish from the hearts of God's persecuted.

As a whole the chapter contains a contrast between the Lamb and the 144,000 sealed Jews, between the nations and the antichrist, between the six angels and their announcements, and between the two sickles and their vintage.

First Word: The Singers and Their Song (Revelation 14:1–5)

They sang a new song before the throne. (Revelation 14:3)

In these five verses we have one of the most remarkable scenes of Revelation. Here is a bright and gladdening vision, a calm after a storm: from the tyranny of the beast to triumph with the Lamb! This is indeed a welcome transition. Let us now consider these saints, who are no longer exposed to trial but are seated in a position of royalty.

Their Savior—The Lamb

Prominence is given to the Lamb on Mount Zion, around whom this singing multitude gathers. The book of Revelation is essentially a book of the Lamb. Some twenty-seven times our Lord is depicted in this way. And it is as the *slain* Lamb that He is seen. Because of His scars, sovereignty is to be His. In this chapter we have an anticipative vision of Christ's coming in power. The bleeding lamb is now the Lamb upon His road to ultimate victory. His chosen ones had been as lambs among wolves, and the flock had been harried by the wild beast. But they overcame through the blood of the Lamb and are now happily at His side.

Their Station—The Throne

This distinguished multitude is found standing on Mount Zion, the selected seat of the earthly thousand-year reign of Christ and His saints. The Lamb has left His position in the midst of the throne and is now on Mount Zion. Here is the seat of royal power, of God's intervention in grace, of God's sovereignty, all in respect to Israel. "Zion," named only once in Revelation, is an extremely interesting term. Out of about 110 times that Zion is mentioned in the Bible, 90 are in terms of the Lord's great love and affection for her, so that the place has very great significance. To the Jew, Zion is rich in sacred memories (Isaiah 2; Psalm 2:6). At long last God's King is on Mount Zion, and surrounding Him are His purchased ones as loyal and loving subjects!

Their Number—144,000

A specific number of purchased ones is stated; the question is, Who are these sealed singers? Is this great multitude the same group as the 144,000 in chapter 7? One expositor suggests that this group in chapter 14 represents only a portion of the great harvest of redeemed Tribulation saints, a "first installment" marked by high spiritual services. Similarities between these two companies include the same number, 144,000; the same location, Mount Zion; the same seal on their foreheads; and the same deliverance from trouble.

The repetition of the number, however, does not prove that these companies are one and the same. Walter Scott suggests, "The 144,000 here witnessed are of *Judah*; a similarly numbered company of all *Israel* (7:4) forms a separate vision . . . They are Jews who steadfastly maintained the right of God and of the Lamb; now they are publicly owned of Him . . . 144,000 Jewish saints who occupy the leading place in the earthly millennial kingdom." The number 144,000 indicates governmental number and fullness.

Their Seal—A Badge of Blessedness

In contrast to the 144,000 in chapter 7, who are sealed as "the servants of our God," this amazing 144,000 in chapter 14 are sealed on their foreheads with the Lamb's name and the name of His Father. A seal, of course, represents a sign of ownership and a guarantee of preservation. Of their "beautiful badge of blessedness," William Newell suggests that it proclaimed their ownership, exhibited their character, and announced their destiny.

The seal of these confessors of Christ is in contrast to the mark of the beast on each of his worshipers. "It has occurred to us," says Newell, "that the presence of the heavenly seal in the foreheads of the remnant from chapter 7 onward is so evident to men that Satan is forced to undertake to break its influence by demanding the opposite seal in the foreheads of his devotees. And especially may this be true when we reflect that God preserves (as in 9:4) those who have His seal from woes to which others are subject."

Their Song—A New Song

The voices from heaven are as the voice of many waters and of a great thunder. As is the voice of God, so is the voice of the heavenly choristers, who are in accord with those on Mount Zion. The harp-singing multitude in heaven and the preserved company of Judah form one grand choir. Harps, associated with song (5:8; 14:2; 15:2), set forth the choral praise of the redeemed and heavenly host. The song and the harp are so beautifully blended that they are spoken of as one voice.

The song that the heavenly harpists know and only the 144,000 can learn, is called a new song. The old song was related to creation, "while the morning stars sang together, and all the angels shouted for joy" (Job 38:7). This new song has redemption as its central theme. That is why it is referred to as the song of Moses and the Lamb. God and the old song are united. The Lamb and the new song are conformed. God's past ways of power toward Israel, combined with His present grace toward them and us, appear to be the thought in the song of Moses and of the Lamb (15:3).

A. R. Fausset, in commenting on this new song, says, "The song is that of victory after conflict with the dragon, beast, and false prophet; [it was] never sung before, for such a conflict had never been fought before; [it was] therefore *new*: till now the kingdom of Christ on earth had been usurped. They sing the *new song* in anticipation of His taking possession of His blood-bought kingdom with His saints." The form of the word "sing" in the Greek indicates continuous singing.

We must not forget that the 144,000 rejoice because they were "purchased from among men" (14:4). We have the double phrase "redeemed from the earth" (a sinful place) and "purchased from among men" (a sinful race). This high position is the privilege of the 144,000 because they had been purchased, not because they were victors over the beast. The angels cannot sing this new song, for they do not know personally what it is to come out of the great Tribulation and to have their robes washed white through the blood of the Lamb (7:14).

Their Separation—Not Defiled

In 14:4–5 we have a wonderful description of the walk and witness of this victorious part of Judah, who has emerged out of the great Tribulation and now stands in triumph with the Lamb on Mount Zion, the seat of royalty and of sovereign grace. A fearsome test has been theirs. The grossest corruption, open idolatry, proud boasting, daring blasphemy, and open wickedness had surrounded them, but like the Jews in Sardis, this 144,000 emerged with garments undefiled.

They have not defiled themselves with women: We are to understand this in a spiritual sense (see Matthew 25:1) in contrast to the apostate church (14:8), which was spiritually a "harlot" (17:1–5; also Isaiah 1:21 contrasted with 2 Corinthians 11:2; Ephesians 5:25–27). So, "not being defiled with women" means not being led astray from faithfulness to the Lord by the tempters who jointly constitute the spiritual harlot. They may be Nazirites unto God as touching their relation to women, as some have suggested. But such an interpretation would confine this defined company to men only. Does the language not imply that the 144,000 represent those who lived and walked in spiritual purity in a scene abandoned to all that was vile? They had "kept themselves pure." Virgin love—undivided heart affection for the Lamb—was theirs as the rest of the world followed the beast. They had a separation, thorough and unqualified, from their sinful surroundings. They were virgin souls, clad in stainless purity.

They follow the Lamb: Nearness to the Lamb on Mount Zion is the fitting reward for their loyalty to Him while they were on earth. All around them were those who had wandered after the beast and his prophet, but the obedience of the 144,000 was as full and unquestionable as their separation from the world. Following the Lamb in His rejection, they now share His royalty. "Follow" is in the present tense, implying an unending obedience.

They are the firstfruits: While similar language is used of the church, we are not to confuse the "firstfruits" here with the redeemed saints forming the new creation. "Firstfruits to God and the Lamb" are kingdom words rather than mere salvation words. "Purchased from among men," these 144,000 form an earnest purchase—a pledge—from among men for the reign of heaven on earth. They form a sample of the full and final harvest.

No lie is found in their mouths: Lying, wonders, and falsehoods characterize the days of the antichrist. "The lie" (that Satan is God and the beast is his Christ, and therefore must be worshiped) was generally believed, but in the mouths of the 144,000 no lie was found. They were truthful in word and way. In spite of fierce persecution they confessed the true Messiah (1 John 2:21–27) and remained true to His Word.

They are blameless: In outward conduct and ways before men, these saints on earth were without fault. This fitting and condensed epitome of the practical character and life concerns their life on earth. In all their ways they refused to conform to the edicts of the beast. In respect to the sincerity of their fidelity to the Lamb, they were without fault. They were not absolutely and in themselves blameless but were regarded as such on the grounds of the Lamb's righteousness, in whom alone they trusted and whom they faithfully served and followed. What a joy this remnant is to God and to the Lamb!

Second Word: An Angel—Good News (Revelation 14:6–7)

He said in a loud voice, "Fear God and give him glory." (Revelation 14:7)

We now come to God's public witness against the reign of the antichrist and to the fast-approaching judgment he deserves. The term "another angel" (14:6) implies a new turn in the unfolding drama; each successive angel announces events within that drama (7:2; 8:3, 13; 10:1). This first angel was seen "flying in midair," appearing in the sight and sound of all people on earth. Previously, an eagle "flying in midair" (8:13) announced woe, but this angel "flying in the midst of heaven" announced joy. This flying angel is a messenger of mercy and shows grace in judgment. He represents the last call to earth dwellers to repent.

A Glad Announcement—Good News

We must not forget that this angel does not proclaim an announcement of doom but the gospel (14:6), which means good news. He announces the good news of the everlasting kingdom of Christ, which will begin immediately after the judgment of evil forces (announced as imminent in 14:7). While the human preachers of the gospel of the kingdom will be converted Jews, angels are commissioned to providentially expedite the declaration of the good news during the last days of the prophetic week.

In unmistakable language this mighty angel urges people to turn from the beast to God. The hour of divine judgment has come, and men must repent of their gross idolatry if they do not want to endure the wrath of the bowls. Here is an urgent call to fear God, which is the beginning of wisdom, and to give glory to Him rather than to the beast and his image. The creator of all things pleads for the last time for man's allegiance. Even as the human race is described under a fourfold designation—nations, tribes, tongues and peoples—so creation is here stated in four terms—heaven, earth, sea, and fountains.

A Great Audience—"To Those Who Live on the Earth"

The angel preaches his gospel all over the earth, and all classes of people hear his message. Whether there is a general response to the angelic call we are not told. Our Lord declared that some people are so abandoned to the rejection of God that they would not believe even if someone rose from the dead and went to them with a message of grace. A great preacher like Noah had little success in warning the multitudes of coming judgment. Deaf to his entreaties, they lived on in their corrupt ways until the flood came and took them all away.

Third Word: Another Angel—Babylon Falls (Revelation 14:8)

Fallen! Fallen is Babylon the Great. (Revelation 14:8)

The prominence of angels in this chapter indicates that they have a major role in the providential and governmental economy both prior to and during Christ's millennial kingdom. In 14:8 we are given a preface of events to come. It is a preliminary and preparatory announcement of the judgment described in chapters 17–18. The destruction of Babylon is being celebrated in heaven, where judgment is treated as already accomplished.

The intensity of utterance in the repetition "Fallen! Fallen is Babylon" is not mere Hebraism but speaks of a double judgment. Both as a system and as a city, Babylon is to be destroyed. The word "is" indicates the anticipation of sure destruction. From heaven's standpoint Babylon *is* fallen, even though its actual doom has not yet occurred.

Babylonianism, as we shall show more fully later, represents a vast system that enslaves professing Christians. It is characterized by worldly pride, idolatry, and spiritual adultery. The reason for Babylon's fall is given in the words, "made all the nations drink the maddening wine of her adulteries" (v. 8). The wine of the wrath of God is the consequence of her fornication. Because she made the nations drunk with the wine of her fornication, she herself shall be made drunk with the wine of God's wrath. Here we are given the ultimate fulfillment of Isaiah 21:9: "Look, here comes a man in a chariot with a team of horses. And he gives back the answer: 'Babylon has fallen, has fallen! All the images of its gods lie shattered on the ground!'"

There are three distinct subjects in this awesome phrase: wine, wrath, and fornication. Babylon's wine: "Babylon was a gold cup in the Lord's hand; she made the whole earth drunk" (Jeremiah 51:7). Babylon's wrath: "This is what the Lord, the God of Israel, said to me: 'Take from my hand this cup filled with the wine of my wrath and make all the nations to whom I send you drink it'" (Jeremiah 25:15). Babylon's fornication: "The kings of the earth committed adultery with her, and the merchants of the earth grew rich from her excessive luxuries" (Revelation 18:3). The white heat of God's anger, held back through the ages, is now about to be turned loose upon accumulated corruption.

Fourth Word: Another Angel—Unending Torment
(Revelation 14:9–12)

A third angel followed them and said, "... he, too, will drink of the wine of God's fury." (Revelation 14:9–10)

The terrible doom of worshipers of the beast, as announced in these verses, is fearsome in the extreme. Judgment, unequaled in its severity and proportioned to the guilt and horrible iniquity openly practiced, is now about to fall. With a great voice this third angel declares the unending torment of all who have followed the beast.

The Worship of the Beast

Six times over in Revelation the worship of the beast, the devil incarnate, is described as directed to his image. Christ came as "the radiance of God's glory and the exact representation of his being" (Hebrews 1:3). But now unrelieved torment is to overtake those who have deliberately chosen Satan's false christ, who has commanded all earth people to worship his image. Just and inevitable retribution will be individual. Retributive justice will be meted out to each and every person who follows the beast and carries his mark.

The Wrath of God

No alleviating circumstances are to be allowed. With a loud voice, so that all can hear, the angel declares that the outpoured wrath is to be "full strength." A. R. Fausset writes:

> Wine was so commonly mixed with water that to mix wine is used in Greek for 'to pour out wine,' [but] this wine of God's wrath is undiluted; there is no drop of water to cool its heat. Nothing of grace or hope is blended with it. This terrible threat may well raise us above the fear of man's threats. This *unmixed* cup is already *mingled* and prepared for Satan and the beast's followers.

The Wail of the Doomed

"Burning sulfur" (14:10) is a symbol of unutterable anguish (Isaiah 30:33; Revelation 20:10), and this eternal doom is to be visited upon the impenitent. Burning sulfur, says William Newell, "is [a] most terrible substance . . . in its action upon human flesh—in torment when it touches the body. Combined with fire, it is absolute agony, unutterable anguish! And it is meant to be so, for it will be the infliction of divine vengeance unlimited."

The eternal doom of the beast worshipers is described in the dreadful language of 14:11: "And the smoke of their torment rises for ever and ever. There is no rest day or night." No cessation, no alleviation of anguish can be expected. Such endless horror and ceaseless agony baffle our comprehension. May grace and power be ours to warn sinners of the inevitable, eternal punishment awaiting all who are not covered by the blood of the Lamb!

Adding to the horror felt by the wicked is the consciousness that the holy angels and the Lamb are onlookers. This will intensify the pungency of the curse. These holy witnesses of doom will not be found gloating over the terrible suffering of the lost. Their presence will indicate the awful and holy approval of a divine sentence. The holy angels, once witnesses to the horrible evils of the beast and his followers, will now witness God's vengeance. Every tormented person will realize that the angels are observing their anguish. And so also will the Lamb, whom they had once openly defied and whose blood they had wantonly rejected. The association of holy angels and the Lamb indicates that they both work together in executing the vengeance of the holy God.

Fifth Word: A Voice from Heaven—The Blessed Dead (Revelation 14:13)

> Then I heard a voice from heaven say, "Write: Blessed are the dead who die in the Lord from now on." (Revelation 14:13)

In contrast to the self-doomed rebels we have God's patient elect, who cry for deliverance from the adversary (Luke 18:7). The twofold mark of the faithful remnant in a time of unequaled tribulation is the keeping of the commandments of God and the maintaining of faith in Jesus. Now their faith and patience are fully rewarded.

What a welcome relief this benediction is! It comes as a break between so much judgment and doom. We pause and draw a fresh breath after a revelation of unspeakable torment. But once we leave this beautiful description of the saints' everlasting rest, we find ourselves again in the terrible atmosphere of wrath and vengeance.

John's meditation was broken by the command to write. The blessedness of the faithful had to be placed on record forever. What the apostle set down must be stored up in the heart. The command to write is repeated twelve times in Revelation, to indicate that all the things it refers to are matters of importance.

While the message John heard has an application to all saints, it has a special relation to those who are to be martyred for their faith. In many funeral manuals this comforting verse is given as one of the Scriptures for recitation at the burial of the Christian dead. But a particular class of martyred saints at a particular junction in human history is intended in this benediction. "From now on" intimates that the end is imminent and that the blessing is just about to be entered. Martyrdom under the beast is the subject. All who die *in* the Lord were willing to die *for* the Lord.

But after these terrible tortures that only the beast is capable of inflicting there comes rest. Rest will come through dying. For the beast worshipers there will be no rest day or night, but for the faithful unto death there is eternal life, eternal rest. The rest from toils and weariness and satanic antagonism will not include rest from activities for those who follow the martyred into heaven. The place of rest is not to be a place of idleness. It will offer the highest form of spiritual service. All believers who are cut short in their Christian service here on earth will be amply utilized by the Lord in heaven.

Sixth Word: Another Angel—Harvest Is Ripe (Revelation 14:14–16)

The harvest of the earth is ripe. (Revelation 14:15)

Armageddon is now about to begin, and we are given a comprehensive summary that succeeding chapters will amplify. Introducing this paragraph, Walter Scott says:

Judicial judgment is about to sweep the guilty earth with the broom of destruction and clear it of evil. The harvest and the vintage are the familiar figures employed to express God's closing dealings. The former is discriminating judgment, the latter unsparing from the tares. In the vintage the tares are alone in the prophetic scene, and form the subjects of the Lord's righteous vengeance.

The Reaper of the Harvest

The heavenly Reaper whom John sees is without doubt the Lord Jesus Christ, referred to as "a son of man." It is under this title that Christ deals with the state of things on the earth and judges the ungodly (Matthew 25:31–33; John 5:22–27). Because of His connection with the human race, Christ exercises all those characteristics entitling Him to universal dominion.

Introducing the vision of the Reaper, John uses "then another angel" (14:15), since he is about to deal with subjects of unusual interest. The first object attracting the apostle was a white cloud, which is a familiar object in Mediterranean lands. This cloud was akin to the bright cloud of the transfiguration of Christ (Matthew 17:5). Clouds symbolize the divine presence (Ezekiel 10:4; Revelation 10:1). White is a prominent color in Revelation and indicates the purity and absolute righteousness of the Reaper in all His actions.

Seated upon a white cloud is the Creator of all clouds. Making this cloud His chariot, He rides to His grim task. Sitting on the cloud suggests calm, deliberative judgment. With no undue haste the Reaper reaps His harvest.

The golden crown upon His head is a garland of victory, not His diadem as King. Christ's full victory is described in detail in 19:11–21, where many crowns encircle His brow, indicating His royal dignity and rights. Here Christ's crown of gold expresses divine righteousness in victorious action and is no imitation crown. Divinely conferred, its Wearer exercises royal authority.

The sharp sickle in the hand of the heavenly Reaper is symbolic of His rights over the harvest. The Mosaic law commanded that no one could "put a sickle to his [neighbor's] standing grain" (Deuteronomy 23:25). Christ with a sickle implies that He will reap the field over which He has authority. The "sharp" sickle indicates that the reaping will be quick and thorough. It is significant that the national emblem of the Soviet Union was the hammer and sickle, both of which were used with dreadful effect to gather a harvest for the godless creed of Communism. But God will yet use His hammer— His Word (Jeremiah 23:29)—to smash the hordes of the northern confederacy (Ezekiel 38:15). Then His sickle will reap a harvest of judgment.

"Another angel came out of the temple in heaven" (14:17). Distinct from those already mentioned, this angel comes out of the temple and calls for immediate action on the part of the Reaper. He does not command the Son of Man but is only a messenger announcing to the Son the will of God the Father, in whose hands are kept the times and seasons. All along Christ had expected such a message (Hebrews 10:12–13; Psalm 2:7–9); now He hears it. God is roused to action, and the angel comes out of the temple; the Sower of the judgment is about to overtake the earth. The temple and the throne, used often in Revelation, represent the presence and authority of God.

The Harvest Is Ripe

The Son of Man acts promptly, since the harvest is "ripe" (14:15). The word could also mean "overripe" or "dried up." The Greek word used here is the one used of the fig tree in Mark 11:20. In Luke 23:31 the adjective form is used: "What will happen when it is dry?

"The time to reap has come" (14:15) is an ominous declaration taking us back to the Old Testament prophets, who describe a harvest time for overripe workers of iniquity at the end of Gentile dominion. Joel 3:13 says, "Swing the sickle, for the harvest is ripe. Come, trample the grapes, for the winepress is full and the vats overflow—so great is their wickedness!" This can only mean that the "ripe" are not the saved saints ripe for glory, but the wicked who are overripe for judgment.

One brief sentence is sufficient to describe the terrible end of all that the proud had boasted of: "the earth was harvested" (v. 16). And what a harvesting! It is the awesome Second Coming of the King of Kings in His great day of wrath.

The Son of Man uses the angels as His actual reapers (Matthew 13:39), and they act swiftly in His harvest work. A separating process is used: discrimination between wheat and tares, good fish and bad. No actual execution of punishment appears in this harvest, for that is accomplished in the vintage. This harvest is one of discriminating judgment prior to the establishment of the kingdom. Though described as a single act of reaping, these events cover a considerable time and employ various agencies of God.

Seventh Word: Another Angel—God's Wrath (Revelation 14:17–20)

Blood flowed out of the press, rising as high as the horses' bridles for a distance of 1,600 stadia. (Revelation 14:20)

Two angels are in the vision of the vine of the earth and its judgment. In 14:17 there is the temple angel with his sharp sickle. Corresponding to the description given of the Son of Man in 14:14, this second angel signifies the association of angels with Christ in His judicial work.

The angel "came from the altar" (14:18). What kind of an altar is not stated. If it represents the brazen altar (the altar of judgment), then the thought is one of pure, unmingled judgment—divine judgment upon the vine of the earth (Deuteronomy 32:31–35). But if the altar stands for the altar of incense, it indicates the incense-accompanied prayers of all saints, which bring down God's fiery judgment upon their foes (8:3–5; 9:13). The cry of the souls of martyrs under the altar (6:9) is now to be fully answered. The false prophet did great wonders and brought fire down from heaven, but now the altar angel, having power over fire, moves against all the godless of earth. The tares are now to be cast into the furnace of fire (Matthew 13:40–42).

The subject of the judgment is the earth and its grapes (v. 18). These grapes are not what the Creator expected, considering how carefully He cultured them. The expression "the clusters of grapes from the earth's vine" in some renderings covers the whole religious system in the coming visitation of God's wrath. The grapes of widespread apostasy are "wild grapes" and must be turned into "grapes of wrath." Into the great winepress of the wrath of God must go both apostate Jews and apostate Gentiles. This is the day of God's vengeance, and mercy will not be shown (Isaiah 63:1–3; Jeremiah 25:15–16; Joel 3:12–13). Christ, the true Vine, deals with the grapes of iniquity produced after centuries of cultivation. Such grapes are fully ripe for burning. The phrase "fully ripe" (KJV) as used in 14:18 means "come to their acme."

"Outside the city" indicates where God's fullest vengeance will be poured out. Jerusalem is the city, and the valley of Jehoshaphat (where the battle of Armageddon is to be fought) is just outside the city. "Multitudes, multitudes in the valley of decision! For the day of the LORD is near" (Joel 3:14). "Outside the city" can also imply that the setting in which was shed the blood of Christ and of His people will also be the scene of divine judgment upon all Christ's rejecters.

The description John gives us of rivers of human blood reaching up to the bits of the horses for a distance of two hundred miles is gruesome. "Blood flowed out of the press" (14:20) is symbolic language testifying to the terrible slaughter of the godless when the Lord tramples on them in His fury. Manifesting His power, God will trample vast masses into a bloody pulp. The beast and the false prophet, along with all their deluded followers and worshipers, will be exterminated forever.

As we watch the movements of opposing armies in our own day, it seems as if the East will soon become a very important theater of war. On every side of Israel tremendous forces are poised. Is such a gathering of powers a forerunner of what will happen when the Deliverer of Israel will crush the embattled nations of the earth? Without doubt the earth is becoming ripe for God's vintage in its strongest form, and as we see this day approaching, it is imperative for us to warn the ungodly to flee from the wrath to come. Today is still the day of grace, and as it lingers we must beseech the wicked around us to be reconciled to God.

8

Seven Golden Bowls

Revelation 15–16

I saw in heaven another great and marvelous sign: seven angels with the seven last plagues. (Revelation 15:1)

The Seven Plagues (Revelation 15:1–8)

We now approach two chapters of exceptional awe. Having considered the instigators of earth's horrible iniquity, we come to the terrible judgment of the bowls. Severe and final chastisements are about to be inflicted in sharp and rapid succession. As the sin of man reached its climax in the man of sin, so now the judgments of God are to fall from the God of judgments. Within the chapters before us we have the details regarding God's judgments preceding His great day of wrath. As we shall see, the pouring out of the seventh bowl completes the wrath of God. Then follows the wrath of the Lamb.

Of this double wrath, William Newell says: "Remember constantly that Christ must come Himself, at the last, and tread the winepress alone in His anger (Isaiah 63:3–5). The wrath of God is general, worldwide, and in view of man's iniquity and idolatry. The wrath of the Lamb is particular, against antichrist and his king, and [against the] armies gathered for the double purpose of cutting off Israel from being a nation (Psalm 83:4) and of making war against the Lamb . . . (Revelation 19:19; Zechariah 12:10) to prevent His rescue of beleaguered Israel." In chapter 15 we have the preparation for the bowls; in chapter 16 the pouring of the bowls.

The sign or wonder of chapter 15 extends to the end of chapter 16. In fact, 15:1 is a summary of all that follows. The angels do not receive the bowls until 15:7, but the opening verse anticipates their having them. The "sign" completes a trio of signs: the "great and wondrous sign" of the woman (Israel) in 12:1; "Another sign" of the dragon, the antagonist of Christ and His counsels, in 12:3; and here, "another great and marvelous sign." All three signs are seen in heaven, God's immediate dwelling place. This third sign (more solemn than the first two because of its association with God's wrath upon the beast) is "great" in that something of outstanding importance is to be revealed. "Marvelous" indicates that divine patience is exhausted and that terrible visitations of divine judgment are about to overtake earth's apostates.

Chapter 15 revolves around three weighty phrases: the wrath of God (15:1, 7), the harps of God (15:2), and the glory of God (15:8).

The Wrath of God (15:1)

With them God's wrath is completed. (Revelation 15:1)

Seven angels and seven plagues form the expression of God's wrath. Occurring six times in Revelation (14:10, 19; 15:1, 7; 16:1, 19), the expression "God's wrath" (or "God's fury") is indeed fearful and should strike terror in the hearts of all unsaved people now on earth.

The "seven angels" (distinct from the seven highly honored angels connected with trumpets) come out of the temple (15:6), the immediate residence of God and the angels. Out of the temple of old, priests came as ministers of grace. Now angels emerge as ministers of judgment.

The temple or tabernacle of "the Testimony" (15:5) is a suggestive phrase. With Israel this was a pledge of God's presence with His people and His provision for them. Now the holiness of God demands punishment of the wicked, so we have the "Testimony" of God's judgment against the beast and all the enemies of His people. David Brown says, "The tabernacle of the testimony appropriately here comes to view, where God's faithfulness is avenging His people with judgments on their foes about to be set forth. We need to get a glimpse within the Holy Place to understand the secret spring and the end of God's righteous dealing."

These seven angels are clothed in a way that befits the righteous character of their mission and resembles the Lord (see 1:13). By consulting with 19:8, we find that the pure linen indicates righteousness, while the golden sashes around their chests suggest the work of judgment compatible with God's holy nature.

The expression "seven last plagues" (15:1) or "seven plagues, which are the last" suggests finality and completion, thus the appearance of "seven" is especially appropriate. We have come to the final cycle of judgmental visitation. Of course, the bowls do not bring the end of divine wrath, since further strokes of vengeance are to fall when Christ comes in person (19:11–21). At this point we have the conclusion of God's providential judgments. These bowls are filled up, or completed, meaning finished or consummated. To God the future is as certain as the past, so sure of accomplishment is His Word.

The Harps of God (15:2–7)

They held harps given them by God and sang the song of Moses. (Revelation 15:2)

This preface to the last of the devastating judgments of God includes a beautiful description of the victorious martyrs who are with the Lord. The text of 15:2–4 is taken up with victory, praise, and worship. Heavenly choral praises are represented by the harp, whose combination of solemn, grand notes and soft, tender strains indicates the praise and worship of God (Psalm 33:2). The harps of God—God's instruments, musicians, and theme—were part of the heavenly instruments, used solely for the praise of God. The two groups of harp singers (14:2 and 15:2) appear to represent the same victorious host.

The setting for the harpers is likened to a sea of glass mingled with fire. In the sea of glass Walter Scott sees a fixed state of holiness, of inward and outward purity. The sea suggests vastness, and glass suggests a solid calm or settled, unruffled peace. A sea of glass expresses smoothness and brightness. This heavenly sea is crystal (4:6), showing that the calm of heaven, unlike earthly seas that are ruffled by winds, is crystallized into an eternity of peace. Pictured as standing beside the sea of glass, the martyrs have come to their rest as well as to this new position as conquerors-worshipers.

The sea of glass mixed with fire introduces another element. These saints have emerged victorious from their fiery trial. We have three foes to face—the world, the flesh, and the devil—but the singers had a fourth foe to defy—the beast. Victory was gained over the beast, over his image, and over "the number of his name." Their victory is thorough and complete.

The song accompanying the harps has the ring of great poetry. It is a song of victory like that of Moses after crossing the Red Sea. Two songs are combined: the song of Moses, bondman of God, and the song of the Lamb. The song of Moses is the triumph over evil by God's judgments. It is a song celebrating the overthrow of Pharaoh and his hosts at the Red Sea (Exodus 15:1–18). (This Mosaic song must not be confused with the prophetic one in Deuteronomy 32:1–43.) The song of Moses, magnificent as it is, only celebrated an earthly redemption. The grace and glory in the song that was sung on the eastern bank of the Red Sea were associated with power over Israel's foes in Egypt, by God's judgments.

The song of the Lamb is different. This song, led by the Lamb as the Captain of our salvation, implies the exaltation of the rejected Messiah, of the suffering One. Sung by the faithful slain remnant amidst unfaithful and apostate Israel, it celebrates what God and the Lamb have done for the victorious sufferers in heaven.

This double song magnifies God in several ways. First, His works are praised. The phrase "great and marvelous" (15:3; also 15:1) implies the vindication of the justice of God, so that He may be glorified at the grand end of His dealings. In the combined divine title "Lord God Almighty" we have a vast reservoir of strength—consoling to the saint but foreboding to the enemies of God.

Second, the ways of God are extolled as being "just and true" or "righteous and true." In the chastisement of His enemies God will act in harmony with His own character. This equitable judgment will be meted out by the "King of nations" (NRSV; not the "King of saints," as in the KJV). The point at issue in the Lord's controversy with the earth is whether He or Satan's man, the beast, is the king of the nations. On this eve of the bowls descending on the kingdom of the beast, the victorious singers hail the Lord as the true King of the nations.

The worship of God also contributes to this remarkable song. The two "fors" supply the reasons why the Lord should be glorified: "*For* you alone are holy!" The singers at the glassy sea celebrate the holiness of God. They fear Him and glorify Him as the only One entitled to be called holy. The beast set himself up as God, but the victorious choir chose holiness in the face of a world gone over to sin but where all true holiness now reigns.

"All nations will come and worship before you" (15:4). God's judgments will strike fear into His foes. Anticipating the universal dominion of the Lord, the saints celebrate the worldwide recognition of His supremacy. Here we see the fulfillment of such prophecies as Isaiah 2:2–4; 56:6–7; Zechariah 14:16–17.

"*For* your righteous acts have been revealed." Because He is righteous even while He dispenses judgment and vengeance, God should be glorified. These are indeed most beautiful words that come from those who passed through the horrors of the torment of the beast.

Commenting on this unique scene, F. B. Meyer says:

Those who were brought up under the dispensation of Moses, and the followers of the Lamb in the present dispensation, together with all holy souls who have overcome, shall constitute one vast choir. But search the Song of Moses as you will, you will fail to find one note that equals this in sublimity. Here are the saints of God, trained in distinguishing the niceties of righteous and holy government and behavior, enabled from their vantage ground in eternity to survey the entire history of the divine dealings, adoring Him as King of the ages and acknowledging that all His ways had been righteous and true. What confession! What an acknowledgment!

The Glory of God (15:8)

The temple was filled with smoke from the glory of God and from his power. (Revelation 15:8)

This paragraph opens with the dwelling of God and closes with the glory of God. Because everything in the paragraph is connected with the glory of God, let us examine these verses with this thought in mind.

The word "temple" is used because of what it represents symbolically, namely, the dwelling place of God, where He is approached and worshiped. Out of the temple come the seven angels having the seven plagues, which represent God's final visitation of judgment upon the nations.

The presentation of the bowls to the angels by one of the living creatures indicates that these living creatures are the executors of the judicial government of God. These dignified beings are deep in the understanding of God's purposes and therefore are present to the angels' previews of dreadful events. God's work of judgment has three steps:

1. The angels are commissioned and equipped in the sanctuary (15:6).
2. The angels receive the golden bowls full of God's fury from one of the living creatures (15:7).
3. The angels cannot take a step in the act of judgment until God gives the command (16:1).

All this suggests that the works and ways of God even in judgment are calm and measured—what we would expect of the One "who lives forever and ever." It is the *eternal* God who is about to plague the guilty earth with His fury. We must never forget that He is glorified in judgment as well as in grace.

Before we leave this preparatory chapter we are introduced to God's smokescreen to cover everything within the sanctuary for the time being. Smoke, of course, is symbolic of God's presence (Exodus 19:18; Isaiah 6:4). No one could enter the temple because of God's presence in His manifested glory and power during the execution of the bowl judgments. Smoke from the glory and power of God filled the temple. Moses could not enter the tent of testimony (and the priests could not enter the temple) because of the glory of the Lord (Exodus 40:34–35; 1 Kings 8:10–11). Here we have not glory itself but smoke from the glory of God. This smoke is the glory of God manifested in judgment. The finality of this whole scene fills our hearts with utmost awe! God is about to deal with all earth rebels.

The opening verse of chapter 16 is rich with significance. First there is the "loud voice from the temple," which has been variously interpreted. Possibly God's voice is meant, since we are now brought to the bowls of God's wrath. Christ is not mentioned until after God has personally executed judgment. As we have already hinted, Revelation is a book of the voice, which always implies an intelligent understanding of the subject in question. We read of a strong voice, a loud voice, and a great voice. Such adjectives describe the character of the voice and also the nature of the announcement.

Here the great voice comes out of the temple, out of the holy of holies. Because God's holiness demands judgment upon an apostate world, God's wrath burns fiercely: "Go, pour out the seven bowls of God's wrath on the earth." A different command came from Christ as He was about to leave His own: "Make disciples of all nations, baptizing them . . . and teaching them" (Matthew 28:19–20). But now grace is withdrawn. It is no longer the cup of salvation but the cup of the wrath of God.

Pentecost witnessed the pouring out of the Spirit, and with such an effusion there was the manifestation of blessing. But now we have come to another pouring out: unmixed fury is about to descend upon the earth. The fullness of divine wrath is emptied into every bowl, which in turn is poured out without reserve upon a guilty world. The prayer of the suffering Jewish remnant is answered in the seven terrible plagues about to fall: "Pay back into the laps of our neighbors seven times the reproach they have hurled at you, O Lord" (Psalm 79:12).

The golden bowls give a further glimpse into the fury of God. The word for "bowls" indicates the broad-rimmed vessels used in the sanctuary, where they were filled with fragrant incense. Hallowed by temple use and service, the vessels are now filled with God's righteous wrath and devoted to judgment. And their broad upper part would tend to cause their contents to pour out all at once, implying the overwhelming suddenness of the woes.

The First Bowl: Wrath upon the Earth (Revelation 16:1–2)

Go, pour out the seven bowls of God's wrath on the earth. (Revelation 16:1)

There is something expressive about the execution of these seven plagues. The bowls as a whole imply swift action. With a lightning overthrow they destroy the kingdom of the beast, who had invested himself with the world kingdom. Sudden destruction will overtake the beast and his worshipers, and they shall not escape.

The earlier trumpet judgments were limited more or less to the Roman world, but the bowl judgments are to cover the earth and form God's total war upon the world. The bowls are God's answer to Satan and will blast his empire. In the trumpets, Satan's power was released to further his objectives. In the bowls, God unleashes all His power to finish His grim work. Direct control over all the forces of nature is committed to the angels, who in turn execute the judgment that is written.

In the first bowl of wrath we see a plague akin to the sixth Egyptian plague (Exodus 9:8–12), which was the first of the plagues to afflict the bodies of the Egyptians. David Brown remarks:

> The reason why the sixth Egyptian plague is the *first* here is because it was directed against the Egyptian magicians, Jannes and Jambres, so that they could not stand before Moses; and so here the plague is sent upon those who in the beast-worship had practiced sorcery. As they submitted to the mark of the beast, so they must bear the mark of the avenging God.

In this connection we wonder whether "ugly and painful sores" will not afflict the very part of the body bearing the mark of the beast, namely, the forehead and the palm of the hand. "Physical suffering, no doubt, will also add to the anguish endured by men, but the chief and predominating features will be judicial, dealing with the soul and conscience—a suffering far exceeding any bodily affliction." But surely we cannot get away from literal sores—bad, malignant, and suppurated wounds!

The word used for "sore" means an ugly ulcer with a highly offensive discharge. In Exodus 9:8 Moses took soot from a furnace and, in the sight of Pharaoh, tossed it into the air. When it came down upon men and animals it formed terrible boils. Both plagues must be taken literally, as is proven by the fact that pains and sores are still on the people at the time of the fifth bowl (16:11). Hopelessness, as well as hideousness, is implied by these unhealed sores. These wounds are incurable (Deuteronomy 28:27, 35) and must be endured as a foretaste of the anguish of hell.

The Second Bowl: Wrath upon the Sea (Revelation 16:3)

The second angel poured out his bowl on the sea. (Revelation 16:3)

A striking feature of the seven bowls is not only their resemblance to the plagues of Egypt but also to the trumpets. With the bowls, however, there is not the limited judgment of the trumpets. In this second bowl of wrath we are given a picture of a murdered man weltering in his own blood. The sea and all that is within it become blood "like that of a dead man." Under the third trumpet only a third part of the sea became blood (8:8), but here the destruction is complete. Once the judgments are over, only a few people will be left to enter the Millennium.

Because the sea covers the greater portion of the earth, this plague will be widespread in its death-dealing power. Blood, the vivid and terrible mark of death, was shed most plentifully by the beast. But the blood of the martyrs is now avenged. The beast is beginning to reap what he has sown.

It is blood for blood! Words fail to describe the terrible condition as millions of dead sea creatures cover the surface of the oceans. The stench from these horrible, rotting carcasses will be overwhelming. With everything dead in the sea, what pollution and disease such a blood-soaked sea will hold!

The Third Bowl: Wrath upon the Rivers (Revelation 16:4–7)

The third angel poured out his bowl on the rivers and springs of water. (Revelation 16:4)

The third angel, presiding over the waters, empties his bowl upon the sources of the sea. All sources of progress and national well-being come under judgment because commerce and life as a whole are so dependent upon rivers, canals, and streams. We reject the wholly symbolic interpretation of "rivers" as the ordinary life of a nation characterized by known and accepted principles of government, and "springs of water" as the sources of prosperity and well-being. We hold that the guardian angel controlling the actual waters instantly pollutes them.

Two angels combine in this declaration of God's righteous, reciprocal, and retributive judgments. First, the angel in charge of the waters (16:5) uses the peculiar idiom for God's eternity—"You who are and who were." As the Righteous One, God does not overstep in the least degree the just measure of strict righteousness. Apostates had shed the blood of saints and prophets; now retributive justice operates as the murderers of God's people are made to drink blood. A terrible doom is earned. They are worthy of a fearful death, which comes now as a preview of the second death in the lake of fire.

The altar that responds (16:7) is the one on which the prayers of the saints are presented before God, and beneath which are the souls of the martyrs crying for vengeance upon their foes and the foes of God. Thus the angel and the altar, representing the whole of heaven, concede that God's judgments are just and true. Everyone within the heavenly *temple* is on God's side as He acts as the great avenger of His own. The cries of altars from the time of Abel onward are now forever vindicated.

The Fourth Bowl: Wrath upon the Sun (Revelation 16:8–9)

The fourth angel poured out his bowl on the sun, and the sun was given power to scorch people. (Revelation 16:8)

Under the fourth trumpet the sun was darkened by a third (8:12), but here the sun's scorching power is intensified. This is to be the release of God's H-bomb. We do not interpret the sun symbolically in this passage (as the supreme governing authority represented by the revived Roman world), but as the actual sun, from whose heat nothing is hidden (Psalm 19:6). Having complete control over His created works, God intensifies the heat of the sun and thereby causes a terrible death toll. Describing the great and terrible day of the Lord, the prophet Joel declared: "The sun and the moon are darkened, and the stars no longer shine" (Joel 2:10).

Under the first trumpet the trees and green grass were burned up, but now God applies His scorched-earth policy to the bodies of humans. Can we imagine the terrible anguish that multitudes will experience as they are scorched with this great heat? The Greek emphasizes, "*They were seared by the intense heat*," meaning those who in 16:2 are described as having the mark of the beast. As with the plagues of Egypt, so here in these judgment plagues, God's people are immune. As the three Hebrew youths were preserved in the fiery furnace, so the remnant will be guarded by God (Revelation 7:16; Daniel 3:27).

Just as Pharaoh's heart was hardened in spite of the display of God's absolute power over His creation, so here the extreme physical suffering fails to produce any change of heart: "They refused to repent and glorify him." Instead of being crushed by the judgment of God and crying out for mercy, these people only blasphemed the name of God. Deserved punishment coarsens the lips and hardens the heart; the fires of judgment fail to purify. Because it is the kindness of God that leads to repentance (Romans 2:4), those who are not won by grace will never be won at all.

We can only speculate on what might have happened if there had been godly repentance on the part of these people with their burning flesh. Would God, with authority over the plagues, have halted the storm of His wrath and once again blessed the repentance with His favor? The tragedy is the absolute lack of humility and sorrow over sin. Such a double judgment as scorching heat and absence of clear water to drink will fail to produce any change of heart. Because these people are thoroughly reprobate, God gives them up.

The Fifth Bowl: Wrath upon the Beast's Throne (Revelation 16:10–11)

> The fifth angel poured out his bowl on the throne of the beast. (Revelation 16:10)

In this fifth bowl of wrath, judgment is poured out upon the throne that was set up in arrogant mimicry of God's throne. The dragon gave his throne to the beast (13:2). Satan's masterpiece is now smitten in the center and seat of his power. The beast, as a real person, stands condemned as the tool of Satan. And it is clear that the subjects of this mock kingdom, as well as its executive, feel the stroke of divine vengeance. It has been suggested that the beast's throne will be rebuilt in Babylon on the Euphrates River— Satan's ancient capital city in the land of Shinar, where wickedness is to be set "in its place" in the end of time (Zechariah 5:5–11).

At last the impious and insolent challenge, "Who is like the beast? Who can make war against him?" (13:4), is answered forever. Under the beast, Satan builds up a vast empire, but God will not be outdone: He smites the kingdom of the beast with darkness. Because they loved darkness rather than light, physical darkness as black as that of the Egyptian plague (Exodus 10:21–23) now falls upon the followers of the beast. This horrible darkness suggests the darkness they are to endure forever.

Such unrelieved darkness causes people to gnaw their tongues in anguish. This judgment seems to run concurrently with the effects of previous plagues. Pains and sores out of the first bowl are rendered more appalling by the darkness. The expression "gnawed their tongues" is the only one of its kind in the Bible and indicates the most intense and excruciating agony. Such an action suggests rage over the baffling of their hopes and the overthrow of their ruler and kingdom. They meditate on revenge but are unable to effect it; hence their fury. Suffering from mental and physical anguish, they bite their lips and tongues.

Note that the part of the body these rebels sinned with is the very part now afflicted with anguish. They blasphemed the God of heaven, the One controlling light and darkness. Terrible oaths went forth from their lips against the name of God and against God Himself. Now these blasphemers gnaw their tongues!

Even the accumulation of plagues, rather than a mere succession, fails to produce a change of heart, for again we read that "they refused to repent of what they had done" (16:11). Their will is unbroken. No tears of penitence flow. Abandoned to their evil deeds, even heavier strokes must descend from God to break their stubborn wills.

This bowl of darkness must not be confused with the darkening of the heavenly bodies just before Christ's appearing (19:11–16). Rather, we see in this fifth bowl one of the signs our Lord gave in His description of the Tribulation period (Luke 21:8–36). For the remnant on earth there will be plenty of light, just as the Israelites had light in their dwellings during the Egyptian plagues.

The Sixth Bowl: Wrath upon the River Euphrates
(Revelation 16:12–16)

The sixth angel poured out his bowl on the great river Euphrates. (Revelation 16:12)

Scholars differ over the interpretation of this passage. One commentator suggests that the drying up of the Euphrates is figurative of Babylon itself, which is situated on it. But nothing will suit the context except the literal Euphrates River, whose broad expanse is difficult for individuals or armies to cross. The drying up of this ancient river will allow the Asiatic armies (as described in chapter 19) to march without hindrance to the promised land, of which the Euphrates is the eastern boundary.

The important point to remember is that both the Nile River and the Euphrates River are to be literally dried up (Isaiah 11:15), and Israel will be open to attack from all quarters. With the drying up of the Euphrates, the eastern armies under their respective kings will achieve their objective.

Note the frequent use of "great" in this chapter. Through the miraculous ministry of the beast, the multitudes will become accustomed to great things. Sensationalism will be the order of the day. Great events, with their deceptive influences, will be daily occurrences.

In 16:13–16, which some writers treat as a parenthesis, we have the satanic trinity directing the most gigantic combination of opposing forces ever witnessed on earth. Personally supervised by Satan, mighty world powers gather for their doom.

With the sixth bowl of wrath we again have the trinity of evil—dragon, beast, and false prophet—marshaling all the kings of the earth for their battle, not only against Israel but also against God Himself. "The kings of the earth take their stand and the rulers gather together against the LORD and against his Anointed One. 'Let us break their chains,' they say, 'and throw off their fetters'" (Psalm 2:2–3).

The Three Frogs (16:13–14)

I saw three evil spirits that looked like frogs. (Revelation 16:13)

Although three frogs were the original coat of arms of France, we do not believe in the exclusively historical interpretation of this (or any other part) of chapters 4–22. Because prophecy is frequently progressive or cumulative, a modified view of the principle of interpretation combines the historical and futurist systems. Thus some sections of Revelation can be partially fulfilled without exhausting their significance. They point to complete fulfillment in the future.

These "spirits that looked like frogs" are the antitype to the plague of frogs sent on Egypt. A conspicuous feature of the ministry of the beast will be the great signs and wonders performed by satanic means. The dragon, the beast, and the false prophet are appropriately likened to loathsome frogs. As frogs croak by night in marshes and quagmires, so these unclean spirits in the darkness of error teach lies in the mire of filthy lusts. Frogs were regarded by Greek writers and poets as the proper inhabitants of the Stygian lake, or river of hell. These spirits issue out of the mouths of the unholy three who form hell's trinity (the mouth being the chief seat of influence). From various Scriptures we gather that the mouth is the source and means of destructions (Revelation 1:16; 2:16; 9:17; 19:15; Isaiah 11:4). The dragon is to be consumed with the breath of the Lord's mouth (2 Thessalonians 2:8).

The unclean spirit out of the dragon's mouth symbolizes the proud infidelity opposing the Lord and His Anointed (Christ). The unclean spirit out of the beast's mouth represents the spirit of the world in the politics, whether lawless democracy or despotism, which set humans above God. The unclean spirit out of the false prophet's mouth pictures lying spiritualism and religious delusion rampant in the days of satanic deception.

In this satanic trinity, with its miracle-working ministry, we have a combination of direct hellish power, brute apostate force, and terrible malignant influence for the dread purpose of gathering the millions of earth for war. The final effort of hell to overthrow heaven is at hand, and it results in Christ's taking over the kingship of the world (19:17–21). At His return, He will deal effectively with these three unclean spirits, just as He did with those who antagonized Him while here on earth.

Because the gathering of world kings with the beast is a signal for Christ's coming to destroy His foes, the saints are exhorted to watch for His return. A word of cheer and of warning is sent to the faithful remnant: "Behold, I come like a thief! Blessed is he who stays awake and keeps his clothes with him, so that he may not go naked and be shamefully exposed" (16:15). Here we have a parenthesis of great spiritual importance. It is not a message for the church, even though the underlying principle of blessedness being associated with watching (and shame with careless living) is applicable to saints of all times. Rather, the "behold" and the "blessed" are related to Tribulation saints. Around them will be multitudes asleep in moral and spiritual darkness. Living in a state of false security, they congratulate themselves on their "peace and safety." But suddenly and unexpectedly—as a thief in the night—the Lord will surprise and destroy the peoples gathered by satanic agency against the Lord and His Anointed.

Those who believe that the church is to go through the great Tribulation make much of this verse, but Christ is not coming for His church as a thief. He returns for the church as the Bridegroom, since the church is His bride. With the coming of a thief there is dread and fear that our possessions will be robbed and our goods destroyed (1 Thessalonians 5:2, 4; Matthew 24:43; 2 Peter 3:10). We are not of the night nor of darkness, therefore we have no fear of our Lord's return. Of course, we must endeavor to have garments without stain, and a life without shame and moral nakedness. But the danger for the saints living at the time when the unclean spirits are operating is that of neglect. By neglecting the advent hope, they expose themselves to angels and a godless world as "naked" or publicly lacking divine direction and protection.

Bishop Lightfoot suggests that this exhortation to watchfulness may allude to a Jewish custom in the service of the temple. Twenty-four wards or companies were appointed night by night to guard the various entrances to the sacred courts. One individual was appointed as captain or marshal over the others, and he was called the "man of the mountain of the house of God." His duty was to go around the various gates during the night to see that his subordinates were faithful to their charge. Each wakeful sentinel was expected to hail his appearance with the password, "Thou man of the mountain of the house, peace be unto thee!" If, through unwatchfulness and slumber, this was neglected, the offender was beaten with the staff of office, his garments were burned, and he was branded with shame.

The Battle of Armageddon (16:16)

Then they gathered the kings together to the place called Armageddon. (Revelation 16:16)

How we tremble as we try to visualize what will happen to the nations, combined in their undying hatred toward God and His Christ, as they are gathered by the unclean spirits to the battle of that day of God

Almighty! What universal slaughter! There are times when nations are seized with a passion for war that even historians cannot fully explain. It will be this way with the war against God.

How blindly will the hordes of earth be led against the One who created them! (See Psalm 2; Revelation 17:14; 19:19.) The phrase "they [the unclean spirits of verses 13 and 14] gathered them together" can also be translated, "he gathered them together." If the "he" of some translations is retained, it can stand for *God*, who gives them over to the unclean spirits. No one can read Revelation as a whole without realizing that God is behind the scenes and the actors in the judicial judgment of the book. In righteous retribution He permits the apostate chiefs of the earth to gather the multitudes together.

Because Armageddon will witness the bloodiest battle of all history, we should briefly consider the historical and prophetic significance of earth's most terrible battlefield. Armageddon is situated near the foot of Mount Carmel, the scene of much past slaughter. Armageddon means "mountain of destruction" or "slaughter" and is well named. Actually the name is *Har*, meaning "mountain," and *Mageddon* or *Megiddo*, from a root meaning "to cut off" or "to slaughter." The limited area of Megiddo would forbid the presence of vast numbers of men, but the name can also stand for the larger vicinity of Israel, where the nations of the earth will be crushed by satanic agency.

Megiddo was the scene of the overthrow of the Canaanite kings by God's miraculous interposition under Deborah and Barak (Judges 5:19–20). As an ally of Babylon, Josiah was defeated and slain at Megiddo (2 Chronicles 35:22–25). The mourning of the Jews at the time just before God shall intervene for them against all the nations is compared to the mourning of Josiah at Megiddo (Zechariah 12:11).

Why is Armageddon chosen as the gathering place? Because the nations assemble there to crush and exterminate Israel! "With cunning they conspire against your people; they plot against those you cherish. 'Come,' they say, 'let us destroy them as a nation, that the name of Israel be remembered no more.' With one mind they plot together; they form an alliance against you" (Psalm 83:3–5). God, however, overrules and intervenes. Though the nations fling themselves with combined might against the Lord and His people, divine fury is unleashed and destruction overtakes the arrogant hordes. Israel is delivered and her cruel foes are slain. In the complete overthrow of the nations, the sovereignty of the earth, as well as Israel's right to her own land, is decided.

The Seventh Bowl: Wrath upon the Air (Revelation 16:17–21)

The seventh angel poured out his bowl into the air. (Revelation 16:17)

All the previous bowls are preparatory to the final outpouring of God's wrath (19:11–16). Then, and not until then, will the rebels be crushed and removed from the earth (Matthew 13:40–43). In the sixth bowl we have the gathering of the nations of the earth to Israel for actual warfare against God and the remnant of His people (Isaiah 11:15–16). Now comes a destruction exceeding in magnitude anything ever witnessed since the expulsion from the Garden of Eden.

The seventh angel poured his bowl *into the air.* Because air is essential to life, we have here divine judgment visiting the life breath of the people. And because Satan is "the ruler of the kingdom of the air" (Ephesians 2:2), we also have in this bowl the consummation of judgment upon all the pernicious influences of the devil. Thus Satan's realm suffers under this awful plague. The "loud voice" is the voice of God, as in 16:1, except that here the temple and the throne unite. In the temple He *resides,* while on the throne He *reigns.* The divine voice cries, "It is done!" meaning that the whole series of plagues is now complete. It is done! It is come to pass. Compare God's voice in this final consummation with Christ's voice on the cross when the work of expiation was completed: "It is finished!" The Savior's "it is finished" was rejected, paving the way for the Judge's "it is done."

The end of God's wrath has come. Later will come the fearful exhibition of the Lamb's wrath. Under this seventh bowl, God gives Babylon "the cup filled with the wine of the fury of his wrath." The phrase "fury of his wrath" suggests a fierce storm and driving wind, both of which are referred to in Jeremiah 30:23–24. Here the fact of Babylon's overthrow is stated. In Chapters 17 and 18 we have a detached expansion of the brief summary given under this bowl.

Tokens of Wrath (16:17)

A loud voice from the throne, saying, "It is done! (Revelation 16:17)

The almighty power in judgment, expressed through "flashes of lightning, rumblings, peals of thunder, and a severe earthquake," is a formula of divine visitation calculated to strike terror in human hearts. These signs and tokens of retributive anger are visited upon the earth in the form of the greatest earthquake the earth has ever experienced. All earthquakes up until this point will fade into insignificance alongside this unparalleled upheaval (see Hebrews 12:25–26).

City Split into Three Parts (16:18–19)

The great city split into three parts. (Revelation 16:19)

So destructive is this vast earthquake that Jerusalem is divided into three parts. Rome and all the great cities of the earth are reduced to ruins. All the sovereignty over the kings of the earth that Rome and Babylon represented is forever destroyed. "Babylon the Great" is singled out as being ripe for a "severe earthquake" (16:18) and a "terrible plague" (16:21). The place and its pride are doomed to eternal destruction (Jeremiah 51:62–64), a doom celebrated in heaven (Revelation 19:1–4).

Adding to the terror of the hour is the banishment of islands and mountains. Under the sixth seal, each of them was "removed from its place" (6:14). Here they "fled away" and "could not be found." What a massive catastrophe!

The crowning act of judgment is the descent of enormous hailstones over the earth. Hail, as we have shown, is a symbol of divine wrath (Isaiah 28:2; Ezekiel 38:22). (For other hailstones, see Revelation 8:7; 11:19). No one can fully imagine what the sudden, disastrous effects of this last hailstorm will be like. The crushing, overwhelming nature of this judgment becomes clear when we remember that the hailstones are "a talent of weight" each. A talent is 103 to 180 pounds, thus the severity of judgment is frightful in the extreme (Job 38:22–23; Psalm 105:32).

But these judgments call forth blasphemy instead of repentance! Hardening of conscience is the effect of persisting in sin. The tragedy is that people do not become broken and repentant but remain unchanged. With the display of God's judgmental power, they should have turned and glorified Him. Instead they perish, cursing God.

9

Seven Final Judgments
Revelation 17–20

The fury of the wrath of God Almighty. (Revelation 19:16)

In the highly dramatic chapters we are now to consider, Christ as the Conqueror moves swiftly in the subjugation of all His foes. What fast-moving action we have in this section! How majestic is the scene of our omnipotent Lord taking to Himself His power and reigning supreme! Once He rises to deal with all antagonistic forces, none will be able to withstand His might. With a rod of iron He will break the strongest enemy. Proud, arrogant rulers, both hellish and human, are to be dashed in pieces as a potter's vessel. Whether it be systems, cities, or citizens, everything and everyone contrary to His will and rule are to fall before His withering look and judgments. Although He is the gentle Lamb, Christ now reveals His lionlike power.

What a memorable occasion that was when Jesus went into the synagogue at Nazareth, took the Old Testament scroll, and read from Isaiah the passage He related to His own ministry:

The Spirit of the Lord is on me,
    because he has anointed me
    to preach good news to the poor.
He has sent me to proclaim freedom for the prisoners
    and recovery of sight for the blind,
to release the oppressed,
    to proclaim the year of the Lord's favor. (Luke 4:18–19)

Then He rolled up the scroll without reading the next phrase, "the day of vengeance of our God." But in Revelation chapters 4–20 the day of vengeance and tribulation emerges.

Zephaniah, a prophet who testified beforehand (1 Peter 1:11) of future events, described "the great day of the Lord" this way:

> A day of trouble and distress, a day of wasteness and desolation, a day of darkness and gloominess, a day of clouds and thick darkness, a day of the trumpet and alarm, ... the day of Jehovah's wrath. (Zephaniah 1:14–18 ASV)

The First Judgment: Babylon (17:1–19:16)

> Come, I will show you the punishment of the great prostitute. (Revelation 17:1)

An introductory word is necessary on the close relationship between chapters 17 and 18, since each chapter deals with Babylon from a different viewpoint. Brief notices of Babylon's destruction are given in 14:8 and 16:19, but chapters 17 and 18 fill in the details of God's judgment upon a guilty religious system. Both chapters should be read together: chapter 17 for the destruction of *ecclesiastical* Babylon; chapter 18 for the destruction of *political* Babylon.

Judgment of Ecclesiastical Babylon (17:1–18)

> I saw a woman sitting on a scarlet beast. (Revelation 17:3)

Ecclesiastical Babylon is mystical, corrupt, apostate—the delight of kings and the mother of prostitutes. It is fitting that one of the seven angels responsible for pouring out the seven bowls of wrath should explain to John the judgment already pronounced upon Babylon (14:8; 16:19). Two significant phrases seem to divide this seventeenth chapter: "I will show you the punishment" (17:1) and "I will explain to you the mystery" (17:7).

A woman and a city are both used as symbols of the church (2 Corinthians 11:2; Revelation 21:2, 9–10), *and both figures are used in this description of apostate Christendom.* In 17:18 the woman is identified as the city: "The woman you saw is the great city that rules over the kings of the earth." The scarlet woman, one of the profound marvels of Scripture, is Satan's masterpiece of counterfeiting. What a travesty the mother of harlots is of the true church! The true church is a chaste virgin; the apostate church is a prostitute. The true church offers the cup of salvation; the apostate church holds the golden cup full of abominations. The true church is purchased by the blood of Christ; the apostate church is drunk with the blood of martyrs.

The woman "sits on many waters." Later, John is told: "The waters you saw where the prostitute sits are peoples, multitudes, nations and languages" (17:15). The "many waters" typify the vast multitudes of the human race over whom the woman has cast her spell. Ancient Babylon got its wealth by means of the Euphrates River and its numerous canals for irrigation. The apostate church fattens on the nations she governs.

Jeremiah's "You who live by many waters" (51:13) indicates that the great prostitute rules and dominate the nations religiously, just as the beast upon which she rides does politically. Representing a vast religious system, the woman's following is a universal one. The great prostitute and the beast are companions in wickedness and apostasy. Combined, they represent ecclesiastical and governmental power.

"I saw a woman sitting on a scarlet beast" (17:3) means that the prostitute not only exercises religious dominion over the multitudes, but she is able to manage and guide the beast. All vassal kings and human rulers, especially within the revived Roman Empire, are under her sway. Civil and political power are subservient to her rule and supremacy. Such thorough and complete subjugation over the vast imperial and apostate power headed up in the beast is already in the making.

Two contrasting ideas are represented by the woman and the beast. We can express the opposite this way: The woman personifies corruption of the truth; the beast personifies open defiance of God. The woman embodies all that is licentious; the beast embodies all that is cruel and ruthless. Thus corruption and violence, which brought about the flood (Genesis 6:11), are to reach their climax in the woman and the beast. "Sitting on a scarlet beast" is a prophecy that the apostate church will be carried and supported by the nations and will rule and reign with temporal power.

The seven hills on which the woman sits (17:9) picture seven kings or successive forms of political government. Of seven Roman emperors, five "have fallen" (which can mean death by violent means) before John's day. The five are usually listed as Julius Caesar, Tiberius, Caligula, Claudius, and Nero. The sixth, who reigned as John wrote Revelation, is the blasphemous Domitian, who was eventually assassinated. He can be looked upon as the one who "is." The emperor who had not yet come in John's day will be the seventh Roman head. The beast will be the eighth. Though distinctive in character and work, he continues the autocratic rule of the seventh head. The woman dominates this last sovereign expression of every anti-Christian movement and sect then in existence, consolidated and controlled by Satan.

The beast is to be the head of a federated empire. Executive power, commencing with Nimrod, will conclude with the beast, both of whom stand related to Babylon. God is to permit executive power in the prophetic earth, meaning the nations clustering around the Mediterranean Sea with allies from the empire of the Caesars. These will form the federation of the beast. All these nations "dwelling on the earth" are earthly minded. The beast's dominion is both external (extending to all nations) and internal (conforming to the world).

The Babylonian system of paganism was a union of religious and civil government and of outward forms and meanings. Secret initiation rites were used, and worshipers were consecrated by rituals of cleansing, even when they were guilty of practicing evil. The woman, the mystery of iniquity, is the symbol of a pagan religion with a priestcraft dominant over all civil power. Her machinations are secret and internal, while those of the beast are manifest to all. In the conflict for supreme authority and control, the beast is victorious.

The removal of the prostitute will mean the lifting of a spiritual, mental, political, and financial burden from the nations. Although they are to rejoice over her destruction, yet they committed fornication with her and gave her reverence.

The woman has titles "written on her forehead" (17:5). The first, "mystery," implies a spiritual fact hitherto hidden and incapable of discovery by mere reason, but now revealed. The union between Christ and His church is a mystery. In contrast to the mystery of godliness will be the mystery of iniquity. This part of the mystic name stamped indelibly on the woman's forehead fittingly describes the terrible system she represents—a travesty of the true church. Christ's place of supremacy over the nations is usurped. Instead of being the depository of all that is true and holy, the woman is shown as the embodiment of error and iniquity.

The second title, "Babylon the Great" refers to that city's terrible reputation and its embodiment of widespread confusion. This description of the woman suggests a widespread system of spiritual evil, representing the culmination of all evils operating against the true church while it was on the earth.

The Babylonism of Revelation 17 is the ecclesiastical system of the apostate church. It is the state religion of the beast. Such a system is called "Babylon the Great" to distinguish it from the Babylon of Nebuchadnezzar, known as "Great Babylon."

The name "Babylon" means confusion and is associated with Babel and its unfinished tower. As used of the woman, it represents apostate Christendom from the divine standpoint. From God's view, such Babylonianism is the mystery of abomination. Professing Christianity, minus a regenerate membership and wholly without God, is to expand into the full outline of the scarlet-clad Babylonian woman. It is a religious Babylonianism that the rulers of earth will find to be a heavy burden. Ultimately it will cause these leaders to join the beast in an attempt to free themselves from a system that has made them its slaves.

What is the meaning of the final title, "mother of prostitutes and of the abominations of the earth"? In ancient Rome harlots wore on their brow a label with their name. Forehead names are worth tracing and contrasting. The redeemed have the name of God on their foreheads (14:1). The prostitute's name on her forehead is another sample of Satan's mimicry. All the names borne by the woman are in sharp contrast to the miter of the high priest with its wording "holy unto the Lord." As "the mother of prostitutes," her offspring will be numerous. Apostate Christendom will give rise to all kinds of religions, idolatries, and arts used by Satan to turn people from God. It will be religion at its worst and the source of all that is morally loathsome.

Apostate Christendom will also give rise to "abominations on the earth" because of the amalgamation it will offer. The parable of the woman mixing leaven until all the meal was penetrated aptly describes the poison of an evil system about to permeate the religious world.

Babylon, as we have already seen, means mixture or confusion. "Bab-el," meaning "the Gate of God," was the rendezvous for lawless sinners. God intervened, however, with the mixture or confusion of languages and scattered the people abroad. Abraham was called out from such an apostate civilization to begin a new race. Thus ancient Babylon, chief of idolatrous cities, is a fitting emblem of the monstrous guilt and extensive influence of latter-day apostate Christendom. But the destruction of this evil system will come when the beast challenges the woman's claim of supreme authority and control.

Two phrases describe the abominable nature of the great whore: "the wine of her adulteries" (17:2) and "the filth of her adulteries" (17:4). Fornication is illicit intercourse, and spiritual fornication is tantamount to idolatry: "They committed adultery with their idols" (Ezekiel 23:37). The solemn indictment against the inhabitants of the earth is that they have allowed themselves to succumb to the seductive glitter and gaudy display of the prostitute. Kings and people are depicted as ensnared by the corrupt and licentious charms of the scarlet-clad woman. But all who drink of her cup, even though it is golden, must perish with her.

John portrays the woman sitting on a scarlet-colored beast and having in her hand a golden cup filled with the abominations and filthiness of her adulteries (17:4). It was the same with Babylon of old. While still in all its glory it had its doom proclaimed by Jeremiah: "Babylon was a gold cup in the LORD's hand; she made the whole earth drunk. The nations drank her wine; therefore they have now gone mad" (Jeremiah 51:7).

As the scarlet beast is full of names of blasphemy (17:3), so the golden cup is "filled with abominable things and the filth of her adulteries." The twin coils of idolatry and corruption are to characterize the last phase of apostate religion, and the worldwide influence of this monstrous harlot can be gathered from the fact that she makes others drunk with the wine of her fornication.

In order to show him the woman astride the beast, the angel carried John away "into a desert." What does this mean? One explanation is that the splendor of the woman and the beast captivates the heart and intoxicates the senses of all people except for the faithful remnant, to whom this gaudy show is as desolate as a desert, for God is not in it.

The "I will show you" of 17:1 changes to the "I will explain to you the mystery" of 17:7. John now receives the divine interpretation of "the mystery of the woman and of the beast she rides." The woman and the beast are treated separately (17:7–14, 15–18) since they are distinct, though they are companions in wickedness and apostasy. The woman pictures ecclesiastical power and the beast personifies civil power. Four phases of the beast's history are explained to John. In four brief, crisp sentences he learns of the course and consummation of the greatest empire of the world: "was"; "is not"; "out of the Abyss"; and "go to his destruction" (17:8).

"The beast, which you saw, once was" signifies the *past*. Here we have the ancient Roman Empire as it existed in imperial form up to John's day and until its destruction in A.D. 476. Under a long succession of imperial rulers the beast existed as one vast consolidated empire. Even though the beast is an actual person, he is also used as the figurehead of an apostate system, just as the woman is. Thus the beast (or the empire he personifies) is an integral part of biblical prophecy.

"The beast, which you saw, once was, now is not" (17:8), signifies the *present*. Even though the countries incorporated within the Roman Empire still remain, the consolidated empire as such is nonexistent. Fragments of the old Roman life and law characterize many of the nations that were once part of this mighty empire.

"The beast, which you saw, once was, is not, will come up out of the Abyss and go to his destruction." This signifies the *future*. In lifting the veil, God enables John to look down the corridor of centuries and behold the satanic revival of the Roman Empire. Leaping over time, John sees in vision form the eve of such a revival: "... *will* come up." The beast himself arises at the beginning of seventieth prophetic week. His empire emerges in the middle of this week. Out of heaven comes the bride of the Lamb, but out of the abyss comes (as an astonishment to all) the empire of the beast.

In this marvelous survey of the beast's future we are given a glimpse into the final phase of apostate Gentile civil power. The hour of vengeance is at hand. The beast and his Babylon are about to be destroyed. Emphasis is given to their everlasting doom in the repeated phrase "go [or "is going"] to his destruction" (17:8, 11). In 17:11 the "he" is emphatic in the Greek. Peculiarly and preeminently *he* is marked out for destruction. This little horn, with eyes like a man and with a mouth speaking great things, is to be cast alive with his companions into the lake of fire (19:20). The empire itself is destroyed by Christ at His coming, when He will lay hold of the kingdoms of the world and will fashion them into His world empire.

Twice over we are told of a guilty, deluded world wondering over the appearance of the beast (13:3; 17:8). But such a marvelous phenomenon does not amaze the elect, who understand the exact character of the beast. Only those whose names are not written in the book of life behold and wonder at Satan's handiwork. The elect have the mind of wisdom and therefore understand the prophetic significance of what is written.

Among the prominent features of the beast are its political history and war with the Lamb. The seven heads have already been mentioned. The ten horns, we are told, represent the ten kings or their kingdoms. Whereas the seven heads express successive forms of government, the ten kings are contemporaneous, covering actual territory at the time of the beast and indicating his empire in a ten-kingdom form.

The respective heads of these kingdoms receive power as kings, which means they reserve their kingly rights. They have the title of kings, but they do not have undivided kingly power. Bowing implicitly to the will of the beast, these ten kings give their power and strength to the beast. With one mind they carry out his will and become his dependent allies.

These ten kings reign "one hour" (17:12) with the beast. The length of their reign is measured by the reign of the beast, with "one hour" indicating a definite time of short duration. The beast, though setting himself up as a king of kings, is quickly deposed by the true King at His coming. The victory of the Lamb over the beast and his coalition of kings is swift and complete.

In verse 17:14 the full and final victory of Christ, described later in 19:19–21, is anticipated by the angel. This war and wrath of the Lamb is specific: against the antichrist and his kings, gathered for the double purpose of cutting off Israel from being a nation (Psalm 83:4) and of making war against the Lamb as an expression of their hatred for Him.

In the phrase "the waters you saw, where the prostitute sits" (17:15) there may be a blasphemous parody of Jehovah sitting upon the flood. The waters that John saw earlier (17:1) are explained as typifying "peoples, multitudes, nations and languages." Here we have the immense moral influence of apostate Christendom over vast masses of humanity.

Yet, abject desolation awaits the apostate church! "The beast and the ten horns ... will hate the prostitute" (17:16). Determined to rid himself and his empire of the subtle and impoverishing influences of the harlot, the beast now turns and casts the harlot from her exalted seat. The rulers of the federated empire strip the harlot of all her seductive, gaudy ornaments. The nations combine with their masterful head in hatred of the harlot. Her downfall comes because of a sudden change in the enslaved peoples. Not only is there loathing for the harlot and plunder of all her wealth and finery, but her flesh is eaten. "Flesh" here is in the plural and signifies masses of flesh— earthly possessions, the fullness of carnality. But the beast and the ten kings, once the harlot's admirers and slaves, are now her bitter foes. They gorge themselves on her gathered possessions.

Next the harlot is burned with fire. This graduated punishment may refer to the legal punishment of abominable fornication. In ancient times harlots were sometimes burned. God's permissive will comes into focus in the perfect agreement between the ten kings and the beast. At the back of the alliance of nations and their union with the beast (and the final overthrow of the harlot) is the will of God. He has decreed the destruction of Gentile dominion and apostate Christendom, and God will triumph. God can even use evil men to accomplish His purposes. The wrath of man can be made to praise Him, as Walter Scott observes:

> God works unseen, but not the less truly, in all the political changes of the day. The astute statesman and the clever diplomat are simply agents in the Lord's hands, though they know it not. Self-will and motives of policy may influence in action, but God is steadily working toward one end: to exhibit the heavenly and earthly glories of His Son. Thus, instead of kings and statesmen thwarting God's purpose, they unconsciously forward it. God is not indifferent, but is behind the scenes of human action. The doings of the future ten kings in relation to Babylon and the beast—the ecclesiastical and secular powers—are not only under the direct control of God, but all is done in fulfillment of His words.

At critical times like this, we must keep our eyes open for evidences of God's overruling hand among the nations.

There is a Stranger in the council hall
Where nations meet to plan the peace again.
He sits unnoticed by the farther wall,
His eyes upon the leaders among men.
His ears attend their clearly laid designs
For living in to-morrow's homes and marts,
And down beneath their spoken words and lines
He hears the inner voices of their hearts.

And when the delegates of all the world
Have cried their million wants, and lists are long
And after blue-prints, charts and plans are hurled
In varied protest at the core of wrong,
He is our hope; He is the peace we seek.
O listen, world, and let the Stranger speak!

Judgment of Political Babylon (18:1–24)

The kings of the earth ... committed adultery with her. (Revelation
18:9)

Next we turn to the judgment of material Babylon. History, both
biblical and secular, provides us with an adequate description of the ancient city of Babylon, which reached its greatest glory and magnificence
during the reign of Nebuchadnezzar (604–562 B.C.). With its high walls,
towers, avenues, gardens, and palaces, Babylon of old must have exerted
a fascination that was compelling and unsurpassed. That its fortunes
have been both wonderful and woeful is a fact emphasized by prophets
and historians alike. At present there is no Babylon, leading some expositors to affirm that all Old Testament prophecies of its destruction
have been fulfilled, and that therefore it cannot be rebuilt. Today the territory covered by the biblical Babylon is known as Hillah.

Babylon, where Alexander the Great drank himself to death, was the
third world kingdom to oppress Israel in the times of Gentile supremacy.
Derived from "Bab-el," meaning "the Gate of God," it became "Babel,"
meaning "confusion." Thus the Gate of God became the gathering place
for lawless sinners, and to check spreading apostasy God intervened with
the confusion of tongues.

The history and prophecy of Babylon can be summarized briefly.

1. Nimrod was its founder (Genesis 10:8–10). Its first queen (and symbol of a wicked system and a city) was Semirames I. Being the first of all idolatrous cities, Babylon is the most suitable emblem for the enormous guilt and the extensive and withering influences of apostate Christendom.
2. When Babylon was an inferior kingdom ruled by Assyria, it helped her against Judah (2 Kings 17:24).
3. It is prophesied as being Judah's captor (2 Kings 20:16–18; Jeremiah 25:9–11).
4. It was chosen by God to chasten Judah (1 Chronicles 9:1; Jeremiah 25:9).
5. It was to be severely punished for its sins (Jeremiah 25:12–14; Daniel 5).
6. It will be prominent again as a symbol under the antichrist (Revelation 17:5, 18).

After the destruction of Nineveh, the great metropolis of the world was Babylon. According to the historian Herodotus, it had a hundred gates of solid brass, with walls thirty-five feet high and so thick that six chariots could ride abreast on top of them. Prophets foretold Babylon's destruction (Isaiah 13:1–22; Jeremiah 50:1–46). Alexander the Great tried to restore Babylon, but God had declared, "I will sweep her with the broom of destruction" (Isaiah 14:23) and it has remained a ruin ever since.

Babylon was the divine instrument of judgment upon Egypt, Judah, Edom, Moab, Ammon, Tyre, Zidon, Assyria, Hazor, and Nineveh. Isaiah, Jeremiah, and Ezekiel are remarkably definite in the statements upon Babylon and her relation to Judah.

The Babylon of the book of Revelation has the same relation to the Babylon of the prophets as the New Jerusalem has to the Jerusalem of the prophets. In Revelation both cities are spoken of in a mystical sense; in the prophets they are spoken of in their literal sense. Because we have no record of a Christian church amid the ruins of ancient Babylon, the Babylon from which Peter sent his first epistle must have been Rome (1 Peter 5:13), where his spiritual son, Mark, was with Paul (Philemon 24).

The revival of Babylon as an actual city is a disputed question. Many Bible scholars affirm that all references to Babylon must be symbolical. Scofield, for example, states,

> The notion of a literal Babylon to be rebuilt on the site of ancient Babylon is in conflict with Isaiah 13:19–22 . . . The prophet has a near and far view, and predicts the destruction of the literal Babylon then existing: with a further statement that, once destroyed, Babylon should never be rebuilt. All this has been literally fulfilled.

Likewise, Jeremiah presents a double prophecy against Babylon: the overthrow by the Medes and Persians and then the prophecy of a future enemy (Jeremiah 50:1–7). This second prophecy describes the regathering of Israel and Judah—definitely a future event. In Jeremiah 50:8–16 the plagues are similar to those of Revelation 18. The past and future of Babylon are before us again in Jeremiah 50:21–46. In Jeremiah 51:1–10 we have language identical to that used in Revelation 14:16; 16:17–21; 18:4–24. Ancient Babylon with all its mysticism and paganism will be destroyed (Revelation 14:8; 18:1–24; Isaiah 21:9).

Zechariah, another Old Testament prophet, used symbolic language to predict the return of Babylonianism (Zechariah 5:5–11). The "measuring basket" (in Hebrew, "ephah") is a three-peck measure; it symbolizes commerce going forth throughout the earth. The "cover of lead," a 158-pound weight, symbolizes the heaviness of the traffic and the richness of the business. The "woman" symbolizes the wickedness in the measure. The "wickedness" (Hebrew *resha‘*) indicates the restless, fallen human nature as manifested in all lawlessness and unrestraint. The "stork" (an unclean bird) and the "wind" in the wings represent the speedy accomplishment of material Babylon as the great business hub of the world.

Old Testament prophecies of Babylon provide a mixture of past and future destinies, but John presents a wholly prophetic declaration of doom. Chapter 17 gives us the description of the power and perdition of mystical Babylon. Chapter 18 records the continuation of the seventh bowl (see 16:17–21). The opening phrase, "After this," emphasizes the unity of the themes revealed. Thus, while the subject of Babylon is carried over from chapter 17, chapter 18 offers a distinct and subsequent revelation: after the perdition of ecclesiastical or mystical Babylon comes the destruction of commercial or material Babylon.

The authoritative angel announcing Babylon's doom (18:1) is not John's guide of 17:1, 7, 15. Various features of this important angelic announcer should be noted. First of all, he descends "coming down from heaven," suggesting the heavenly character of Babylon's judgment and the interest that heaven shows in the affairs of the earth. Whoever the human agents may be in the overthrow of Babylon, it is heaven that ultimately judges her. His "great authority" suggests that there are orders and degrees among the angelic hosts. Some angels are more distinguished than others, and some receive authority to act for God in unusual circumstances. That the angel here is no ordinary one is clearly evident from the fact that "the earth was illuminated by his splendor" (18:1). So recently has this angel come from the presence of God that in passing he flings a broad belt of light across the dark earth.

Is there a thought here of inherent glory, as well as of gather glory? In view of two other passages (8:3 and 10:1), it has been suggested that this angel may be none other than Christ Himself. Combining these three passages, we have Christ, the Angel-Priest, on behalf of His suffering remnant (8:3), Christ, the Angel-Redeemer, taking possession of His inheritance (10:1), and Christ, the Angel-Avenger of His people, taking vengeance on Babylon (18:1–24).

Because angels "excel in strength" (Psalm 103:20 KJV), the strong cry of this angel announcing the judgment of Babylon is not prospective but retrospective. From His point of view, the mighty, iniquitous system is already destroyed (18:2). The repetition is like the solemn dirge of the damned: "Fallen! Fallen!"

In chapter 17 a corrupt religious system is stripped of possessions and wealth, which in turn are transferred to the treasuries of the empire rulers. But apostate civil authorities triumphing over the great whore face more terrible days than they imposed upon the woman. They will yield themselves and their kingdoms to the bestial and brutal will of the antichrist.

The language used in this opening section of chapter 18 provides us with the reason for Babylon's doom. The illicit intercourse with nations and kings under the guise of religion (chapter 17) passes into illicit intercourse in the realm of commerce (chapter 18). It is almost beyond belief that we can conceive of a city becoming a habitation of demons, whose proper home is in the abyss of the underground world. Besides being the capital of demonism, Babylon is also the center of unparalleled wickedness and degradation. By "every evil spirit" and "unclean and detestable bird" we can understand the varied and highly pernicious agents of Satan, all helping to turn Babylon into a sink of iniquity and an abomination in the sight of a holy God.

Included within this grave indictment against Babylon is judgment upon those nations (covering a wide geographical area) who fell an easy prey to the seductive charms of a godless metropolis. "The kings of the earth" (18:3) are not to be confused with the personal heads of the ten kingdoms. They are the merchants of the earth who traffic with Babylon's luxury, the abundance of which was taken from the great prostitute by civil and apostate powers coveting it. Out of that abundance they offer a tempting bait to all those willing to associate with Babylon for mere worldly gain. But such advancement of temporal interests is short-lived, for these very merchants weep and wail over the vanishing of their source of enrichment.

Of all the plagues smiting the earth, those of Babylon are to be the worst, because in their intensity they are to overtake the city "in one day" (18:8). The plagues of Egypt came by installments, but here death, mourning, famine, and fire are permitted by the strong Judge to come together and to come suddenly (16:19–21).

The heavenly voice calling God's people to come out of the city is different from the angelic voice in 18:1. Possibly it is God Himself inviting His own people to leave the sins and plagues of Babylon (Jeremiah 50:4–9; 51:5–8, 45). Such a call for separation is applicable at all times wherever the Babylonian spirit and principle are found (2 Corinthians 6:17). "Come out of her, my people, so that you will not share in her sins, so that you will not receive any of her plagues" (18:4). Lot's wife, lingering near the polluted and doomed cities, perished because of her lingering (Genesis 19:29). This earnest call suggests that even in an apostate city God has His own people, but their only safety is in separation from it.

By "her sins" (18:4–5) we are to understand the utter and terrible corruption of the morals of Babylon, a condition requiring God's stern judgment: "for her sins are piled up to heaven." In the first Babel confederacy, heaped-up stones tried to reach heaven (Genesis 11:4). Here, heaped-up sins do reach heaven. What a monument of shame! A tower not of stones but of sins—sins so bold and impious that they call for heaven's stern and unsparing judgment.

The executioners of God's wrath were commanded to mete out a full compensation to Babylon: "Mix her a double portion from her own cup" (18:6). The cup of destruction is to be filled "double." The cup of luxury and prominence must give way to the cup of torment and humiliation. Death must take the place of life; mourning must dethrone exaltation; famine must sweep away delicacies; fire must consume all of Babylon's boasted works. The Levitical law speaks of a double recompense for full acquittal (Exodus 22:4, 7, 9). Vengeance here goes beyond the "eye for an eye." In God's retributive justice, measure is doubled. But such terrible judgment will not be mere spiteful vindictiveness. Like all divine judgments, it will be deserved and just.

A unique description of the confident boast of security is before us in the words "the glory and luxury she gave herself" (18:7). Presumption is added to Babylon's many crimes. The city is judged not only for conduct but for character. Haughtiness is indicated by a boastful, queenly state. But whatever her hope of retrieving former grandeur, Babylon's doom is sealed: "She will be consumed by fire." The mighty God is to be Babylon's Judge. The doom of Babylon is certain because of the justice and power of God.

One cannot read Revelation 18:9–19 without realizing the luxurious centralization of the great city of Babylon. The wealth of nations increases, and universal influence is exercised from such a capital. Potentates, merchant princes, and all who go down to the sea in ships share in Babylon's prosperity, and all alike are caught by surprise in the holocaust of destruction. Let us separate the three classes affected by Babylon's ruin.

Kings lead in the general mourning, since they profited most by Babylon's worldwide commercial influence (18:9–10). And by these "kings of the earth" we can understand chiefs and rulers generally—not only the ten kings associated in chapter 17 with the beast. All rulers associated with the licentiousness and luxury of material Babylon up to the hour of its overthrow are found wailing over its burning. Under the impact of the great earthquake (16:17–21) these corrupt rulers will flee from the doomed city in a frenzied state, crying,

"Woe! Woe, O great city,
  O Babylon, city of power!
In one hour your doom has come!" (18:10)

Thus God's judgments inspire fear even in the most worldly.

Because commerce plays a large part in the greatness of the city, the merchants are among its chief mourners (18:11–16). The varied items of merchandise in these verses indicate what a great commercial metropolis Babylon becomes in about three years after the harlot has been abolished. In the days of the antichrist, markets will be controlled from this great trading post of the nations. At this crossroads of the world all business is to be centralized. The wording here suggests luxury in the extreme. Everything a person could possibly lust after is provided in this universal emporium. Expensive jewelry, costly furniture, unusual perfumes, delicious banquets, crowded markets, rich fabrics—all are here. Buying and selling, unbridled passion, pleasure and musical resorts will reproduce the days of Noah and of Lot.

Altogether some twenty-nine items are singled out, proving that a great world market will be seriously affected by the ruin of Babylon. No wonder the millionaire merchants of the earth, whose affluence came from silver, stones, sheep, slaves, and souls, will weep and wail over the destruction of all the sources of their wealth. Merchandise will be completely ruined. Everything catering to pride and prosperity will perish in the unexpected and sudden blow from the divine hand.

As a world center of finance and commerce, Babylon will engage in an extensive sea trade. Ships loaded with all kinds of merchandise will travel to and from its ports. The pathetic cries of shipmasters and sailors are occasioned by the fact that the desolation of Babylon means the end of all seagoing traffic and consequently the end of their livelihood (18:17–19). No wonder all who were made rich by ships in the sea weep and wail and cast dust on their heads!

To all the seafarers nothing was equal to Babylon: "Was there ever a city like this great city?" (18:18). It was the epitome of great worldly prestige and power. By policies, diplomacy, and unholy ends it had gained worldwide influence. By sword and money its domain had been spread far and wide. But all such unholy greatness is swiftly banished by Him who is able to cast the mighty from their seats of power (Luke 1:51–53).

Gathering together the lamentations of the monarchs, merchants, and mariners, we have an insight into the terror of Babylon's judgment. The double "woe" of the monarchs ends with, "In one hour your doom has come" (18:10). Here we have the swiftness of divine action. The stroke of vengeance from the hand of God is sudden and unexpected. The merchants give their viewpoint of Babylon's ruin: "In one hour such great wealth has been brought to ruin" (18:17), indicating the complete banishment of prideful material prosperity. The double "woe" of the mariners gives us another phase of the anguish experienced over the city's downfall. "In one hour she has been brought to ruin" (18:19). Loaded with riches one moment, the next moment she is stripped bare of all her coastlines.

By a direct visitation of God, Babylon's destruction is complete (18:22–24). The singers and players are silent, for nothing but cries of anguish are heard. Craftsmen who prostituted their art to further the sensuous worship of apostate Christendom cannot repair the damage. All illumination will fail, for not even the light of a candle can be found.

In this remarkable section of Revelation we have a striking illustration of Scripture interpreting Scripture. We read of a mighty angel taking up a stone like a great millstone and casting it into the sea crying,

> "With such violence
> the great city of Babylon will be thrown down,
> never to be found again." (18:21)

Going back to Jeremiah, we have the prophet instructed by God to bind a stone to the book, cast it into the midst of the Euphrates River then say: "So will Babylon sink to rise no more because of the disaster I will bring upon her" (Jeremiah 51:64).

Turning to Daniel's prophecy of the final world empire, we find him predicting the time when "the rock cut out of a mountain, but not by human hands" will completely destroy the image representing the great Gentile age (Daniel 2:44–45). The sea into which the boulder is thrown (18:21) is a symbol of the restless, turbulent Gentile nations; "the great city Babylon" is the final expression of Gentile monarchy and dominion. Thus it is not difficult to see in Christ the Stone out of the mountain of God, destroying a godless civilization.

Babylon is distinguished in Scripture as being subject to the Lord's vengeance, since she is prominent as the enemy and enslaver of His people. The martyrdom of the righteous, commencing with the death of Abel and gathering intensity throughout the ages, reaches its final concentration of martyrdoms and reign of terror in Revelation 17 and 18. But the destruction of both Babylons avenges the blood of the saints and culminates the wrath of God (18:24).

The announcement of Babylon's destruction (18:21–24) is preceded by a divine call to the saints to delight in God's judgment (18:20). "Rejoice over her, O heaven!" is the opposite of the rejoicing in 11:10, where the godless rejoice over the death of the two witnesses. Rejoicing over Babylon's ruin may not appear to be very heavenly, but the execution of righteous justice always elicits the approval of God's own people. Heaven rejoices over just vengeance upon the great harlot and the beast. In many of the imprecatory psalms, the righteous sigh for judgment to overtake the wicked; here those sighs are answered: "Rejoice, saints and apostles and prophets! God has judged her for the way she treated you" (18:20).

This call to rejoice anticipates the hallelujah chorus (19:1–8) that comes between the second and third judgments. What the notables of earth mourn over, the multitude in heaven rejoices over. It is significant that the first "hallelujah" in the New Testament arises over the judgment of the great prostitute (19:1–2). The four hallelujahs—uttered by the great multitude, the four beasts, and the twenty-four elders—constitute a cry of victory that ascribes praise to God. At last the eternal desolation of Babylon as prophesied in Old Testament Scriptures is an accomplished fact (Isaiah 13:1–22; Jeremiah 50:13, 23, 29–40; 51:24, 37, 60–64).

The eternally ascending smoke (19:3) testifies that the doom of Babylon is an everlasting witness to the righteous judgment of God poured out upon all fornication and upon the martyrdom of His people. The word used for "up" in reference to the ascending smoke of 19:3 means "keeps on going up" and is somewhat different from the ascending incense of 8:4. Some writers see this passage as indicating that the eternal lake of fire will be visible to earth dwellers in the new earth after the millennium (Isaiah 66:22–24; Revelation 14:9–11). "The light of a lamp will never shine in you again" (18:23).

Interlude—Hallelujah! (Revelation 19:1–16)

I heard what sounded like the roar of a great multitude in heaven shouting: "Hallelujah!" (Revelation 19:1)

The opening phrase of chapter 19, "After this I heard," describes a turn of events and the climax of the previous chapters. Vengeance is at last enacted. The doom of Babylon indicated in 14:8 is now fully accomplished.

Briefly reviewing this hallelujah section, which celebrates the utter and eternal ruin of Babylon, we note that the same destruction is viewed differently in heaven and on earth. On earth a dirge of sorrow is heard, but in heaven a paean of praise arises. That beautiful word "hallelujah," meaning "praise Jehovah," rolls through the vault of heaven. In the Greek text, the definite article appears before each of the three divine possessions: "the" salvation (divine deliverance from judgment); "the" glory (divine moral glory in judgment); "the" power (divine might displayed in judgment).

The foundation for the triumph of the redeemed and heavenly hosts is the divine truth and righteousness: "true and just are his judgments" (19:1). In all God's dealing with His creatures, whether in grace or in judgment, God's essential attributes are conspicuously displayed.

The second "hallelujah" is related to the finality and perpetuity of a divinely executed judgment. Two further "hallelujahs" swell the volume of praise. God is the Judge of Babylon, as Christ is the Judge of the beast. At last an angelic voice summons all the servants of God to join in antiphonal praise to God, and their united voices are like the roar of a mighty waterfall. From God's throne, the very center and source of judicial action, the call goes forth to praise, "For our Lord God Almighty reigns" (v. 6).

Let us now look at this title given to God, "our Lord God." He is the Lord of creation, of compassion, and of completion. He is *our God.* When the Apostle John wrote these words there were hundreds of false gods in Rome, but He is *"our God."* This is the final song in the Bible, and it is fitting that it should be a song of the total triumph of God over all His enemies. It corresponds to the first song in the Bible (Exodus 15:1–21), especially 15:11: "Who among the gods is like you?" There is a challenge in these songs. In Psalm 42:3, 10 the voice of unbelief asks, "Where is your God?" This is the question many people are asking today. But in that day the tables will be turned; all people will finally recognize that God is upon His everlasting throne.

Our God is all-powerful; He has no limitations. This is one of His supreme attributes. The devil cannot claim this, nor can any dictator, nor will the antichrist. Omnipotence belongs to *God alone.* In Ephesians 1:19–20 the Apostle Paul writes of "his incomparably great power . . . which he exerted in Christ when he raised him from the dead." Paul then proceeds to Christ's exaltation "far above all rule and authority."

God's love is both omnipotent and everlasting (Jeremiah 31:3). His purpose is also omnipotent; it cannot be thwarted, no matter how the nations or the invisible forces of evil may seek to do so. God's will is also omnipotent, the mightiest thing in the universe. We can only exclaim in these days of tragic suffering upon the earth, "Alleluia, for the Lord God Omnipotent reigneth." (19:6 KJV).

Our God also has kingship over all the universe. Not merely does He live, but He *lives and reigns.* When this supreme fact grips us, nothing else matters. Our God's throne is intact; the Apostle John heard a great multitude saying, "Let us rejoice and be glad and give him glory" (19:7). Amid all that is bringing desolation and death on this earth, let us keep the eye of faith upon that throne, which can never be shaken.

The nineteenth chapter of Revelation is an interlude in which John turns aside to describe all he heard and saw of the reaction in heaven to the manifestation of divine vengeance. Its three sections are clearly marked: the four hallelujahs (19:1–6), the marriage supper of the Lamb (19:7–10), and the return of the Redeemer in glory (19:11–21).

The Hallelujah Choruses (19:1–6). These four hallelujahs (19:1, 3, 4, 6) constitute the only place in the Bible where this word is used. The repeated Old Testament phrase "praise the Lord" is a translation of the Hebrew "hallelujah" and was first uttered over God's punishment of the wicked (Psalm 104:35).

The four hallelujahs are the response of the host of heaven and the godly saints of earth to the divine destruction of Babylon. The first two are an extension of the previous section in which heaven rejoices over the doom of Babylon, and these hallelujahs come from a mighty host in heaven who praise God for His true and righteous judgments. The third is echoed by the twenty-four elders and the four living creatures, who add a loud "amen" to their tribute of praise. The fourth comes from the multitudes of earth and from creation as they bless God for His omnipotence.

"Hallelujah! For our Lord God Almighty reigns." (Revelation 19:6)

The Wedding Supper of the Lamb (19:7–10). The wedding supper of the Lamb is a precious revelation to the hearts of God's people. What a moment this will be when the church of the Firstborn is forever united to Him who bought her with His own blood! This is to be the marriage supper of the Lamb. Our presence there will be the result of His grace, and only those washed through the blood of the Lamb will be present at this nuptial celebration.

This supper will be one of delight—though "the great supper of God" (19:17) will be one of destruction. At this supper the fowls of the air will eat the flesh of kings, while at the marriage supper of the Lamb the saints will feast with Christ, the King of Kings. Our beautiful wedding garments represent the righteousness that the Lamb imputes and imparts to all His saints.

Blessed are those who are invited to the wedding supper of the Lamb! (Revelation 19:9)

The Return of the King of Kings (19:11–16). As to the identity of the Rider of the white horse, there is no doubt: He is the Redeemer returning in glory. His names correspond to all that He is in Himself, and to the nature of His judgments. He is called Faithful and True, the Word of God, King of Kings, and Lord of Lords.

The diadems encircling His brow are royal ones, different from the mock ones on the head of the beast. The striking phrase "robe dipped in blood" (19:13) refers to the blood of Christ's enemies, who are not sprinkled with the blood of Calvary. "Word of God" offers one of the strongest arguments for His incarnation (see John 1:1, 14; 1 John 1:1–3). Jesus Himself is the final and perfect revelation of God (Hebrews 1:1–4).

Zechariah predicted the Second Coming: "Then the LORD will go out and fight against those nations, as he fights in the day of battle. On that day his feet will stand on the Mount of Olives, east of Jerusalem, and the Mount of Olives will be split in two from east to west, forming a great valley, with half of the mountain moving north and half moving south" (Zechariah 14:3–4).

Jesus described His Second Coming in Matthew 24:27–31:

For as lightning that comes from the east is visible even in the west, so will be the coming of the Son of Man. Wherever there is a carcass, there the vultures will gather. Immediately after the distress of those days

"the sun will be darkened,
    and the moon will not give its light;
the stars will fall from the sky,
    and the heavenly bodies will be shaken."

At that time the sign of the Son of Man will appear in the sky, and all the nations of the earth will mourn. They will see the Son of Man coming on the clouds of the sky, with power and great glory. And he will send his angels with a loud trumpet call, and they will gather his elect from the four winds, from one end of the heavens to the other.

On His robe and on his thigh he has his name written: "KING OF KINGS AND LORD OF LORDS." (Revelation 19:16)

The Second Judgment: The Kings (Revelation 19:17–21)

The kings of the earth and their armies gathered together to make war. (Revelation 19:19)

The promise and prophecy given to Christ by His Father was that when He came to reign He would dash His enemies to pieces (Psalm 2:9). Here in the battle of Armageddon, with its terrible carnage, is the fulfillment of that fearful prophecy concerning the catastrophe overtaking Gentile world powers. Before us is the terrible Day of the Lord predicted by the prophets (Joel 2:11). We must also note in this connection Ezekiel 38 and 39, dealing with the end-time period of Gentile dominion.

In the gathering for the supper of the great God, John gives us a bold and powerful picture of the battlefield after the victory of Christ—"a sacrificial feast spread on God's table for all the vultures of the sky." (For the habits of vultures, look at Matthew 24:28.) In this grim conflict there are some interesting contrasts to observe.

Opposing the armies of the beast and the kings of the earth are the armies of the Rider on the white horse, and there is never any doubt about the outcome (19:19–21). Fowls eat up the flesh of the mighty men of earth (19:21). Even the escaping few are captured by the sword of the One sitting upon His horse. In connection with Satan's effort to destroy the Jewish remnant, God graciously protected "the rest of her offspring" (12:17), but these people fleeing from the armies of kings cannot escape the vengeance of the King of Kings.

The Third Judgment: The Beast (Revelation 19:20–20:10)

Thrown alive into the . . . lake of burning sulfur. (Revelation 19:20)

At last this "abomination that causes desolation" (Matthew 24:15) and "man of lawlessness" (2 Thessalonians 2:3) reaps the harvest of his diabolical hatred of God and His saints. As earth's last and most terrible tyrant, he suffers a well-deserved punishment. We read that "the beast was captured" (19:20); this Greek word for "captured" means to take hold of forcefully, to apprehend (as a police officer lays hold of a criminal). Who is it that seizes the beast and his companion in crime, the false prophet? None other than the strong Son of God, with eyes as a flame of fire, flashing with righteous anger!

"The two of them were thrown alive into the fiery lake of burning sulfur" (19:20). They were not allowed to die, nor were they slain, but were *thrown alive* into everlasting punishment. The three Hebrew youths in the book of Daniel were cast alive into the fiery furnace, but God withheld the action of the fire and graciously preserved alive the courageous young men. But the beast and the false prophet are cast alive into a fire from which there is no deliverance.

As for the lake of fire, we do not claim to know all that is implied by such eternal suffering. Granted that the language may be symbolic, the reality must be far more terrible than the figure used. Jesus was a "hell-fire" Preacher. To Him, eternal punishment was a terrible reality, though He had no pleasure in the eternal misery of sinners. He died upon the cross that men might not perish but have everlasting life instead. It is our urgent task to warn the lost to flee from the wrath to come.

The Fourth Judgment: The False Prophet (Revelation 19:20–20:10)

> The lake of burning sulfur, where . . . the false prophet had been thrown. (Revelation 20:10)

United in their defiance of God, these two powerful and pernicious persons are now united in their doom. The false prophet, although the murderer of multitudes who would not worship the image of the beast, will not be permitted to die. Even his professed miraculous power cannot now save him from being cast alive into the lake of fire. No doubt the everlasting punishment of the false prophet will be all the worse because of his religious pretensions. The doom of the beast and the false prophet represents the end of a false statecraft and a false priestcraft. Both these personages suffer together because they fought together against the Lamb.

The Fifth Judgment: Satan (Revelation 20:1–3, 10)

> He seized . . . Satan and bound him for a thousand years. (20:10)

At long last the head of the serpent is forever bruised (Genesis 3:15). The victory secured over the devil at Calvary is now completely operative. Cast out of heaven in ancient times because of his rebellion, then cast out of the air to the earth (12:9), the devil is now cast into the bottomless pit for a thousand years (20:3). His liberty to walk about devouring souls (1 Peter 5:8) is now abolished as an angel from heaven chains Satan, binds him, confines him in the abyss, and seals his prison. John says that the dragon was imprisoned "to keep him from deceiving the nations anymore until the thousand years were ended. After that, he must be set free for a short time" (v. 3).

Satan's thousand years in the abyss will produce no change in his evil character. Once released, he will prove himself to be the same old devil. But while he is confined, the earth will breathe a purer air, and Christ's millennial reign will cause peace and righteousness to cover the earth as the waters cover the sea. Six times the phrase "a thousand years" is mentioned, and this period is the glorious kingdom age predicted by the prophets and by Christ and His apostles.

After his final, postmillennial work of deception the devil is "thrown into the lake of burning sulfur . . . [to] be tormented day and night forever" (v. 10). There he joins the deluded devotees who had already endured the flames for a thousand years. With them he enters into eternal torment (20:10). At last the trinity of evil imitating the Trinity of heaven reap their unrelieved doom. The devil, along with the beast and the false prophet, are together forever in the lake of fire. No wonder the devil strives to keep people from reading this final book of the Bible! It is heavy with his deserved doom, and he does not want those he deceives to know of his terrible future.

The Sixth Judgment: Gog and Magog (Revelation 20:7–9)

Gog and Magog—to gather them for battle. (Revelation 20:8)

The mention of Gog (the prince) and Magog (the land) takes us back to Ezekiel 38, where Gog represents the nations forming the great northern confederacy. We have now come to the final revolt of the nations and to their destruction. Some people ask why the Lord would release Satan from the bottomless pit after Christ's prosperous thousand-year reign during which the roaring lion is chained. Why set Satan free even for a little while to head up a massive revolt? The only answer is the Lord wants to prove the utter depravity of human nature.

One would think that after a thousand years of Christ's blessed and beneficial reign no one on earth would want to revolt. But even as Adam sinned in the most perfect environment of the Garden of Eden, so large numbers of these millennial dwellers rebel against Christ in spite of the peace and provision accompanying the King's reign. Of course, He rules them with a rod of iron, and they *must* bow before Him. But their instant response to Satan's call reveals that their obedience to Christ is only feigned; they recognized His power only because they have to.

Judgment, however, is swift: fire comes down from heaven and devours the multitudes (20:9). Fire, as we know, is related to all God's judgments, even the judgment of the saints at the judgment seat of Christ "the fire will test the quality of each man's work" (1 Corinthians 3:13). In this final conflict there is no battle, no fighting. The Almighty God sends a consuming fire to immediately destroy all the deceived and brutalized nations. The last attack against God and against "the camp of God's people, the city he loves" (20:9) ends in complete failure, and hell enlarges its mouth to receive the hordes of earth whom the devil has deceived and led in rebellion. No wonder we go on to read of a new earth—one without a devil forever!

The Seventh Judgment: The Great White Throne
(Revelation 20:11–15)

Then I saw a great white throne and him who was seated on it. Earth and sky fled from his presence, and there was no place for them. And I saw the dead, great and small, standing before the throne, and books were opened. Another book was opened, which is the book of life. The dead were judged according to what they had done as recorded in the books. The sea gave up the dead that were in it, and death and Hades gave up the dead that were in them, and each person was judged according to what he had done. Then death and Hades were thrown into the lake of fire. The lake of fire is the second death. If anyone's name was not found written in the book of life, he was thrown into the lake of fire. (Revelation 20:10–15)

Law courts have witnessed some tense and terrible scenes, but the most famous and fearful of these pale into insignificance alongside the staggering scene of the final judgment we are now to consider. This judgment, which occurs after the millennium and the final disposition of Satan and the present heavens and earth, will be the most solemn and awful ever witnessed. At last the eternal Judge is to settle all accounts. Having dealt with Satan, the god of the world, Christ now prepares to deal with the sinners of the world. At last the end of the world is reached, for creation flees from the face of the One sitting upon the throne. Some refer to this as a general judgment, but Revelation knows no general judgment. Any judgment in this book is particular. All people from all ages of earth's history, whether good or bad, are not to gather at this great scene. It is only for the wicked dead, just as the judgment seat of Christ is only for believers.

John's vision is in two parts, indicated by the repeated phrase "I saw": he saw the throne and its Judge (20:11), and he saw the dead and their judgment (20:12–15). Revelation is a book of thrones and judgments. In 19:11–21 we have Christ's judgment against living persons. Here in 20:11–15 we have the judgment of the dead. In 4:2 we have the throne in heaven, from which earth is governed. Matthew 25:31 speaks of "his throne in heavenly glory," which is related to Christ's judgment of the living nations. But among the thrones of Scripture, "the great white throne" (Revelation 20:11) is the most dreadful and hopeless of all.

What kind of throne is this one, set up not on earth nor in the heavens? It is not the throne of a sovereign about to reign and rule, but that of a Judge about to pronounce doom upon the guilty. Set up for a specific purpose, it is not a permanent throne, for it ceases to be as soon as its judgments have been meted out to the condemned. At this throne the position in Pilate's day will be reversed: then the Creator was judged by the creature, but now the creature appears before the Creator for sentencing. In Pilate's hall God stood speechless before man, but here man is speechless before God. He who stood condemned before the earthly tribunal will now decide the destinies of the human race and will reveal the principles of divine government.

Having rejected the great salvation offered by Christ, sinners are now made to stand before God's great white throne. It will be great for several reasons: because of the dignity of the Judge Himself; because of the greatness and unparalleled solemnity of the occasion; because of the vastness of the scene: here is the dawn of eternity; because of the eternal consequences involved; and because of the great destinies it will decide.

The throne corresponds to the character of its Occupant. "The LORD reigns forever; he has established his throne for judgment. He will judge the world in righteousness" (Psalm 9:7–8). The Infinite One, before whom the finite must stand, is holy and righteous in "the day of God's wrath, when his righteous judgment will be revealed" (Romans 2:5). There will be no unfair, unjust treatment, such as He Himself received at Pilate's hands. Being white, the throne symbolizes the purity and righteousness of the judgments of the Judge. It is white because of its immaculate purity. Here we have the un-dimmed blaze of divine holiness, purity, and justice. How terrible it will be for sinners to face the unapproachable light of the Lord's presence!

The Judge

The Father . . . has given him authority to judge because he is the Son of Man. (John 5:26–27)

The Judge is the Lord God, even the Savior. Since salvation was planned by God, was achieved by Christ, and is applied by the Holy Spirit, all three Persons of the Godhead may be at the judgment of those who despised such a salvation. Christ, however, is left to pronounce the solemn judgment of the lost (see John 5:22; 2 Timothy 4:1).

With eyes as a flame of fire, Christ will search and scorch those before Him (Revelation 1:14; 19:12). Everyone and everything will wither as those eyes gleam with righteous judgment. They will not sparkle with mercy then, for with majesty unlimited the Owner of those piercing eyes has earned the right to dispose of the destiny of His willful creatures. "With justice he judges"; "true and just are your judgments" (19:11; 16:7).

In 12:13–16 Israel is forced to flee from "the face of the serpent" (KJV); in 20:11 "earth and heaven" (KJV) flee from the face of the Savior, who is now the Judge. Once that face was spat upon, buffeted, and marred beyond human recognition, but now it is adorned with fearful majesty. And in this countenance sinners will read their doom.

How different will be the church's sight of that face! "They will see his face, and his name will be on their foreheads" (22:4). And Christ's saints are to be honored by participation in this judgment. "To carry out the sentence written against them. This is the glory of all his saints" (Psalm 149:9).

The Case

Whoever does not believe stands condemned already. (John 3:18)

The courts of democratic countries attempt to offer criminals a fair trial. This court in heaven, however, is not set up to discuss the pros and cons of any sinner's case but to carry out a sentence already declared. Unsaved people, here and now, are condemned already (John 3:18). In that future day the dead will be raised and made to stand before the Judge, not to be judged as to their guilt or innocence, but to receive the ratification of a condemnation already pronounced.

> Whoever believes in him is not condemned, but whoever does not believe stands condemned already because he has not believed in the name of God's one and only Son. (John 3:18)

> Whoever believes in the Son has eternal life, but whoever rejects the Son will not see life, for God's wrath remains on him. (John 3:36)

This judgment is called "eternal" (Hebrews 6:2) because its consequences are eternal. It also acts as a guarantee that sin will never be allowed to invade God's new creation. The children of God are happy to know that they will never face such condemnation: "Therefore, there is now no condemnation for those who are in Christ Jesus" (Romans 8:1). By our acceptance of Christ, who bore our condemnation, we are saved from sin and its just and eternal punishment.

Several objects of judgment are enumerated in the awesome account of the great white throne, and it is important to note these respective judgments.

The earth and the heaven (KJV): There will be a quick disappearance of the old creation because the One sitting upon the throne was its Creator, and therefore it immediately obeys His command. Why will the earth vanish? Because it was the scene of sin and rebellion, and it bore the stain of the Judge's blood. Humans held onto it for many centuries, but now it flees away. Why does the heaven also vanish? The aerial heavens cannot remain, since they were polluted by Satan, the prince of the power of the air. How can the heavens continue if they are not clean in God's sight? Among the new creations are a new heaven and new earth (Revelation 21:1; see also Isaiah 65:17; 66:22; 2 Peter 3:7, 10–13; Hebrews 1:10–11, 12).

The fallen angels: Because the chief rebel has been dealt with (20:10), Christ now proceeds to deal with all those whom Satan influenced. While we have no direct proof in the narrative that Satan's host of evil spirits are to appear at this throne, we feel that they will be judged at this time. "And the angels who did not keep their positions of authority but abandoned their own home—these he has kept in darkness, bound with everlasting chains for judgment on the great Day" (Jude 6). If, as Paul affirms, we are to judge angels (that is, fallen ones), then it would seem as if the saints will be at this tribunal in a judicial capacity. It is not hard to understand why Satan hates the book of Revelation and attempts to keep people from reading and studying it! He does not want them to know of his terrible doom as well as the stern punishment awaiting his angelic and human dupes.

The dead: By this group we are to understand all the dead in sin, whether dead spiritually or physically. The godless on earth at the time when this throne is set up are immediately transferred to it, while the dead in hell are raised and made to appear with them. Here they stand like condemned prisoners at the bar, awaiting their sentence of doom.

The dead in Christ were raised at His return for the church (1 Thessalonians 4:16). But the resurrection here is not "out of" the dead (for believers); it is the final resurrection of all the wicked dead for their final disposition. All the wicked dead before Christ came to earth will have the book of the law to judge them (Romans 2:12; 3:19). All the wicked dead since Christ will be judged by the gospel of grace (Romans 2:16; John 3:18–19; 12:48). All the wicked dead after Christ's Second Coming will be judged by the everlasting gospel. Infants and mentally incompetent will not be there. Because they never had any conscious accountability, the blood of Christ, which covers Adamic sin, guarantees their presence in heaven.

All ranks and degrees of sinners are to appear at this awesome throne, as indicated by the phrase "great and small" (Revelation 20:12), a phrase occurring five times over in the book of Revelation. Now we have various classes and distinctions, social and racial. But all distinctions are to be swept away as the Judge takes His seat, for He is no Respecter of persons. The proud and mighty, as well as the insignificant, are to enter the lake of fire. In 21:8 we are told who will find their place "in the lake which burneth" (KJV).

The fearful: These people were full of fear while on earth. They were always afraid to confess Christ, to identify themselves with the gospel and to live for the Lord. Their hearts failed them. Though courageous enough in other realms, they were cowards when it came to receiving Christ as their Savior.

The unbelieving: Here we have a numerous class, found in all ranks. Jesus Himself declared that travelers on the broad road are many. It is sad to realize that so many men and women are unbelievers. So many of our centers of secular learning produce polished pagans. The natural mind simply will not receive and believe the message of the crucified and risen Savior.

The abominable: By this group we are to understand all who are morally filthy. The corruption of Noah's days is here again. Wars bring with them the liberation of detestable forms of sin.

The murderers: Statistics inform us that murders are on the increase. Jesus called Satan a murderer and the parent of all who destroy the lives of others. What a day of reckoning awaits those butchers and executioners in the world who wantonly kill innocent men, women, and children!

The fornicators: Fornication implies sexual immorality of every kind. Adultery, incest, and idolatry are cited as fornication (Matthew 5:32; 1 Corinthians 5:1; 2 Chronicles 21:11 KJV). Unscriptural doctrine is likewise likened to spiritual fornication (Revelation 19:2 KJV).

The sorcerers: We have already drawn attention to the fact that this word is connected with our English word "pharmacy." Long ago drugs played an important part in witchcraft, and once again we have a drunken, drugged, doped society! In this category we can place all those who are identified with spiritism and demonism.

The idolaters: Many people assume that idolaters are those who worship idols of wood and stone. But there are countless numbers of idolaters around us who worship themselves, their money, their businesses, their sports. What is an idol? An idol is anyone or anything taking the place of God in our lives.

The liars: Every kind of liar must stand before God's throne. Satan, the father of lies and the master liar, is already in the lake of fire, and now his children are about to follow him. All who are contrary to God and His Word are liars.

None of the foregoing people will be able to appeal against their judgment. They will be only too conscious of their guilt. While the punishments will be proportional in intensity to the sins committed, the duration of punishment will be eternal in every case.

The sea: In his description of the new creation, John declares that the sea exists no more (21:1). This meant much to John, who in his Patmos prison knew that the Aegean Sea separated him from those to whom he loved to minister. But what is the full implication of this phrase about the sea giving up the dead that were in it? Is "sea" to be treated as symbolic of the unsettled condition of humanity, and therefore descriptive of the surrender of the seething masses to judgment? Or are we to accept the usual interpretation that all those drowned at sea are to emerge from their watery grave? To our mind it seems that the next phrase, "death and Hades gave up the dead that were in them," covers all who died and were buried in the earth or sea.

George Pember, in his stirring book *Earth's Earliest Ages,* suggests that the sea is the prison of vast numbers of demons who followed Satan in his expulsion from heaven and who, when the sea was formed, were confined within it. This may be the darkness and chains referred to in Jude 6. With the passing of earth and heaven, the sea will also vanish, and therefore all beings within this liquid tomb must appear before Him who made the sea.

Death and Hades: Death, or the grave, held the bodies of the lost, while Hades held their spirits. Now bodies and spirits are united, and their eternal bodies of shame and in their eternal spirits the condemned go out to the death of death. But at last this monster is destroyed: "thrown into the lake of fire" (20:14). Hades or hell is the present abode of the lost. But this temporary abode gives way to the more fearful, eternal judgment of the lake of fire. Such a resurrection is spoken of as one of shame (Daniel 12:2); of the wicked (Acts 24:15); of condemnation (John 5:29). How different will be the resurrection of the saved at the return of Christ (see 1 Thessalonians 4:16–17; Philippians 3:21; 1 Corinthians 15).

Death and hell quickly follow their occupants into the lake of fire (20:14). Brought into existence because of Satan's work, they now follow him into eternal perdition. Because the keys of hell and death dangle at Christ's waistband, He is able to act as He likes with such abodes. "I am the Living One; I was dead, and behold I am alive for ever and ever! And I hold the keys of death and Hades" (Revelation 1:18). Thus the lake of fire becomes the final depository of all that was contrary to God and to Jesus Christ. The terrible term "the lake of fire" occurs five times in Revelation, and we should consider the significance of this final abode of Satan, the beast, the false prophet, the dead, death, and hell. Surely such striking language suggests the finality and eternity of unspeakable, unrelieved doom!

Some argue that the language is only figurative and that actual flames are not meant. If this is so, then the reality symbolized must be even more terrible than the figure. "Remember," says Broadus,

> that language may be highly figurative without being fictitious. Only ascertain what the figures of Scripture were designed to mean, and that meaning is as certainly true as if stated in plain words. Thus the fire that cannot be quenched may be called a figure, if you choose; yet it assuredly means that in hell there will be something as bad as fire, as torturing as fire to the earthly body—nay, the reality of hell, the most impressive imagery that earthly things can afford.

To this we may add the fact that Christ never made idle threats, and when He spoke of eternal fire, He was warning against a real punishment vividly described by figures of the most extreme suffering.

This judgment of fire was prepared for the devil and his angels: "Then he will say to those on his left, 'Depart from me, you who are cursed, into the eternal fire prepared for the devil and his angels'" (Matthew 25:41). They are the last to endure the torment of flames.

Truly the language used of the eternal condition of the lost is sufficient to strike terror into the heart of every sinner: the lake of fire; the second death; outer darkness; blackness forever; wailing and gnashing of teeth. The teaching of our Lord makes it plain that the torment is to be eternal (Mark 9:43). In the lake of fire, full consciousness will make anguish more intense. There is no purgatory, no probation, no ultimate escape. "And besides all this, between us and you a great chasm has been fixed, so that those who want to go from here to you cannot, nor can anyone cross over from there to us" (Luke 16:26). All the condemned "will be tormented day and night for ever and ever" (20:10).

The repeated phrase the second death is easily explained. The first death was physical—the final separation of the spirit from the body. The second death is eternal—the final separation of the spirit from God. Over the saved this second death has no power (20:6). Donald G. Barnhouse, in *God's Last Word,* remarks: "As though to give one final word of comfort to those whose names are written in the Lamb's book of life, and one final word of warning to those who know Him not, the distinction is once more clearly drawn. Whoever was not found written in the book of life was cast into the lake of fire."

The Verdict

Many will say to me on that day, "Lord, Lord, did we not prophesy in your name, and in your name drive out demons and perform many miracles?" Then I will tell them plainly, "I never knew you. Away from me, you evildoers!" (Matthew 7:22–23)

We now come to the somewhat difficult question of the various records that John mentions as being before the Judge as He deals with the condemned persons standing at the throne. "Books," "another book," "the book of life" (20:12, and elsewhere), and the "Lamb's book of life" (21:27) are terms to be distinguished and interpreted.

"Books" (20:12) implies that more than one set of records is in heaven. By these books we can understand the record of the works of the people about to be judged. "The dead were judged according to what they had done as recorded in the books" (20:12). The Lord is keeping a faithful record of the thoughts, deeds, and words of sinners. Nothing is too trivial to set down.

This is not a general judgment; the merits of each person will be considered, "each person ... according to what he has done" (20:13). The rich man of Luke 16 died, went to Hades, and cried out, "I am in agony in this flame." But Abraham replied, "Son, remember!" And the rich man remembered past and lost opportunities. He remembered what Moses and the prophets had said. He remembered the message of God's Holy Word. He remembered, but now it was too late!

While a person may have a good record, evidently it is Christ's insertion of his name into "the book of life" (20:12) that counts. "However, do not rejoice that the spirits submit to you, but rejoice that your names are written in heaven" (Luke 10:20). It is not the absence of works but of a name that condemns. "Many will say to me on that day, 'Lord, Lord, did we not prophesy in your name, and in your name drive out demons and perform many miracles?' Then I will tell them plainly, 'I never knew you. Away from me, you evildoers!' " (Matthew 7:22–23).

Christ has control of this register, as indicated in Revelation 3:5 (see also 13:8; 17:8; 21:27). The Lamb's book of life is the golden record of those belonging to the Lord. Names in this book were written long before the events of the great white throne. Donald G. Barnhouse notes the following points on the various books in heaven:

"Books" is a plural form. There is more than one set of books kept in heaven. There are at least two records in heaven concerning the believers in the Lord Jesus Christ. There is one which is the roll of the elect chosen in Christ before the foundation of the world, and this is called "the Lamb's book of life" (Revelation 21:27) or simply "the book of life" (Philippians 4:3; Revelation 13:8, etc.). It was of this that the Lord spoke to His disciples when He told them that they were to rejoice that their names were written in heaven (Luke 10:20). There is another book concerning the believers which is the record of all their thoughts and meditations concerning their Lord. We read of this in the beautiful passage in Malachi, "Then they that feared the Lord spake often one to another; and the Lord hearkened, and heard it, and a book of remembrance was written before Him for them that feared the Lord, and that thought upon His name" (Malachi 3:16). It is very possible that this book contains the difference between those who are saved plus the reward of having a crown, and those who are saved so as by fire with all their works burned away (1 Corinthians 3:14, 15).

In our passage it is evident that there are books which concern the unsaved ... The easiest to describe is the book of the records of the life and works of the unsaved. Here we read in no uncertain terms that the deeds of the unbelievers are recorded in heaven. How this is done we do not claim to know or venture to guess. It is hidden to God, but there should be no difficulty in believing this when man himself is able to record great symphonies and speeches in wax, and reduce whole libraries to microfilms. The fact is there. God states it. The unbeliever may scoff at it, but he will be judged by it. Then there is another book which definitely concerns the unbeliever, and which is called also "the book of life," though it is evidently very different from the Lamb's book of life! The names of the unbelievers are in this book, but are blotted out of the book. This is evident from a study of certain passages of the Scriptures.

It would seem that there is a book, something like a census record, in which the names of every individual to whom physical life is given are recorded, and that these names are blotted out of the book, leaving at the end a checklist which would be identical with the list in the book of the elect, chosen in Christ before the foundation of the world. We have already seen (3:5) that one of the promises made to the born-again ones (for who is the overcomer but he that believes that Jesus is the Son of God—1 John 5:4, 5) is that their names shall never be blotted out of the book of life. This would indicate that some names are blotted out, and since the names of the elect cannot be blotted out, it must be the names of the lost are in that particular book, along with the names of the saved, and that the names of the lost are blotted out. This would be further indicated by the statement in the last paragraph of the Bible (Revelation 22:19) that the names of those who subtract anything from the whole of God's revelation in the Scriptures shall be subtracted from the book of life.

SECTION THREE:
"I AM MAKING EVERYTHING NEW"

■   ■   ■

Revelation 21–22

Ages to Come

10

Seven New Things

Revelation 21:1–22:5

*Then I saw a new heaven and a new earth, for the first heaven and the
first earth had passed away.* (Revelation 21:1)

With Satan and sin and sinners forever removed, with death and hell
vanquished, and with Christ recognized and revered as Lord of all, a perfect age begins in which God becomes all in all. At last the eternal state
appears. Gloom has been banished, and glory begins. An everlasting
sunrise ushers in a new creation, for the world's last dark day has gone.
Human history has been consummated and God's new order is now
introduced.

These last chapters of Revelation compose a fitting close to God's
eternal purpose and marvelous provision for His own people (Ephesians
2:7). Here we are at the goal of all revelation! Satan's purpose throughout the ages was to separate God from humanity, but God is ultimately
victorious. At long last every divine purpose for humanity's eternal
well-being is realized and every divine promise is fulfilled.

In sublimity of language, the description John gives of the transpor-
tation of the glorified to the pinnacle of eternal peace stands unsurpassed. The moral competence of the apostle to behold and grasp the
glories of eternity was not in himself but was in the Holy Spirit. Under
His absolute control, John lived and moved in another realm of existence
and was thus prepared to receive the vision of the realities of heaven.

Somehow we feel that the chapters before us call for contemplation
more than interpretation, for reverence rather than research. We find
ourselves wishing that more had been recorded of our eternal abode.

One reason for the scarcity of facts regarding the eternal state is the limitation of language to express what John saw and felt. The best of words are only words at best, and a poor medium of expression when it comes to eternal glories. Once in heaven, amid its splendor, ours will be the exclamation of the queen of Sheba: "Not even half was told me" (1 Kings 10:7).

The key phrase of the closing section of Revelation is found in 21:5, "I am making everything new." Some writers suggest that now the millennial and the eternal ages blend into one perfect portrayal of unending glory. (Chronologically, 21:9–27 may precede 21:1–8. Verses 7 and 8 point to a time before the dawning of the eternal age.) The scene presented is indeed magnificent. At last Christ is the Victor of the ages and is about to hand over the kingdom to His Father. And what a thrill this act of surrender will be for both Father and Son! How we need to live more in the future than we do! Like the Apostle Paul, let us learn how to balance the gloomy "now" with the glorious "then."

First: New Heaven (Revelation 21:1)

I saw a new heaven . . . the first heaven . . . had passed away. (Revelation 21:1)

Comparing this entire verse with 20:11, we find the order reversed. At the great white throne earth and heaven fled away. Now it is heaven and earth. And this reversal is significant. In the old creation, which terminates in 20:11, God was intimately related with earth, on which He had a temple for His people. But now, with His people as a temple (21:3), everything is of a heavenly nature.

"Heaven" in 21:1 does not mean God's immediate presence, but the aerial heavens—that is, all that is between the earth and God Himself. The old heaven was where Satan operated from and was therefore not clean in God's sight. The new heaven is to be constituted so differently that the sun, moon, stars, and atmospheric properties will no longer be necessary. At last there will be a sunrise without a sunset.

There are three heavens referred to in Scripture:

1. The third heaven, or actual heaven, is the place to which Paul was caught up into the immediate presence of God. It is the re-

gion of divine glory and the dwelling place of angels and saints (2 Corinthians 12:1–5).

2. The second heaven, or astronomical heaven, is the setting of sun, moon, and starry host (Job 38:31–33).

3. The first heaven, or atmospheric heaven, is the air around and above us. Satan is referred to as the prince of this region (Ephesians 2:2).

Because the first heaven (God's abode) is eternal, it is not subject to any change. "The new heaven" implies the transformation of the aerial and astronomical heavens. With our heavenly bodies we shall be able to roam around the new heaven and the new earth.

A new midheaven is necessary because the present heavens are polluted by Satan's presence as the prince of the power of the air. This is why the stars are not pure in God's sight (Job 25:5). The space between us and God's abode is also cluttered with twentieth-century missiles, rockets, satellites, and miscellaneous orbital debris.

Second: New Earth (Revelation 21:1)

A new earth . . . the first earth had passed away. (Revelation 21:1)

Truly it will pass with little regret. The old earth must disappear because it has witnessed human sin and violence. It has also been soaked with the blood of millions of martyrs, stained by the blood of the Redeemer, and drenched with the tears of godly men and women. The new earth will never experience sin, sorrow, or slaughter. Some scholars suggest that the new heaven is to be the abode of the redeemed saints in glory, while the new earth is to be the abode of the redeemed ones saved in the tribulation who passed into the millennium.

The oceans are conspicuously absent from God's new creation: "There was no longer any sea" (21:1). How John's heart must have been comforted by such a revelation, for on the island of Patmos the apostle was experiencing the separation that the sea can cause! In heaven, however, nothing will cut us off from our dear ones. All who are the Lord's will be together forever.

There is a difference of opinion among Bible scholars as to whether the new creation (which will not appear before the old one disappears) is to be totally new or simply a remaking of the old. Some argue that fire does not symbolize annihilation but purging, and that God will merely purify the old creation, making it a fit habitation for His glorified saints. Other writers say that the language used by the New Testament is definite and emphatic: the old creation is to disappear totally. The expressions "fled away," "pass away with a great noise," and "be burned up" (2 Peter 3:10 KJV) imply (it is contended) not a mere transformation but an obliteration. The old creation is to be laid aside, as an outworn garment is folded up and utterly discarded.

But do not old rags have a way of reappearing as new clothes? When God says, "I am making everything new" (21:5), the word used for "new" is not the one meaning new in time or of recent appearance, but new as to form or quality, of different nature from the old. Thus "the new man" of Ephesians 4:24 (KJV) implies a different man altogether from the first man, Adam. Paul describes a new character of manhood that is spiritual and moral, after the pattern of Christ. And it is so with the *new* heaven and the *new* earth, which will differ completely in form and quality from the original heaven and earth.

But no matter which view we hold, the time from the first creation to the new creation spans the Bible. The first creation is the sphere and scene of first things. Sin, commenced in heaven by Lucifer, has wrecked the first creation. The new creation is altogether different, as shown by a study of John's "no mores." Human language is inadequate to describe all that he sees in heaven, so he tells us what will *not* be in heaven:

1. No hunger or thirst (7:16)
2. No sun or heat (7:16; 21:23; 22:5)
3. No tears or crying (7:17; 21:4)
4. No sea (21:1)
5. No death (21:4)
6. No sorrow (21:4)
7. No pain (21:4)
8. No temples (21:22)
9. No moon (21:23)
10. No night (21:25; 22:5)

11. No sin (21:27; 22:15)

12. No curse (22:3)

13. No lamps (22:5)

With Satan forever banished, temptation will be forever absent. With the vista of the ages of the ages, we reach a world without tragedy, tribulation, or evil practices, a world that is "the home of righteousness" (2 Peter 3:13). Passages to compare are Matthew 24:35; Hebrews 1:1–12; 12:25–29; 2 Peter 3; Isaiah 34:4; 65:17; 66:22. With such a glorious prospect awaiting us, should we not strive to live with eternity's values in view? Present trials and disappointments are not to be compared with the glory to be revealed in that eternal day.

Third: New Jerusalem (Revelation 21:2, 9–21)

I saw the Holy City, the New Jerusalem. (Revelation 21:1)

In his description of perfect unity, John gives us an insight into the church's governmental relationship to everything else. (Here again we should note John's verbs of experience: I *saw;* I *heard.*) The New Jerusalem is contrasted with the old one. The earthly Jerusalem, the so-called Holy City, is most imperfect, but the New Jerusalem is perfect, holy, and from heaven. As a bride dressed in beautiful bridal robes, the church descends in all her glory. Formed by the wooing of the Spirit in the wilderness below, she was caught up at the return of the Bridegroom and, after her marriage to Him, is now adorned with eternal loveliness.

Some writers believe that Revelation 21:1 is an elaboration of the marriage supper of the Lamb (19:7). The first bride of the Bible (Genesis 2:18–24) can be used as a picture of the church's origin and relationship to Christ. The false bride, the prostitute (17:5), shone in human glory, but the Lamb's bride shines in the reflected beauty and glory of God. Even in the eternal state she lacks any inherent glory: "it shone with the glory of God" (21:11; see also Philippians 3:20–21).

John also likens the church to a city (see also 3:12). William Newell's exposition of the society of the redeemed, as a city, is extremely helpful. Here is an adapted summary of some of his points.

It is a literal city

Everything suggests literalness—gold, streets, dimensions, stones. This city comes *down*, for it is impossible to build a *holy* city here. In this new home of the church all the materials are provided by God. (The prostitute and the city of Babylon are Satan's counterfeit of 21:2, which is a summary of 21:9–11.)

It is a heavenly city

It comes down out of heaven, since it is for heavenly people. Without a heavenly nature (which the Holy Spirit makes possible in regeneration), one cannot respond to his eternal environment. "Instead, they were longing for a better country—a heavenly one. Therefore God is not ashamed to be called their God, for he has prepared a city for them" (Hebrews 11:16).

It is a home city

The city John so fully describes is to be the eternal home of Christ and His own, whose glorified bodies will correspond to Christ's. Others, of course, will also share this glory (21:24–26), but the church will be as a wife at home. The word "dwell" (Psalm 23:6) means to be "at home." What a prospect—at home with the Lord forever!

It is a vast city

The figures used for this city stagger the imagination. The length and width and height of this cubelike city are equal: 12,000 stadia (about 1,500 miles). Government perfection is suggested by the constant repetition of the number 12. There are twelve gates, angels, tribes, foundations, apostles, precious stones, and pearls. The twelve gates are identified with Israel (21:12) and the twelve foundations with the church (19:14; see also Ephesians 2:20).

It is a glorious city

The glory of God is to be its light: "It shone with the glory of God, and its brilliance was like that of a very precious jewel, like a jasper, clear as crystal" (21:11). The Lamb is to be the lamp—that is, the source of all necessary illumination. There will be no need of natural lights. The mention of a "measuring rod" (21:15) implies that when God measures a thing, He intends to use what belongs to Him. And everything will measure up to *His* requirements for the glorified; His church will be adorned with eternal loveliness.

It is a capital city

God's eternal home is to be in this capital city of the new creation, more resplendent than any renowned capital in the world today. This is the center of divine presence and government in the universe of God and the Lamb. With each view of the city the Lamb is named, and the seven-fold reference to Him (21:9, 14, 22, 23, 27; 22:1, 3) indicates that even though Christ delivers up the kingdom to the Father, He nevertheless shares it with the redeemed.

Fourth: New Fellowship (Revelation 21:3–8)

They will be his people, and God himself will be with them. (Revelation 21:3)

At last the broken fellowship of the first garden (Genesis 3) is fully, completely, and eternally restored. Never again will Satan or humans be able to rupture such fellowship. What is heaven? Is it not a society of perfectly restored souls in ecstatic, unrestrained fellowship with God? Here then is a heaven coming down out of heaven.

But God will not come down to dwell with men until the old creation passes away. This present earth is too corrupt to be God's abode. The phrase "with men" occurs three times, suggesting a blessed and eternal communion between God and men. God's delight is to dwell with the sons of men (Proverbs 8:31). The result of this precious fellowship is a world without tears, for only God is able to dry our tears: "He will wipe every tear from their eyes. There will be no more death or mourning or crying or pain, for the old order of things has passed away" (21:4). What a day!

Fifth: New Temple (Revelation 21:22)

The Lord Almighty and the Lamb are its temple. (21:22)

At long last the shadows give way to the substance (Hebrews 9:23–24). Everything associated with the tabernacle and the temple merely typified the Lord God and the Lamb. Ezekiel's millennial temple was the center of worship for an earthly city, but now everything centers around the throne, to which all have access. In ancient times God had a temple for His people; in this present church age He has a redeemed people as His temple. But John describes the *eternal* age, when God will provide *Himself* as a temple for His own.

When John speaks of the temple of God being opened in heaven, he uses a Greek word for temple that means "the holiest of all" and refers to the shrine of shrines into which the high priest alone entered, and only once a year. God makes good His unchanging grace to His people, and His throne and presence in their midst will gloriously supersede the ark in the tabernacle and the temple of old. This reference, along with the previous one about measuring the temple (11:1–2), implies that the secret abode of the safeguarded children of God is now revealed.

Amid the crash of empires and the passing of the old world, John assures us that all the saints are under the shadow of the Almighty and that access to God requires no intervention of a priest or other mediator. The absence of a temple thus signifies full and free access for all true worshipers. As Walter Scott so fittingly expresses it: "What need of a temple? God in the greatness of His Being, and as the One who has acted and ruled of old, is now revealed in glory by the Lamb. The divine Presence is equally diffused. God and the Lamb make themselves known throughout every part of the vast city of gold."

God has regarded His people as His temple, but now He is their true and living Temple, as well as their true Ark and their everlasting Manna. Around the sacred peak of Sinai, where the first tabernacle was pitched, there were lightnings and thunders—tokens of the holy law that the power of the world had defied. Now the habitation of God is always an open sanctuary to the faithful, but a clouded and lightning-crowned Sinai to all who reject God (Hebrews 12:18–24).

Sixth: New Light (Revelation 21:23–25)

The glory of God gives it light. (Revelation 21:23)

The eternal Holy City is to have a remarkable, supernatural lighting system. It does not need the sun or the moon to shine on it (21:23). Now we have natural illumination provided by sun, moon, and stars. The sun is the source of life and light for all on earth, and the moon and stars are only reflectors. But these heavenly bodies, called into being from ancient times to perform certain functions, now pass away with the old heavens. At present we have artificial illumination, for technology has succeeded very well in lighting up our darkness at night. But in the New City, God and the Lamb provide all necessary light. Christ referred to Himself as the Light of the world, and He will be the Light of the eternal world. Along with God, He will be the Light of the new world as well as the old. Together they are to provide all necessary illumination. There will be "no night there" (21:25) in that eternal day.

The gates of the new city will never be shut. Police will be unnecessary to guard the city dwellers, since there will be no more thieves. Nations can come and go. All that accompanies sinful darkness disappears. Everything natural and artificial has vanished. Truly the prospect of such perfect provision overwhelms us! Amid the darkness of this present world we are to "shine like lights" (Philippians 2:15), and in the new world we shall still shine as we reflect Christ's eternal glory.

Seventh: New Paradise (Revelation 22:1–5)

Blessed are those who wash their robes, that they may have the right to the tree of life and may go through the gates into the city. (Revelation 22:14)

There are several important features to bear in mind in the study of this chapter as a whole.

1. A book is only valuable in proportion to the truth it reveals. "These words are trustworthy and true" (22:6). Here we have a solemn affirmation as to the veracity of Scripture. An angel

from heaven authenticates the prophecies of Revelation. All the prophets of old were under the control of the Spirit of truth.

2. A book is closely associated with its writer. Five times the name "John" appears as the writer of Revelation: "Write on a scroll what you see" (1:11). This entire book was written by John, who was familiar with writing (see 2 John 12; 3 John 13). Higher criticism may reject the Apostle John as the writer of Revelation, but as Hilgenfield aptly remarks, "An unknown John whose name has disappeared from history, leaving hardly any trace behind, can scarcely have given commandments in the name of Christ and the Spirit to the seven churches." The fivefold use of John's name demonstrates that the John who wrote the Fourth Gospel and the three epistles bearing his name also penned Revelation, as he was divinely instructed to do (1:9, 19; 22:8).

3. A book not sealed is open for perusal and profit. What was sealed in Daniel's day (Daniel 12:4) is now exposed. Let us not forget that revelation means an "unveiling," and this is just what the whole of the book is. The nearer we approach the events recorded in it, the clearer the prophecies become (22:10).

What are the specifics about this new paradise, this garden from which the serpent and sin are forever excluded? Let us briefly note some of them. In the old creation all the rivers ran into the sea, but here we have a river without a sea—a river responsible for fertilization and vegetation in the new creation. Rivers open the Bible (Genesis 2:10) and close it (22:1). This river flows from the throne, which is its spring and source. The water of this divine river is clear as crystal—totally pure, requiring no treatment to purify it. All thrones give place to the throne of God and of the Lamb (1 Corinthians 15:24–28).

The Bible, which opens with a tree of life in the garden (Genesis 2:9), closes with another tree of life (Revelation 2:22), this one in the midst of a street, signifying no seclusion or exclusion. All are to have access to this tree—its monthly fruits are for the saints and its healing leaves are for the nations. Ezekiel talks of such a tree (Ezekiel 47:12). Because all sickness and death have passed away (21:4), the expression "for the healing of the nations" is better translated as "for the health of the nations."

In Genesis 2:8–15 God created a material home for humans within a garden. But that original garden witnessed satanic rebellion and human transgression (Genesis 3:1–7). Now we have a garden surpassing the first one in every way. Nothing will ever wither or die in it. The curse pronounced by God in earth's first garden is forever removed. The calamity of Eden will not happen again. With sin forever banished, there will be no more curse. The last word of the Old Testament is "curse": "He will turn the hearts of the fathers to their children, and the hearts of the children to their fathers, or else I come and strike the earth with a curse" (Malachi 4:6). But the New Testament opens with Jesus Christ, the One who came to bear the curse (Galatians 3:13), and closes not with a curse (Revelation 22:3) but with a benediction (Revelation 22:21).

The ultimate triumph of Christ can be presented in this way:

In Genesis: "In the beginning God created the heavens and earth."
In Revelation: "I saw a new heaven and a new earth."
In Genesis: "The darkness he called night."
In Revelation: "There shall be no night there."
In Genesis: "Thou shalt surely die."
In Revelation: "Death shall be no more."
In Genesis: "I will greatly multiply your pain."
In Revelation: "Neither shall there be any more pain."
In Genesis: "Cursed is the ground for your sake."
In Revelation: "There shall be no more curse."
In Genesis: "Driven from the tree of life."
In Revelation: The tree of life appears.
In Genesis: Satan appears.
In Revelation: Satan disappears.
In Genesis: Abraham sought the foundation of city.
In Revelation: The city is brought to final perfection and glory.

John goes on to declare that in the new creation God's servants are to be ceaselessly active: "they will reign for ever and ever" (22:5). This means that the saints are not going to sit around playing harps all the time. With perfect, glorified minds and bodies, it will be our joy to serve the Lord as we cannot do now because of the hindering influence of sin. Undreamed-of privileges are to be ours in the land that is fairer than day: we will see His face. Whose face? That of the Lamb (22:4)! Are we living in anticipation of the thrill when for the first time our eyes will behold the King in all His beauty?

> Face to face with Christ my Saviour—
> Face to face—what will it be—
> When with rapture I behold Him,
> Jesus Christ Who died for me?

Speechless wonder will be ours as we look upon that face before which heaven and earth fled away. The greatest wonder will be our transformation into His likeness. "His name," says John, "will be on their foreheads" (22:4). By the *name* we are to understand the character or nature of God. The seal, of course, is the sign of ownership and security. But why the reference to the forehead? The implication is that the seal will be in a place easily seen by others. We are publicly and perfectly to reflect the character of God (7:3).

Before closing his marvelous description of this "Holy City, the new Jerusalem" (21:2), John has another word regarding its radiance of glory and light: "There will be no more night. They will not need the light of a lamp or the light of the sun, for the Lord God will give them light" (22:5). No night, no candle, no sun—just a glorious city of light that stands in contrast to the present world of darkness. Now only half the world can have light at one time, but when the Lord God gives light, it will be diffused everywhere at the same time. Such eternal light is outside the scope of scientific investigation; it transcends our human, finite comprehension. What a city! No night, with its darkness and fear; no candlelight services; no sunrises or sunsets!

The revelation of Jesus Christ is accomplished. The great unveiling of Him as the all-powerful Lamb is both ratified and enforced. After the wonderful panorama of His glory, grace, and government, the Revelation closes with the simplest, sweetest, and shortest of benedictions. In both the prologue and epilogue of Revelation, the Second Coming of our Lord is declared (1:7; 22:20). In the epilogue (22:6–21), concise sentences provide a striking conclusion to this remarkable book. As we examine the words closely, we find that they condense the main themes of Revelation, namely, the certainty of the fulfillment of prophecy and the imminence of this fulfillment.

The angel who appears speaks of himself in the third person and adds a beatitude to the promise of Christ's return (22:6). Parallels with the prologue (1:1–8) are striking.

John, overwhelmed by the astonishing vision and the climatic scene of the Holy City, falls in worship at the feet of the angelic herald. But the angel reminds him that all adoration, praise, and reverence belong to God alone.

Then John is instructed to regard Christ's Second Coming as being near (22:10). The visions John received were not to be kept secret, as if the day were far off. They belong to the present, for Christ is about to appear. Next comes a solemn declaration of the fixed, unalterable fate of a deliberate human choice, with human character continuing to produce its inevitable development and fruit; the doom of the godless is sealed. "Let him who is vile continue to be vile; . . . let him who is holy continue to be holy" (22:11).

In the repeated designation "I am the Alpha and the Omega" (1:8, 11; 22:13) we have striking evidence of Christ's deity. "Dogs" symbolize the offensive, uncontrolled uncleanness of all who reject the cleansing blood of the Lamb and are shut outside the Holy City (22:15). The morning star, shining most brightly just before the dawn, is a fitting symbol of the return of Christ, who will bring the dawn of an age of radiant light (22:16).

Even as a blessing is attached to the proper use of this book, so also a solemn warning is issued against its abuse: a woe upon all who tamper with any of its teachings. This warning refers to the willful perversion and distortion of its great truths. All who love the book must guard its integrity (22:18–19) and must declare the whole counsel of God.

11

Seven Final Things

Revelation 22:6–21

Do not seal up the words of the prophecy of this book, because the time is near.
(Revelation 22:10)

Revelation is a book of lasts. In this last section of the last book of the Bible, seven last things stand out.

First: Final Witness (Revelation 22:6–13)

I, John, am the one who heard and saw these things. (Revelation 22:8)

This may refer to the crowning vision that John had of the new paradise (22:1–7), the consummation of the revelation of Jesus Christ (1:1). But these verbs of experience also confirm the authenticity of Revelation as a whole.

Second: Final Beatitude (Revelation 22:14–15)

Blessed are those who wash their robes, that they may have the right to the tree of life and may go through the gates into the city. (Revelation 22:14)

Previously we described all the beatitudes of Revelation. Here we are reminded that obedience to all God has revealed brings a rich reward (John 13:17). Believers walk on two feet—trust and obedience.

Third: Final Divine Testimony (Revelation 22:16, 18–20)

I, Jesus. (Revelation 22:16)

Alive forevermore, Christ confirms all the prophecies of the book of Revelation, which are divinely designed to reveal Him in all His glory and majesty. The phrase "I, Jesus" declares Him to be the Jesus of all history. What a calm yet emphatic assertion of dignity this is: "I, Jesus, have sent my angel to give you this testimony" (v. 16). The personal pronoun is emphatic.

Also, He is both Root and Morning Star. A root is of the earth and symbolizes His humanity, but the star is from above and speaks of His deity. Revelation is the book of His unveiling, and He is the medium of its communication: "He who testifies to these things" (v. 20). If the words of Jesus mean what they say, then to tamper with any part of this sublime book is tragic. To mutilate any part of it (or any part of the Bible, for that matter) merits divine judgment.

Fourth: Final Heavenly Invitation (Revelation 22:17)

Yes, I am coming soon. (Revelation 22:20)

To rightly understand John's triple use of "come," we must examine each in its context. The first two actually mean "Come Thou!" The first is a double "come": "The Spirit and the bride say 'Come!'" Whom are they addressing? The One who, three times in the chapter, says, "I am coming soon" (22:7, 12, 20). The Holy Spirit speaks through His Bride, the church, and joins with her in response to the voice of Him who is coming as the Morning Star. Then the individual saint (as well as the saints collectively) says, "Come!" Do we have a strong personal desire to welcome the returning Lord? The third "come" is related to the sinner, who as a thirsty one is bidden to come and take of the living waters before it is forever too late.

Fifth: Final Promise (Revelation 22:20)

I am coming soon. (Revelation 22:7)

Before his death, resurrection, and ascension our Lord promised to return for His true church (John 14:1–3), and here for the last time He confirms His promise with the words, "I am coming soon." The Bible is loaded with promises, as I have shown in a companion volume, *All the Promises of the Bible*. But this is the most blessed promise of all.

Sixth: Final Prayer (Revelation 22:20)

Amen. Come, Lord Jesus. (Revelation 22:20)

In another companion volume, *All the Prayers of the Bible*, you will find how prayer permeates Scriptures. John echoes the desire of the saints throughout the ages in his brief but heartfelt supplication, "Amen. Come, Lord Jesus."

Seventh: Final Benediction (Revelation 22:21)

The grace of the Lord Jesus be with God's people. Amen. (Revelation 22:21)

The last book of the Bible, so heavy with wrath and judgments, ends with *grace*, not *curse* (as the Old Testament ends). "Amen!" So be it. The absolute certainty of truth is confirmed, and all the glories of eternity are to be ours through grace alone. Thus the book that begins with "the revelation of Jesus Christ" ends with the grace of the Lord Jesus. As Christina Rossetti expresses it: "All that lies between has not effected towards ourselves its purpose unless we conclude the whole matter in a culminating grace by fearing God and keeping His commandments."

The hour is late, the sands of time are sinking. May we be found living as children of the dawn, with our faces turned toward the eternal sunrise! May the things of earth grow strangely dim in the light of such glory and grace! As we linger amid the shadows, may we be found singing with Robert Murray McCheyne (1813–43):

"I Am Debtor"

When this passing world is done,
When has sunk yon glaring sun,
When we stand with Christ in glory,
Looking o'er life's finished story;
Then Lord, shall I fully know—
Not till then—how much I owe.

When I stand before the throne,
Dressed in beauty not my own;
When I see Thee as Thou art,
Love Thee with unsinning heart;
Then, Lord, shall I fully know—
Not till then—how much I owe.

Chosen not for good in me,
Wakened up from wrath to flee;
Hidden in the Saviour's side,
By the Spirit sanctified;
Teach me, Lord, on earth to show,
By my love, how much I owe.

Conclusion

Now Is the Time of Harvest

Dr. Mateen A. Elass[1]

It is no easy task to peer ahead through the veils of time to assess the condition of both church and world when the Lord returns in triumph at the Second Coming. Our work is made significantly easier by the teachings of the Scriptures, but even so, the appropriate biblical texts provide us mainly with tantalizing hints or vague teachings concerning the extent and effectiveness of evangelism as the Second Coming approaches. In this essay, we will look at those Scriptures that deal with the church's call to evangelism and the extent to which the world is won to Christ as the end of history draws near.

Evangelism and the End Times

Though the term "end times" is commonly used to refer to that period of time immediately preceding the Second Coming of Christ, in the New Testament it is understood more broadly as the indefinite period extending from the resurrection and ascension of the Lord until His triumphal return to consummate history. Thus, the early church understood itself to be living in the end times and was filled with expectancy over the Lord's imminent return. This means, among other things, that over the last two thousand years Christians in every generation have been living in the end times, and the mission of the church to take the gospel to the whole world has been understood in that context. To speak about evangelism in the end times, then, means to speak about the church's primary mission as it has existed unchanged from the birth of the body of Christ at Pentecost until now, and its ongoing, unchanging mission until the Parousia.[2]

This divine charter is found in countless places in the Scriptures, as early as God's covenant election of the people of Israel. Abraham's descendants were chosen by grace not only to belong to God and not only to receive His divine blessing but also to carry out a divine mission on behalf of the world. Old Testament scholar H. H. Rowley writes, "Election is for service. And if God chose Israel, it was not alone that He might reveal Himself to her, but that He might claim her for service."[3] What is this vocation to which the Old Testament people of God are called? It is principally to live according to God's code of holiness, thereby witnessing to the world God's salvation and glory (cf. Isaiah 43:10, 21; 44:8; 49:3). Israel is given positive responsibilities as God's primary agent for announcing and modeling His work of worldwide redemption. In Isaiah 42:6–7 God announces:

> I, the LORD, have called you in righteousness;
>   I will take hold of your hand.
> I will keep you and will make you
>   to be a covenant for the people
>   and a light for the Gentiles,
> to open eyes that are blind,
>   to free captives from prison
>   and to release from the dungeon
>   those who sit in darkness.

It comes as no surprise that Jesus, when announcing the inauguration of His ministry (cf. Luke 4:14–21), quotes from a sister passage, Isaiah 61:1–2. By this He indicates His intention to fulfill through His life's work what Israel as a nation had failed to accomplish in her vocation as the servant of Yahweh:

> The Spirit of the Lord is on me,
>   because he has anointed me
>   to preach good news to the poor.

He has sent me to proclaim freedom for the prisoners
   and recovery of sight for the blind,
to release the oppressed,
   to proclaim the year of the Lord's favor. (Luke 4:18–19)

During His ministry, Jesus begins to gather around Him disciples to be trained as agents of this mission. In Matthew 9:35–10:16 our Lord not only traverses Israel "preaching the good news of the kingdom" but authorizes His twelve disciples to carry out this same mission. As a result of this, they are called apostles ("sent ones") for the first time (Matthew 10:2; cf. Mark 6:30; Luke 6:13). Jesus justifies their involvement by declaring that "the harvest is plentiful but the workers are few. Ask the Lord of the harvest, therefore, to send out workers into his harvest field" (Matthew 9:37–38). For three years He continues to carry out this call of His Father and train His followers as harvesters. Finally He lays the foundation for its eternal success with His own death and resurrection. Then as the risen Lord, Jesus commissions His followers to expand the mission by their becoming a light to the nations.[4]

Perhaps the most famous example of this charter is found in Matthew 28:18–20, known popularly as the Great Commission. On the basis of Jesus' complete authority as Lord, His recruits are given the task of making disciples from among all the nations, and they are given the assurance that Jesus will continue to be with them (in the person of the Holy Spirit) "to the very end of the age." One clear implication of this Great Commission is the assumption that the mandate to evangelize the world remains in force from the beginning of the church's life until Christ's return at the consummation of all things.[5] The proclamation of the gospel is for all people groups at all points of history. A second implication is that the promise of Christ's presence with the church in her mission will ensure its success. Through the outpouring of His Spirit upon the community of faith, Jesus both authorizes and energizes His followers to reach the ends of the earth with the gospel.[6]

For this reason, theologians have always insisted that one of the essential marks of the true church is her apostolicity; i.e., that she is *sent* in mission to the whole world. Where the church in any age does not evidence this calling, she has lost one of the major reasons for her existence. But where the church places the mission of world evangelism at the heart of her existence, there she flourishes in her obedience to Christ. Hence as Jesus speaks of the approaching end, he emphasizes that since no one knows when the Son of Man will return, each believer must be ready and watching, ever at his post doing the work to which God has called him (Matthew 24:42). Significantly, the call to bear witness to Jesus is at the top of the Christian's work list.

The Witness of the Church to Christ in the End Times

It remains now for us to consider what the Scriptures say concerning the effectiveness of the church's witness to Christ as the end of time approaches. To do so, we will review the relevant chapters in the Synoptic Gospels (Matthew 24–25; Mark 13; Luke 21) as well as material found in Paul and Revelation.

In the parallel Synoptic accounts, four things stand out as characteristic of the last days. *First,* there will be many counterfeit spiritual movements competing with the church for the allegiance of human hearts. Jesus declares in Matthew 24:4–5 (par Mark 13:5–6; Luke 21:8), "Watch out that no one deceives you. For many will come in my name, claiming, 'I am the Christ,' and will deceive many." While this indicates that the end of time will likely see an increased spiritual hunger within the human race, it also implies that the masses will not have much true spiritual discernment—"many will be deceived." Jesus is particularly concerned that those already within the fold are not misled during this time.

Second, there will be an increase of severe persecution against God's people. This, together with false prophets arising within the church, will cause many to leave the faith. So Jesus says, "You will be handed over to be persecuted and put to death, and you will be hated by all nations because of me. At that time, many will turn away from the faith and will betray and hate each other, and many false prophets will appear and deceive many people" (Matthew 24:9–11; cf. Mark 13:9–13; Luke 21:12–19). The parallel accounts in Mark and Luke highlight the fact that the persecuted, when brought before political authorities, will become witnesses in a way they had never envisioned—empowered and inspired by the Holy Spirit in what they say. Yet this wave of persecution and accompanying tribulation will be so fierce that according to Jesus no one would survive if God had not decided to intervene to shorten this time period "for the sake of the elect" (Matthew 24:22).[7]

Third, there will be a strong moral decline in the world outside the church, which will have a deleterious effect on love for God in the hearts of many within the church. Jesus says, "Because of the increase of wickedness, the love of most will grow cold, but he who stands firm to the end will be saved" (Matthew 24:12–13).[8] Along the same lines, the Apostle Paul expects that the time will come (presumably as the end draws near) when people will not endure sound doctrine, even within the church. "Instead, to suit their own desires, they will gather around them a great number of teachers to say what their itching ears want to hear. They will turn their ears away form the truth and turn aside to myth" (1 Timothy 4:3–4). Timothy is nevertheless admonished by Paul to keep his head in the midst of all this and to "do the work of an evangelist, discharging all the duties of [his] ministry" (verse 5).

Last, in the Gospel accounts Jesus predicts that the gospel of the kingdom of God will be proclaimed in all the world as a testimony to all people groups; then the end will come. Though this declaration tells us much of God's intention that news of His glory in Christ be spread to all the inhabited world, it says nothing concerning the extent of positive or negative response by the evangelized. Though we know from Matthew 24:31 (cf. Mark 13:27) that the elect will be gathered from the four corners of the earth, we are told nothing of the size of this group.[9] For hints about this we must turn elsewhere.

The "Full Number" and "All Israel"

In Romans 9–11, the Apostle Paul deals with the question of Israel's recalcitrance before the gospel in light of God's promise to keep Israel as His people. Despite knowing that the bulk of Israelites of his day have rejected Jesus as their Messiah, Paul states clearly that God's Word (i.e., His saving promise to Israel) has not failed (9:6). The rest of Romans 9–11 is devoted to proving this point. In Romans 11 Paul offers his final reason why God has not failed in His faithfulness to Israel, even though many of the apostles' Jewish contemporaries had hard hearts. At the end of time, Paul says, after "the full number of the Gentiles" has come into the fold, "all Israel will be saved" (11:25–26). Two questions naturally arise as we seek to interpret this text: what is the significance of the term "full number" and what does Paul mean by "all Israel"?

A few scholars have speculated that by "full number" Paul could mean the Gentile world as a whole. This presupposes a close parallel with Paul's usage of the same Greek word *(plērōma)* in 11:12, where the "fullness" of Israel most likely means her return to God en masse. Paul then would be saying, "A hardening has come in part upon Israel until the Gentile world as a whole is saved, then Israel as a whole will be saved." Such a view is possible, although Paul gives us no clear indication here that he envisions a complete turning of the Gentile world to God. But even if such were the case, Paul would no doubt continue to maintain (as he has throughout Romans 9 up until this point) that this pattern conforms to God's electing purpose and that the full number of those who come in do so as a result of having been elected by God to salvation. There is no thought of universalism here, as if all humanity—past, present, and future—is finally saved by God. Rather, Paul envisions only the possibility that as the end approaches, more and more Gentiles will turn to Christ until the vast majority among the nations (i.e., the Gentile world as a whole) comes to faith, after which "all Israel will be saved."

However, it is more likely that "full number" in 11:25 gets its sense of "fullness" not from the largeness of its size (which may or may not be) but from the fact that it contains the total number determined in advance by God. The use of *plērōma* in Galatians 4:4 provides an apt parallel. In its context there, "fullness" must refer not to the completion of time as a whole but to the reaching of a particular point in time decreed by God. For this reason, most scholars generally agree that the term "full number," while signifying a numerical quantity, refers either to the total number of those chosen from among the Gentiles throughout the ages or to that portion of the total still to come to faith between Paul's day and the ingathering of Israel.[10] Unfortunately, we learn nothing from Paul here about whether the "full number" of Gentiles to be saved by the end of history is extremely large or not. Thus, we can say nothing on the basis of this passage concerning the effectiveness of the church's work of evangelism in the last days.

Concerning the phrase "all Israel" in 11:26, we are a bit better off. Paul affirms that after the Gentile mission is completed all Israel will be saved. "Israel" here undoubtedly refers to that group represented in the previous verse, i.e., the ethnic Jewish nation that "experienced a hardening in part, until the full number of the Gentiles has come in" (11:25). But does "all Israel" then mean ethnic Israel comprising every individual Jew alive at the time of Christ's return, or ethnic Israel as a whole, without regard to every particular Israelite?

There are obvious cases in the Septuagint and extrabiblical Jewish writings where "all Israel" does not demand or imply numerical entirety, as well as passages where such a notion is necessarily excluded.[11] Further, as we have noted concerning Paul's thought in verse 25, "fullness" or "the full number" does not necessarily connote entirety; it may just as well mean "completeness." If we are correct that in verse 25 "the full number of the Gentiles" means the completed number from the Gentile nations of those predetermined by God according to election and if we should see a positive correspondence between this full number in verse 25 and "all Israel" in verse 26, then it becomes highly likely that for Paul "all Israel" does not mean every Israelite alive at the end of history. Rather it means the full number of those chosen by God—though, as the flow of his thought makes clear, these include the vast majority of hardened Israel.

What then can we say about Paul's perspective on the degree of human response to the gospel as the Second Coming approaches? It seems that the apostle envisions a time of large-scale conversions to Christ immediately prior to His return. Though we cannot be sure that the number of Gentiles represented in this activity will be enormous, we can say with confidence that an extensive spiritual revival will take place within ethnic Israel, and Jews en masse will turn in repentance and faith toward the risen Lord.

Some have argued more generally that Paul optimistically envisioned the conversion of the whole world to Christ. They point to such passages as Romans 11:32 ("For God has bound all men over to disobedience so that he may have mercy on them all") and Colossians 1:19–20 ("For God was pleased to have all his fullness dwell in him [Christ], and through him to reconcile to himself all things, whether things on earth or things in heaven, by making peace through his blood, shed on the cross"). From these they argue that we are to expect the world eventually to turn to Christ. But when seen in the context of Paul's thought generally, such passages are tempered by Paul's certain declarations that the destiny of the enemies of the gospel is destruction (e.g., Romans 2:5–16; 2 Corinthians 11:13–15; Galatians 6:7–8; Philippians 3:19; 1 Thessalonians 5:3). Likewise, we are reminded of Jesus' teachings in Matthew 7:13–14, where He indicates that the road to destruction is broad and many walk down it to the wide gates of hell, whereas the road leading to life is narrow and few travel it to the small gates of heaven. Though the gospel is broadcast to all the inhabited earth, though the divine invitation goes out to all, only a relatively small percentage in the end seem to find heaven as their home ("Many are invited, but few are chosen" [Matthew 22:14]).

In any case, we are peering now into areas that are beyond our certain knowledge. The number of the elect, be it great or small, is God's business. Likewise, the degree to which the world responds to the gospel is ultimately in God's hands, not ours. Our task as Christians is simply to be willing instruments in the service of God's mission of reconciling lost sinners to Himself. As workers, we go out into the harvest field, which God in His sovereignty has caused to ripen according to His own often inscrutable good pleasure. Our call to evangelism today is the same one given to Christians in the first century—the same one given to those in generations after us, should the Lord tarry. We are to be about our task, with excitement and devotion sparked by our intimacy with the Master, empowered and inspired by the might and wisdom of the Holy Spirit, obedient to God as we witness with humility to Jesus Christ wherever we are placed. May God grant His church to be at her post with Christ returns in glory! May we reach the ends of the earth with His irresistible love. Amen. Come Lord Jesus!

Endnotes

1. Mateen A. Elass has served as Minister of Adult Education at First Presbyterian Church of Colorado Springs since 1994. An ordained Presbyterian minister, he has served in several churches prior to his present position. He teaches regularly as an adjunct professor for Fuller Seminary and Knox Seminary in Colorado. He received a Ph.D. in New Testament studies from the University of Durham, England, as well as a M.Div. and a M.A. in Biblical Studies from Fuller Theological Seminary.

2. The term "parousia" is a loan-word from biblical Greek, and originally meant "presence" or "coming." In the New Testament, it serves as a technical term denoting the Second Coming of Christ.

3. H. H. Rowley, *The Biblical Doctrine of Election,* London: Lutterworth Press, 1950; p. 43.

4. To the Hebrew mind, the terms "Gentiles," "nations," and "people groups" are synonymous.

5. The apostle Paul understood that the purpose of the church was to make known the saving works of God. So he speaks in Ephesians 1:9–10 of God's having now made known the mystery of His will "according to his good pleasure, which he purposed in Christ, to be put into effect when the times will have reached their fulfillment—to bring all things in heaven and on earth together under one head, even Christ" (cf. also Colossians 1:20).

6. The apostle John in the fourth Gospel is the only one to record Jesus' words concerning his understanding of the work of the Holy Spirit. In John 16:8–11, we find: "When he comes, he will convict the world of guilt in regard to sin and righteousness and judgment: in regard to sin, because men do not believe in me, in regard to righteousness, because I am going to the Father, where you can see me no longer; and in regard to judgment, because the prince of this world now stands condemned."

In Acts, Luke opens with a scene in which the risen Lord speaks his last words to the disciples before ascending to heaven. His final sentence serves as the climax of his commission to the fledgling church: "You will receive power when the Holy Spirit comes upon you; and you will be my witnesses in Jerusalem, and in all Judea and Samaria, and to the ends of the earth" (Acts 1:8). The rest of the book of Acts is Luke's attempt to demonstrate how, through the inspiration and power of the Spirit, this mandate is carried out as the gospel moves from the center of Jewish faith (Jerusalem) to the center of secular power (Rome).

7. Interestingly, the reason given for God's intervention is the fate of the elect; i.e., in order to keep the chosen from falling away due to relentless suffering, God shortens this period of tribulation.

8. In 2 Timothy 3:1–5, the Apostle Paul offers what seems to be a commentary on Jesus' teaching in Matthew: "But mark this: There will be terrible times in the last days. People will be lovers of themselves, lovers of money, boastful, proud, abusive, disobedient to their parents, ungrateful, unholy, without love, unforgiving, slanderous, without self-control, brutal, not lovers of the good, treacherous, rash, conceited, lovers of pleasure rather than lovers of God— having a form of godliness but denying its power. Have nothing to do with them." See also 2 Thessalonians 2:12 where Paul links unbelief with delight in wickedness.

9. Second Peter 3:9 also emphasizes God's intention that all have a chance to hear and respond to His invitation in Christ: "The Lord is not slow in keeping his promise, as some understand slowness. He is patient with you, not wanting anyone to perish, but everyone to come to repentance." However, we learn nothing here concerning the size of the group that ultimately benefits from God's patience.

10. According to the rabbis, after the fall of Adam and Eve the precise number of humans was decreed until the day of judgment, which could not take place until that number was reached. The *Syriac Apocalypse of Baruch* 23:4–5a, demonstrates this understanding of a fixed numbering of the human race which must be reached before God's judgment and reward is meted out: "For when Adam sinned and death was decreed against those who were to be born, the multitude of those who would be born was numbered. And for that number a place was prepared where the living ones might live and where the dead might be preserved. No creature will live again unless the number that has been appointed is completed." (Translation by A. F. J. Klijn in *The Old Testament Pseudepigrapha*, James H. Charlesworth, ed.; 1:629.)

Even more telling is the account of 4 Ezra 4:35–37, where in reply to Ezra's impatient cry, the Most High points to a future date when the number of the righteous will be completed. "Did not the souls of the righteous in their chambers ask about these matters, saying, 'How long are we to remain here? And when will come the harvest of our reward?' And Jeremiel the archangel answered them and said, 'When the number of those like yourselves is completed; for he has weighed the age in the balance, and measured the times by measure, and numbered the times by number; and he will not move or arouse them until that measure is fulfilled.' " (Translation by B. M. Metzger in *The Old Testament Pseudepigrapha*, 1:531.) Parallels with the thought of a fixed number of elect may also be found in Revelation 6:11; 7:4; and 14:1.

11. Cf. 1 Samuel 7:5; 11:15; 13:20; 2 Samuel 15:6; 18:17; Deuteronomy 31:11; Judges 8:27 where a subset within Israel, standing as a representative group for the nation, is called "all Israel." In passages such as 1 Samuel 18:16; 2 Samuel 2:9; 3:21; and 2 Chronicles 12:1, "all Israel" denotes a portion of the twelve tribes. And in *Mishnah Sanhedrin* 10:1 (Danby, 397), the bare assertion, "All Israelites [Hebrew: *kol yisra'el*] have a share in the world to come," is followed by a list of individuals and groups within ethnic Israel that "have no share in the world to come."

Appendix

Numerology in the Book of Revelation

Bible numerology is a fascinating aspect of Bible study, yet one that many people seem to neglect. From earliest times, educated people have found great delight in the study of numbers, and the strange fancies and extravagant speculations in the use of certain numbers reveal the superstition and philosophy of the ancient heathen world. Many of their assertions as to the significance of some numbers were completely false. Though speculation has no place in the Holy Spirit's use of numbers, Scripture numerology provides a great aid in the discovery of moral, dispensational, and prophetic glories.

"One thing God has spoken, two things have I heard: that you, O God are strong, and that you, O Lord, are loving" (Psalm 62:11–12). Ellicott observes that this is the usual Hebrew mode of emphasizing a numerical statement, and one growing naturally out of the structure of the verse, which loves a climax. Solomon also uses the numerical climax when he enumerates six things that God hates and then the seventh, which He abhors most of all (Proverbs 6:16–19). Confining ourselves to Revelation, let us trace the literal and symbolic significance of the numbers employed by the Holy Spirit through John to express many facets of truth.

One

There is universal agreement as to the significance of this number. In all languages it is the symbol of unity, and in Scripture it is the sign of divine unity and absolute supremacy. "You shall have no other gods before me" (Exodus 20:3). Such a command asserts that there is in God a sufficiency that needs nothing and an independence that admits no other.

In Ephesians 4:3–6 the Apostle Paul describes a complete circle consisting of seven distinct unities: one body, one spirit, one hope, one Lord, one faith, one baptism, one God. We can see more deeply into these unities by remembering that three is the sign of divine manifestation and seven, of spiritual completeness. The first three unities are the inward manifestations of God, since only believers are included. The second three unities are the outward manifestations of God, since profession is contemplated. The unity and supremacy of the whole is maintained by "one God . . . who is over all and through all and in all."

Bullinger, in his most erudite work, *Numbers in Scripture,* says, "As a cardinal number, *one* denotes *unity;* as an ordinal it denotes *primacy.* Unity being indivisible, and not made up of other numbers, *one* is therefore independent of all others, and is the source of all others. *One* excludes all difference, for there is no second with which it can either harmonize or conflict. . . . The *first* is the only one. There cannot be two *firsts.*"

The unity of the governmental attributes of Jehovah can be seen in the golden cherubim, which were one measure and one size (1 Kings 6:25). Does not the professing church need to be recalled to the meaning of this divine number? Is she not gradually slipping away from the unity of Christ's one sacrifice of Himself and her unity of worship—one altar?

Among the thirty-six references to "one" in Revelation we have these four conspicuous phrases:

1. *"The Holy One"*
   "the one who sat there" (4:3)
   "the One who is and who was" (11:17)
   "one 'like the son of man'" (14:14)
   "the Holy One" (16:5)

2. *"No one" or "the one"*
   (3:7; 3:8; 5:3; 5:4; 13:17; 14:3; 15:8; 22:8)

3. *"One purpose"*
   "they have one purpose" (17:13)

4. *"One hour"*
   "for one hour will receive authority" (17:12)
   "in one hour" (18:10; 18:17; 18:19)

The "one hour" in the foregoing passages cannot be limited to an hour of exactly sixty minutes. Probably the repeated cry is the same period spoken of as "a little while" (17:10) or "one day" (18:8). Such a brief period indicates the terror and suddenness of God's judgment. "One purpose" (17:13) refers to the unity of the kings in subjection to the authority and will of the beast. Each of the twelve gates was made up of "a single pearl" (21:21). Although each pearl was distinct and different, there was unity in variety—unity but not uniformity.

Two

While "one" affirms that there is no other, "two" declares that there is another. Hence it takes a twofold coloring, according to the context. One writer suggests that the figure can mean responsibility, weakness, or grace. The "two" may be one in testimony and fellowship though different in character. We are tempted to linger over the pairs we find in Scripture, such as the two tablets of testimony (Deuteronomy 4:13), and thereby to prove that in the majority of references this number is the expression of ample and competent testimony.

Consider the ministry of the two prophets (Elijah and Elisha) and the two soldiers (Joshua and Caleb), who were faithful witnesses to the truth of God's Word. In the coming days of the great Tribulation, testimony to Christ will be borne by a fearless pair who are described as "two witnesses" (11:3), "two olive trees" (11:4), "two lampstands" (11:4), and "two prophets" (11:10).

The two hearts of these courageous warriors beat as one in their full testimony and in their devotion to the cause of Christ. When two are united in holy marriage, we speak about them being "one." Married to Christ, the two martyred witnesses were one in testimony, ridicule, death, resurrection, and ascension.

Three

This number has a sacred association because it represents the Trinity—Father, Son, and Holy Spirit (Matthew 28:19). Paul uses the phrase "these three" when he deals with the Christian graces of faith, hope, and love (1 Corinthians 13:13). Occurring very frequently in Scripture, "three" offers the expositor of the Word a wealth of material for pulpit or classroom treatment. Here, for example, are a few instances to whet the appetite:

Three men who appeared to Abraham (Genesis 18:2)
Three cities of refuge (Deuteronomy 4:41)
Three times a year (Deuteronomy 16:16)
Threefold priestly blessing (Numbers 6:24–26)
Threefold cry of the seraphim (Isaiah 6:3)
Three calls to earth (Jeremiah 22:29)
Three times of prayer (Daniel 6:13)
Three denials of Christ (Mark 14:72)
Three measures of meal (Matthew 13:33)
Three days and three nights (Matthew 12:40)
Three times Peter saw the vision (Acts 10:16)
Three times Paul besought the Lord about the thorn in his flesh
     (2 Corinthians 12:8)

The triad is a most integral part of Scripture and can usually be regarded as the sign number of what is divine (as in the case of Paul's frequent salutation of grace, mercy, and peace). Divine testimony and divine completeness are often emphasized by this number. In certain Scriptures, however, three can be regarded as the sign of resurrection in things moral, physical, and spiritual: the third day in creation; the third day in Christ's resurrection; and the third day in Christ's revival.

Just as three dimensions of length, breadth, and height are necessary to form a solid object, so the number three can be treated as the symbol of the cube, and therefore a representation of something that is solid, real, substantial, complete, and entire. Altogether, Scripture has four perfect numbers suggesting completeness: three, representing divine perfection; seven, representing spiritual perfection; ten, representing ordinal perfection; and twelve, representing governmental perfection.

The introductory section of Revelation is specially marked by this great divine seal of three:

- This Revelation is divinely given, divinely shown, divinely sent (1:1).
- John bore record of the divine vision (everything he saw), the divine Word of God, the divine Witness (the testimony of Jesus Christ) (1:2).
- The divine blessing is on the reader, the hearer, the keeper (1:3).
- The divine Being is the One who is, who was, who is to come (1:4, 8).
- The coming Lord is presented as the divine prophet (faithful witness), the divine priest (firstborn from the dead), the divine king (ruler of the kings) (1:5).
- The people of God are divinely loved, divinely cleansed (freed from sins), divinely consecrated (made a kingdom of priests) (1:5–6).
- Christ is presented as divinely eternal (the First and the Last), divinely living, divinely powerful (holding the keys of death and Hades) (1:17–18).
- The divine Revelation is threefold: what you have seen, what is now, what will take place later (1:19).

Four

Because global events are prominent in Revelation, the number four or fourfold, the sign of universality, is used eighteen times in the NIV: four living creatures (4:6; 4:8; 5:6; 5:8; 5:14; 6:1; 6:6; 7:11; 14:3; 15:7; 19:4); four angels (7:1; 7:2; 9:14; 9:15); four corners of the earth (7:1; 20:8); four winds (7:1).

When the world or the whole scene of creation is contemplated and when largeness and breadth of scope are in view, four is the number that is used, since it is associated with the earth's four directions and four seasons. As to those inhabiting the earth, they are made up of the four universal monarchies that Daniel depicted as four beasts (Daniel 7:4–17). The fullness of material blessing on the earth is described in this fourfold way: "Instead of bronze I will bring gold, and silver in place of iron. Instead of wood I will bring bronze, and iron in place of stones" (Isaiah 60:17).

If three is the signature of God, four is the signature of the world, which is made up of the four divisions of nations, tribes, peoples, and languages (7:9). Four, then, is the signature of creation—human and material. An old Jewish saying describes four things that take the first place in the world: man among the creatures; eagle among the birds; ox among the cattle; lion among the beasts.

Five

Although not so frequently used as other numbers, five has its own significance. Weakness in contrast to might is suggested by some references: David's use of five smooth stones to smite Goliath; five chasing a hundred; five loaves to feed five thousand. However, other passages—such as Numbers 5:7 and Matthew 25:2—imply the thought of human responsibility. Five and its multiples occupy a conspicuous place in the measurements and arrangements of those parts of the tabernacle and temple that express human responsibility and testimony toward man. There are five great mysteries: of God, of the Son, of the Spirit, of the creation, of the redemption of the Cross.

In the book of Revelation scorpions are given power to torture those without the seal for five months (9:4–5). In 9:10 the scorpions sting for five months. In 17:10 five weak kings have fallen.

Six

Created on the sixth day, humans are sealed with the number six. Six days they had to labor, and six is the number stamped on everything connected with human activity. The recurring references to six days of labor show the incompleteness of human work—it can never reach a full and final result. Solomon's throne had six steps (1 Kings 10:19). Because of the imperfection of his rule, his kingdom was divided and his glory fell short of perfection. The sixth Commandment relates to murder, the worst sin one person can inflict on another.

Because six is one less than seven, the number of perfection, it implies human imperfection. It is the number of those without God. The six waterpots of stone (John 2:6) witness to human imperfection and the inability of human ordinances to bring blessing. Six, then, indicates human limits—the best that can be done without God.

In Revelation, the four beasts have six wings (4:8), and "666" is "the number of the beast [and] man's number" (13:18). The opening of the sixth seal brings cataclysmic destruction to the universe (6:12). The sixth angel's trumpet releases two hundred million troops to "kill a third of mankind" (9:13–16). The contents of the sixth angel's bowl unleashes the wrath of the dragon, the beast, and the false prophet (16:12–14).

Seven

The constant use in Scripture of the number seven demands careful study by all lovers of the Word. The important role that this number plays in Revelation is proved by the fact that John uses it no less than fifty times in twenty-two chapters. In the Bible as a whole, seven appears more frequently than any other symbolic number. Seven also occurs in several multiples, as in "seventy times seven." At creation God rested on the seventh day.

As previously indicated, seven comes from a Hebrew root meaning "to be full, satisfied, have enough of" and conveys the idea of perfection or completion, either of good or of evil. Paul enumerates seven gifts and seven unities associated with the true church (Romans 12:6–8; Ephesians 4:4–6). There were seven feasts of Jehovah (Leviticus 23).

We have already noted many of the sevens in Revelation. The following list shows the perfections associated with that number.

The seven Spirits of God—perfections of the Godhead (1:4)
The seven golden lampstands (the seven churches)—perfection of light and truth and of professed testimony for Christ (1:12)
The seven stars—perfection in rule and oversight (1:20)
The seven spirits—perfection in illumination of the Spirit (3:1)
The seven seals—perfection of security and authority (5:1)
The seven horns—perfection of divine power (5:6)
The seven eyes—perfection of discernment (5:6)

The seven trumpets—perfection of jurisdiction (8:6)
The seven thunders—perfection of judgment (10:4)
The seven plagues—perfection of divine wrath (15:1)
The seven bowls—perfection of destruction (15:7)
The seven hills—perfection of earthly power (17:9)
The seven kings—perfection of earthly royalty (17:10)

Eight

This number comes from a Hebrew root that means "to make fat," "to superabound," and as a participle implies superabundant fertility or satiating. Because Christ rose on the first day of the week, which is also the eighth day, the number has come to represent resurrection. Eight is also the sign of eternity and of a new epoch (see Genesis 21:4; Leviticus 14:23; 1 Peter 3:20; 2 Peter 2:5; Revelation 17:11).

Ten

Five indicates our responsibility toward humans, and twice five measures our responsibility toward God, as proven by its use in many parts of the tabernacle and in the Ten Commandments. Israel's failure in the wilderness is described as consisting of ten times that they tempted God (Numbers 14:22–23). Pharaoh hardened his heart ten times and experienced the judgment of ten plagues.

As one of the perfect numbers of Scripture, ten signifies the perfection of divine order: nothing is lacking; the whole is complete. Thus in the Ten Commandments we have the complete revelation of the requirements of God. In the physical realm, how perfectly suited we are with ten fingers and ten toes! In the book of Revelation we find ten days of persecution (2:10), ten hours (12:3; 13:1; 17:3; 17:7; 17:16), ten women (13:1), ten kings (17:12).

In our treatment of the seven churches we suggested that the "ten days" of extreme tribulation refer to the ten persecutions endured under successive emperors. The immediate meaning of the phrase, however, is the precious thought that the Lord knew how much His saints could bear and so limited the period of trial accordingly. "He stayeth his rough wind in the day of the east wind" (Isaiah 27:8 KJV).

Eleven

Eleven signifies "the culmination; close to completion." It is mentioned forty-two times in the Bible but only once in Revelation: "the eleventh jacinth" (21:20). Jacob had eleven sons (Genesis 32:22); Joseph in his dream saw eleven stars (Genesis 37:9). The tabernacle in the wilderness had eleven curtains (Exodus 26:8); offerings were made on the eleventh day (Numbers 7:72). The disciples are called "the eleven" in Matthew 28:16; Mark 16:14; Luke 24:9, 33; Acts 2:14. "About the eleventh hour Jesus went out" (Matthew 20:6, 9).

Twelve

This number, with its cognates, occurs over four hundred times in the Bible and is an exceptionally important figure. God has chosen it to signify the perfect administration of divine government in the world, in Israel, and in the church (Matthew 19:28; Revelation 21:12–21). At age twelve Jesus publicly announced His heavenly relationship and His task in a world of need (Luke 2:42). Twelve legions of angels mark the perfection of angelic powers (Matthew 26:53).

In the Old Testament the reader will find much to meditate upon in the frequent use of twelve:

The twelve cakes of showbread (Leviticus 24:5)
The twelve springs of water (Exodus 15:27)
The twelve precious stones in the breastplate (Exodus 28:21)
The twelve sons of Jacob (Genesis 35:23–26)
The twelve stones (Joshua 4:8–9)
The twelve bulls (1 Kings 7:25)
The twelve gates (Ezekiel 48:31–34)

Occurring some twenty times in Revelation, the number twelve pervades patriarchal, apostolic, and national government. Thus we have

The twelve stars (12:1)
The twelve angels (21:12), representing heaven's hierarchy
The twelve tribes (21:12), representing Israel as a nation
The twelve foundations (21:14), representing the faith
The twelve apostles (21:14), representing the church of Christ
The twelve fruits (22:2), representing bountiful provision in heaven
The twelve gates (21:12, 21), representing freedom of entrance
The twelve pearls (21:21), representing the glory of the city

Multiples of twelve also appear. Twelve thousand stadia is the length, width, and height of the new city (21:16). Twelve thousand are sealed from each of the twelve tribes (7:5–8), totaling 144,000, a number that suggests perfection or fullness of God's purpose concerning His people, especially Israel. Twenty-four (twice twelve) means the fullness of authority and representation: the twenty-four elders (4:4) represent law and grace; the twenty-four thrones (11:16) represent power and judgment.

Forty-Two

Six times seven is a number of prophetic significance, conveying the idea of limitation—"trample on the holy city for 42 months" (11:2); "exercise his authority for forty-two months" (13:5). This period represents 1,260 days, or three and a half years, or "time [one year], times [two years] and half a time [six months]" (12:14). It is associated with the antichrist and the time of Jacob's trouble. It is also the last half of Daniel's prophetic week (Daniel 9:25–27). Bullinger remarks, "Being a multiple of seven, *forty-two* might be supposed to have some connection with spiritual perfection. But it is the product of *six* times *seven*. Six therefore, being the number of man's opposition to God, *forty-two* becomes significant of the working out of man's opposition to God."

Scripture Index